FOOD

FOR LIFE

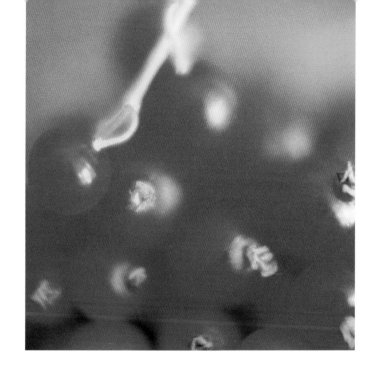

FOOD
FOR LIFE

MICHAEL VAN STRATEN
with recipes by Sally van Straten

Editorial Director Jane O'Shea
Art Director Helen Lewis
Designer Amanda Lerwil
Project Editor Hilary Mandleberg
Production Rebecca Short

First published in 2005 by
Quadrille Publishing Limited
Alhambra House
27–31 Charing Cross Road
London WC2H 0LS

British Library Cataloguing-in-Publication Data. A catalogue record for this book is available from the British Library.

ISBN 1-84400-129-6

Every effort has been made to ensure the accuracy of the information in this book. In no circumstances can the publisher or the author accept any liability for any loss, injury or damage of any kind resulting from any error in or omission from the information contained in this book.

Printed in China

Because precise nutritional requirements are so varied, not only from individual to individual and from one stage of life to another, but also from country to country, where I give figures for Recommended Daily Allowances (RDAs), they are an approximation of various needs. I never consider it important to know precise figures as they are meaningless when you are shopping or cooking. All that matters is that you eat as wide a variety of items from all the food groups to guarantee that you won't suffer from any deficiency diseases. Eating a balanced mixture of the recipes in this book will ensure an abundance of the nutrients needed for optimum health.

CONTENTS

When I trained as a Naturopath in the late 1950s and early 1960s, I quickly became a health-food zealot. Growing up in a traditional Jewish home, food was central to our lives. My mother, like her five sisters, was a wonderful cook and family life revolved around hoards of noisy cousins, a variety of aunts and uncles, a host of in-laws and many 'drop in' friends and neighbours, all sitting down to eat. Whether it was a religious festival, an anniversary, a birthday, the Friday-night Sabbath or a routine workaday meal, my mother cooked.

Not surprisingly, I quickly embraced the austerity of food-reform principles – the forerunner of modern complementary nutritional therapy. I tried every regime. I was a vegetarian, a vegan, a fruitarian. I gave up coffee and tea, forswore forever white bread and white sugar, grew sprouting seeds on the windowsill, and juiced carrots till my skin turned yellow. Naturally I tried force-feeding this new-found nutritional wisdom to my early patients but few of them were compliant. Happily, like St. Paul on the road to Damascus, I was rescued by a dramatic conversion when, in a restaurant in the heart of London's Soho, I succumbed to eating steak tartare – one of my father's favourite foods.

I have never looked back. I qualified as a Naturopath and Osteopath in 1964 and since that time have developed my Food for Life principles. Now, exactly 40 years later, I am still totally immersed in them.

There is nothing strange, eccentric or fanatical about these principles. Anyone can follow them without extra expense or the trouble of committing themselves to an antisocial, unnatural, obsessive and unhealthy extreme regime. The Food for Life principles are all about re-establishing the knowledge of our grandparents and their grandparents. It is the knowledge that, gathered from all around the world, has enabled people to survive the centuries. It is knowledge that will dramatically increase your chances of a long and healthy life whilst at the same time reducing your risks of developing many of the dread diseases of modern civilisation.

All you have to do to guarantee Food for Life is

- eat as wide a variety of foods as possible
- where practical, eat foods in season and produced as close to where you live as possible
- use foods which are as close as possible to the way nature intended them – whole, unprocessed and free from chemical additives
- enjoy what you're eating – guilt-free pleasure is probably the most important thing of all.

No, this does not mean a life of drudgery in the kitchen or a diet of nothing but brown rice, lentils and nut roasts. What it does mean is eating foods that look good, taste wonderful, are quick and easy to prepare, and provide the fullest possible spectrum of essential nutrients and protective phytochemicals. If you can afford and have access to organic food so much the better. If not, all fresh produce is good and there's nothing wrong with good quality frozen fruit and vegetables or canned tomatoes, beans and fish.

Food for Life also means a need to regain our respect for food and revisit our attitudes to what and why we eat. The Slow Food movement that started in Italy is now spreading worldwide. It fosters the small dedicated food producer, the traditional cheese maker, the butcher who turns out wonderful salamis and sausages, the baker for whom bread is almost a religion, the farmer who is passionate about the soil, his livestock and his crops. We should all be searching out the specialist food shop, the local farmers' market, the organic grower on our doorstep, the organic egg and poultry producer in the next village, and local restaurants that use local produce.

It is also vital that we teach our children about food, where it comes from and how to cook it so that their children will not be slaves to the fast-food industry and will not become the next junk-food generation. Children love to cook, they love to plant seeds and watch their carrots and lettuces grow and, most importantly, they love to eat what they've grown and cooked. So don't deprive them of a lifetime of healthy pleasure. If you plant the seed now, it will mature into a lifelong interest in, and love of Food for Life.

"Food for Life will, without question add years to your life and life to your years."

A SHORT HISTORY OF FOOD

The history of our relationship with food is fascinating. Not only is it the history of our emergence, survival and development but it's also the history of our growing intellectual abilities. In the beginning, food meant little more than survival but from the moment people began living in communities, domesticating animals and planting crops, food took on much greater significance. It was used as offerings to the gods, symbols of fertility, the measure of a man's wealth and status – all inextricably tied to the development of civilisation. Through famine and plenty, plague and pestilence, war and peace, the availability of food was the key to survival. Tragically, in the twenty-first-century world we live in, the wheel has come full circle and what we eat is once again linked to survival. But now it's the over-abundance of food that threatens us, bringing new plagues of disease caused by obesity and unhealthy eating patterns. We all have a lot to learn from history.

Seventy million years ago our earliest ancestors were vegetarians and for the next 50 million years lived happily on nuts, berries and fruits. Twelve million years of drought followed, grass replaced forests, and meat-eating became essential. Now Stone Age man was eating nuts, berries and fruits together with leaves, roots and meat. He had become omnivorous.

Ten thousand years ago, as we learned to domesticate animals and cultivate cereals, our diet contained more carbohydrates and fewer fats and proteins for the first time in our existence. Travel, trade and war meant that it slowly evolved still further, but in the last 60 years, the way we eat has been transformed more than in our entire previous history. So, who had the healthiest diet?

The stone age diet

In the Arctic during the Stone Age there was little food apart from polar bears, arctic foxes and seals but in temperate climates, like the Fertile Crescent of the Middle East, agriculture thrived and cereals and milk were commonplace alongside the meat of hunted animals.

Because of growing concerns about the Atkins Diet, which is mostly meat and virtually no carbohydrates, a false interpretation of the Stone-Age diet is now set to be the next big money-spinner. It advocates lots of lean red meat, some fruit and nuts, and no bread, pasta or milk. It rules out cooking fat, cereals and dairy products on the grounds that they are hard to digest and cause allergies. And this is all because believers in the Stone-Age diet insist that people haven't yet had time to adapt to an agrarian diet.

But there is no supporting evidence for this and whilst you will lose weight if you follow this diet, you won't be healthy. We all need to eat some fats and in the Stone Age they ate the fattiest meat possible, starting with the fattest of all – offal. The reason they didn't appear to get cancer, heart disease or arthritis, was because they didn't live long enough. Real Stone Agers ate vegetables, grains, roots, nuts and seeds which, with the meat, is a pretty good starting point for healthy living. In fact, if Stone Age people had eaten this modern version of the Stone-Age diet, they wouldn't have survived at all.

RIGHT Prehistoric cave paintings in Spain

Romans roam the world

As everyone knows the Roman Empire spread across much of the known world and as it did, Roman cooks used local produce both for ordinary meals and for banquets.

Apicius was the greatest of the Roman cooks and his remarkable text on food comprised ten separate book, including: The Careful Cook, The Gardener, Legumes, Birds, The Gourmet, Quadrupeds and The Fisherman. These are still relevant today, even though some of the ingredients may be unfamiliar. Not so his herbs and spices: nutmeg, cloves, cinnamon, pepper, ginger, mint and rosemary were commonplace in the Roman empire. Bread, olive oil, wine, celery, almonds raisins, dates and honey, cider vinegar,

fennel, lamb, oysters, shellfish, wild boar, pork, chicken, geese, duck, pheasant and pigeon were all there to be enjoyed. The street markets of Ancient Rome probably didn't differ much from our street markets today.

Apicius's recipes were extremely healthy. After all, what could be healthier than steamed squash, courgette or pumpkin with beans, rosemary, cider vinegar and olive oil? He also used broccoli, cabbage, spring greens, leeks and all the root vegetables. He gives instructions for steamed and baked fish, trout, mullet, eels, fresh tuna, salmon, sardines and many freshwater varieties. Recipes for shellfish abound in his books and there are a dozen different ways of cooking venison.

Roman cooking has been neglected for almost two thousand years but if we look carefully, we will find that there are still lessons to be learned from it that would improve our diet today.

The highs and lows of the nineteenth century

The nineteenth century was a bleak time for northern European and American nutrition and continued to be so right through to the first decade of the twentieth century. Though there was much prosperity, the divisions between rich and poor were enormous and were clearly reflected in their food.

The wealthy ate gargantuan amounts of food that would make modern-day nutritionists throw up their hands in horror. Liver disease, gout, heart attacks, obesity, high blood pressure, strokes and alcoholism were the result, all of them illnessses that were commonplace in this affluent society.

But the illnesses of the poor were largely caused by malnutrition – rickets, tuberculosis, pneumonia, childhood infections, miscarriage, stillbirth, scurvy, congenital birth defects, and skin conditions.

Though fruit and vegetables, and all kinds of meat, poultry and fish were abundant, the urban poor couldn't afford them. Those living in the country could at least catch their own fish, keep a few hens for eggs and meat, and grow their own fruit and vegetables.

Surprisingly, some of the foods of this period in history were nourishing, if you could get them. There were the soups and consommés, for example, and rabbit and pheasant, which could often be caught in the wild so were popular with rich and poor alike. Simply roasted meat and poultry were the pinnacles of nineteenth-century cooking, particularly when cooked on a spit, rack or trivet so that all the fat drained away from the cooking meat. In some places there was also inexpensive and highly nutritious shellfish, but even for the well off, nutrients were often lacking in the diet as it was the fashion to cook all vegetables to a grey and soggy mush.

Healthy nutrition and the second world war

Life was tough for the troops, Allied and German alike, but it was no picnic for the struggling cooks at home either. American forces had much better food than the European troops and though there was some belt-tightening in the US, Americans never experienced food rationing, which started in Britain on 8 January 1940.

PICK 'N' MIX So how can you benefit from these diets for all ages? The answer is simple. First, you must choose foods you like otherwise you'll never eat them, and lack of enjoyment does nothing for your digestion. Second, you should try and aim for a sensible balance.

Take a leaf from the Stone Age. You do need protein, you do need some fat and you do need some carbohydrates. Unfortunately the suggestion that around 50 per cent of our calories should come from carbohydrates often doesn't make it clear that it's the quality of those carbohydrates that's so important. Refined flour, sugars, high-fat cakes and biscuits, polished rice and processed foods are not the answer. These calories need to come from wholegrains, beans, lentils and root vegetables.

Then look at the Romans. They had wonderful ways with vegetables and consumed large amounts of fish, but they had no sugar, no manufactured fats like margarines, nor any kind of processed food. Just avoid their excesses.

The nineteenth century set an example with its broths and consommés, roasted meat and poultry, and shellfish. Fortunately nineteenth-century levels of poverty are a thing of the past for most of the developed world.

And finally, you could do worse than follow the rules of British wartime rationing. Reduce your total consumption of meat, keep saturated fats to sensible low levels, do away with salt, reduce your sugar intake by two-thirds and you won't go far wrong.

Put these all together and make them the foundation of your family's daily meals and you'll have a diet for all ages.

ABOVE A Victorian family sitting down to dinner

The food situation was even worse in the rest of Europe, especially during the last two years of the war. In occupied Europe, the German army requisitioned most of the food, leaving the local people to fend for themselves. In the agricultural regions of France, Italy, Greece, families were able to survive on whatever local produce they could hide and share amongst family and friends. But in many places attempts at rationing failed because there simply wasn't enough food. In Holland the infamous 'Hunger Winter' of 1944–5 was catastrophic. The Germans forbade the transport of food into the areas which they controlled, the weather was appalling, there was no fuel and official rations were cut to 450 calories a day. Reduced to eating tulip bulbs, rats and the few pets that survived, more than 18,000 Dutch men, women and children died of starvation that winter.

In Britain, things didn't get any easier when the war ended in May 1945. Within three weeks of VE Day, the bacon allowance went from 100g to 75g per person per week, cooking fat from 50g to 25g, and part of the already tiny allowance of meat had to be corned beef. Even bread, which was never rationed during the war itself, became rationed in Britain in July 1946. Most of these controls stayed in place until June 1954 when, more than eight years after the end of the war, meat was finally freely available again in Britain.

The British wartime government published recipes such as Leftover Meat Stew, using carrots, fresh herbs and fat-free dumplings; Pease Pudding made from dried peas, onions, parsley, thyme, one egg, 25g of butter and lots of mint; Vegetable Casserole with leeks, onions and any root vegetables people could get their hands on. There was even a low-fat, low-sugar apple crumble made with oats, a little flour and only 50g of butter.

Despite rationing, these recipes were brimful of health for, ironically, the restriction of meat, fats and sugar played a key role in the improved health of the nation. Heart disease, obesity, diabetes and even some forms of cancer were at levels that Britons would like to enjoy today. If the same rationing were imposed now, virtually every Briton who is overweight would quickly slim down and most people's nutritional status would be greatly improved. There's surely food for thought here as our twenty-first-century waistlines expand, seemingly, beyond control.

NUTRITION MADE SIMPLE

I'm always amazed by the wonderfully healthy eating habits of earlier generations. My mother and grandmother never possessed a nutrition reference book, had no idea about what foods were the best sources of vitamins and minerals, and never gave a thought to the relative balance of fats, proteins and carbohydrates in the food they gave to their families. My mother may have known about vitamin C in citrus fruits, but her mother certainly didn't. Yet in spite of this apparent lack of knowledge, my grandmother raised eight children who all led long, healthy and productive lives and her six daughters fed their families in exactly the same way as she did. The secret was simple – as wide a variety of foods as possible and virtually everything fresh and seasonal. Apart from jams, chutney, pickles and the occasional canned food, there were no other preserved foods around. Nor were there any freezers, instant meals or microwave ovens.

I hope that this section of the book will tell you all you need to know about nutrition and will enable you to plan healthy meals without the need for a calculator or a set of reference tables.

THE KEY BUILDING

This section of the book is all about the major food groups – fats, proteins and carbohydrates. They can be confusing because when you're planning a menu or a shopping trip, you don't think about them: what you think about is food. I call the major food groups the key building blocks because, like the foundations of your house, they are the cornerstones of every cell your body repairs or makes.

For years the focus was on the link between fat and heart disease and the well-established relationship between a diet that's high in animal protein and the risks of blood pressure and bowel cancer. Now it has shifted to the dangers of carbohydrates, so high-protein diets are the rage. As a result of all these fads, supermarket shelves are groaning with low-fat, reduced-fat, low-carb, low-sugar and 'lite' foods, all of which are nothing more than marketing terminology aimed at misleading you, the shopper.

Worryingly, when you're out shopping for food, you end up playing the manufacturers' misleading magic numbers game. For the giant food manufacturers, this game means profits. But they are leading you down the wrong nutritional path and it's even more serious when you're shopping for children's foods.

So what is the magic numbers game? Manufacturers simply add one or two inexpensive nutrients to junk food and fool you into thinking that it's better for you. So breakfast cereal with added vitamins and iron carries the slogan that it's good for healthy bones. It may be, but it's not much good for your teeth or your risk of diabetes as it is 38 per cent sugar. What they also don't tell you is that one bowl is saltier than a bowl of sea water. Fromage frais with added calcium and vitamins has all the nutritional value of milk but turns out to be more than 12 per cent pure sugar.

The magic numbers game is also used by fast-food chains. They play it to emphasise the one or two good nutrients in their products and so distract you from the huge amount of fat, salt and sugar they contain. It allows them virtually to suggest that a burger, fries and coke is a healthy meal for an adult or growing child.

Low-fat and fat-free foods are another instance of the food manufacturers' sleight of hand. They have encouraged the public to believe that the greatest threat to health comes from eating too much fat and that it is fat that is responsible for today's epidemic of obesity. But this is just not true. The number of seriously overweight adults in the USA has rocketed to 35 per cent of the population, yet in recent years the average consumption of calories there from fat has gone down by 6 per cent as Americans

BLOCKS

switched to the heavily marketed low-fat and fat-free foods. Sadly, Americans still eat more fat than is good for them. At the same time, the amount of sugar they get from carbohydrates has rocketed, so that the average American now consumes around 35 teaspoons a day. It doesn't take much to realise that it's the combination of excess sugar and too much fat that's the cause of the obesity.

What is more, the 'low-fat' labels are misleading. 'Low-fat' crisps are still 21 per cent fat and yoghurt is always low-fat – even the richest creamiest yoghurt is no more than 4 per cent fat. But the low-fat claims distract you from all the sugar, flavourings, colourings, preservatives and salt – that goes into these foods.

The most important thing to realise is that any diet which excludes any one of the major food groups is a recipe for long-term disaster. Whether you totally exclude fats or carbohydrates, or follow any extreme dietary programme like macrobiotic or vegan eating, you are making it much more difficult for your body to be provided with sufficient of the essential building blocks.

How can I make sure I'm eating a healthy diet?

There's been lots of talk recently about healthy food pyramids but most people I speak to find it much easier to visualise the healthy plate. This is the way to get the optimum amounts of fats, proteins and carbohydrates, as well as all the nutrients, without feeling deprived, or guilty about the occasional treat.

The plate is divided into five sections, and if you think about it whenever you're shopping or cooking you'll never stray far from the path of good nutrition. A third of the plate is filled with fresh produce – fruits, vegetables and salads. The second third contains carbohydrates like potatoes, pasta, wholegrain breads, brown rice, oats, rye, barley and corn. Divide the last third into two equal-sized wedges of 15 per cent, leaving a tiny 3 per cent sliver. One of the two 15 per cent segments is filled with protein foods for body-building – lean meat, fish, poultry, eggs, beans, lentils, nuts and seeds – and the second with further body- and bone-building foods like milk, yoghurt, fromage frais and cheese. When it comes to the tiniest sliver of plate, that's where you put fats, oils, butter, cream, sugar, chocolate, ice cream, croissants, cakes and biscuits.

Sticking to these proportions will make sure that you get the ideal balanced diet. Even as a rough guide this plate will provide enough carbohydrates for energy, sufficient protein for growth and repair, enough of the essential fatty acids and a very safe amount of other fats. And you can even enjoy your favourite treats.

PROTEIN

Only serious illness or following bizarre diets cause problems with protein levels in the West. Far from worrying about getting enough protein, we should be concerned about consuming excessive amounts as it's now certain that too much animal protein is a factor in cancer, high blood pressure, heart and kidney disease.

What does it do?

Protein is essential for the building of every single one of the body's cells and is constantly being used and replaced.

How much do I need?

Adult men need around 56g a day and women 45g but in the Western world, protein deficiency is extremely unusual, except in people suffering from eating disorders or from serious digestive illnesses, which either prevent them from eating or hinder absorption of the food they eat. Over the years I've analysed thousands of my patients' diets and only a handful have been short of protein, and that includes even those with quite bizarre diets, who aren't getting sufficient protein on a daily basis. In fact, it's far more common to see people with excessively high protein consumption, which might trigger high blood pressure and kidney disorders. And if their high protein intake comes mostly from red meat, they also have an increased risk of getting raised cholesterol, heart disease and bowel cancer.

There are, though, some children with low protein intakes, especially those who are faddy eaters and stick to the same few favourite foods all the time. But don't worry if your youngster wants to live on baked beans, packets of crisps and chips. Though such foods may not be healthy options in other respects, they do provide protein. As little as a hundred grams of each will provide 5g, 6g and 4g of protein respectively. And that's not bad considering that the average 5-year-old only needs around 20g of protein daily.

Where do I get it?

Protein is found in a wide variety of foods. These include cereals such as wheat, oats, rice and anything made from them; eggs, cheese, fish, poultry, meat, nuts and seeds, and all varieties of beans, peas and lentils. Generally speaking, protein derived from animal sources is a complete protein on its own, whereas, with the exception of soya beans, you need a combination of cereals with pulses and legumes for complete protein. Such combinations are commonly seen in ethnic foods

KEY STAGES OF LIFE Because babies, children and teenagers are all growing rapidly they tend to need more protein in relation to their weight than adults. Pregnant women also need extra protein to create the new cells in their growing babies.

like rice and peas (actually black-eye beans) from the West Indies, or chapattis with dhal from India.

But no food is made up of nothing but protein. Vegetables, for example, are only 5 per cent or less protein, and fruits contain very little. Eggs, cheese, fish, meat and poultry, peanuts, beans, lentils, cereals and bread are anything between 10 and 30 per cent but they usually provide over 80 per cent of our daily protein consumption.

The average woman will get all she needs from 100g fish, 500ml milk, two boiled eggs and a slice of wholemeal bread, so you see how easy it is to make sure there's enough protein in your diet.

Who needs extra?

Serious athletes, weightlifters, body builders and, particularly, distance runners, need rather more protein than the average person.

DID YOU KNOW THAT?

• Generally speaking, freezing and cooking do not alter the amount of protein present in foods, though cooking can make a difference. Slightly cooked proteins are more easily digested than raw, but overcook your steak, and the protein in it will be less available as your digestive juices will have more trouble breaking it down.

• The body cannot store protein and any excess is converted into sugars and fats, so the idea that replacing starchy foods with lots of protein is less fattening is a myth and may be harmful. That's just one reason why I, personally, wouldn't ever recommend the Atkins diet to anyone.

• It's not difficult for adults to be healthy vegetarians but it can be more problematic raising a vegetarian child. Of course, millions of people who are vegetarians for religious reasons are not only healthy themselves, but raise extremely healthy children. Getting enough protein for normal growth and repair from completely vegetable- and dairy-based foods is not a problem, but if you give up all animal foods you will need to take more care about getting sufficient iron and vitamin B1.

DEFICIENCY SYMPTOMS Kwashiorkor (common in Third World children)

CARBOHYDRATES

Once and for all, carbohydrates are not fattening. It's what you do to them that does the damage. Complex, unrefined carbohydrates are essential for health.

What do they do?

All the carbohydrate, or starchy foods, are good sources of energy. When they are digested, the sugars they contain are broken down into glucose. Glucose – or blood sugar as it is also confusingly known – is the fuel our bodies run on. The glucose circulating in the bloodstream after a starchy meal is available for instant use. Any surplus is converted to glycogen and stored in the liver, ready to be used when needed. It's the hormone insulin that makes the storage possible.

How much do I need?

Carbohydrates should make up 50 per cent of your daily calorie consumption; most of it should come from complex carbohydrates.

Where do I get them?

Complex carbohydrates are found in cereals and grain such as wheat, rye, corn, oats and rice; they are also in pulses such as peas, beans and lentils; in starchy vegetables like potatoes, sweet potatoes, parsnips, swede, turnip and carrots; and in milk, sugar and honey.

The best carbohydrates come from wholegrain bread, brown rice and whole oats, beans and lentils and fruits. These supply more than just energy; they're also loaded with essential nutrients and are rich in fibre for efficient digestion. But when they are refined or processed, they lose many nutrients and most of their fibre. White flour, for instance, contains less zinc, needed for natural immunity and brain function; less magnesium, required for the nervous system and bone-building; and much less body-building protein.

The same happens to processed (white) rice and corn, while white sugar provides nothing but

DON'T GO TO EXTREMES Vary the carbohydrates in your diet. Most Westerners tend to stick to a few basic foodstuffs, one of which is white flour. Toast or bread for breakfast, sandwiches for lunch, cakes and biscuits for tea, and pasta or pizza in the evening all add up to an awful lot of just one food type. No wonder growing numbers of people are developing sensitivities to wheat and wheat products.

empty calories. Brown sugar and honey at least contain traces of some key nutrients, and honey is an excellent source of protective antioxidants (see page 82). Heidrum Gross and her colleagues at the University of California fed honey to 25 volunteers every day for a month. At the end of the month, blood tests showed that the volunteers had a significant increase in their disease-fighting natural antioxidant polyphenols. The average American consumes in excess of 75 kilos of sweeteners every year: this experiment proves that they would be much better off eating honey.

Who needs extra?

The physically active, athletes, the elderly and people recovering from illness.

DID YOU KNOW THAT? Eat a slice of wholegrain bread, a dish of lentils, or a handful of ripe apricots, and the sugars in them are broken down into glucose quite slowly. But a couple of biscuits, a bowl of refined breakfast cereal or a chocolate bar – all of which are examples of highly refined carbohydrates – provide sugars that are converted very quickly into glucose and that rapidly raise the blood-sugar levels. These are the high-glycaemic foods.

When blood-sugar levels soar, the pancreas pumps out lots of insulin to counteract the effect, then you end up with hypoglycaemia – low blood sugar. So lots of refined sugars for breakfast means a slump in the middle of the morning, poor concentration, the jitters and sugar cravings.

This type of eating is also thought to lead to high blood pressure, obesity, diabetes and heart disease, as well as very disruptive behaviour in children.

Blood-sugar levels which yo-yo up and down are also known to increase the storage of fat in body cells, and this pushes up your weight. For six years, Professor Walter Willett at Harvard University studied 100,000 men and women, none of whom had diabetes when he started his study. At the end of the study the people who'd eaten the most high-glycaemic foods – white bread, white sugar, jam, sweetened breakfast cereals, and so on – proved to have a 50 per cent greater risk of developing Type II diabetes (see page 54) than the others. And the women eating large amounts of high-glycaemic foods were even more likely to develop Type II diabetes than the men.

So, whenever possible you should eat wholemeal bread, brown rice, oats, all the other wholegrain cereals and lots of pulses, and you should save the white flour, high-sugar content and other refined carbohydrate foods for occasional treats.

DEFICIENCY SYMPTOMS Constipation • Fatigue

FATS

Fat is bad seems to be today's message. Fats gives you heart disease, clog up your arteries, cause high blood pressure, are linked to breast pain, bowel cancer, obesity and a host of other health horrors. Everywhere you look there are adverts, posters and food labels screaming 'low fat' – as if you'd expect your breakfast cereal, a loaf of bread or carton of pure fruit juice to have much fat in the first place.

What do they do?

It's true that too much of the worst kind of fat means raised cholesterol, high blood pressure, heart disease and an increased risk of some cancers, but too little fat causes poor absorption of the fat-soluble vitamins A, E, D and K – essential for natural resistance to infection, for healthy skin, eyes, heart and circulation, and for strong bones and normal blood clotting.

How much do I need?

You should get no more than 33 per cent of your calories from all the fat in your diet – 10 per cent from saturated fat, 6–10 per cent from polyunsaturated fat and 12 per cent from monounsaturated fat, but don't forget the vital essential fatty acids too (see page 24).

However, fat provides more calories than the same weight of any other food – around 900 calories per 100g compared with 400 calories per 100g of protein or carbohydrate, and that's

DON'T GO TO EXTREMES Don't go overboard with sunflower seed oil. Although it has been much publicised as a healthy alternative, you shouldn't use it with abandon. It is more than 60 per cent Omega-6 and has virtually no Omega-3 (see page 24). True, it's extremely low in saturated fat, but its high levels of Omega-6 mean you should use it sparingly.

regardless of whether the fat comes from olive oil, butter, margarine or cooking fat. And because the body uses far less energy to store calories from fat than calories from starches and proteins, surplus fat calories are the most fattening.

Where do I get them?

Most shoppers now look for leaner cuts of meat, lean mince, and lower-fat varieties of foods, but it's the hidden fats that cause the problem – those

DID YOU KNOW THAT? 'Low fat' labels have become the latest marketing tool of the food industry to persuade you to buy yet more processed, packaged, frozen and generally low-nutrient, factory-produced meals. These often have little reduction in their calorie content compared with the full-fat equivalent.

buried in sausages, salamis, hot dogs, burgers, ready meals, takeaways, meat pies, cakes, biscuits, Danish pastries, sweet and savoury snacks, and mayonnaise. Read the labels and you'll see just how bad they are.

How do I choose?

Here are the fat facts which will help you make the wisest choices:

Saturated fats

These are nearly all animal fats from meat and meat products, poultry, lard, dripping, butter, cream and cheese. It's these fats that can lead to an increase in cholesterol, which in turn blocks the arteries and causes heart disease and raised blood pressure. Though there's little direct evidence that saturated fats play a role in the development of cancer, many experts believe that lower consumptions reduce the risks – especially of bowel cancer.

Trans fats

These are manufactured from polyunsaturates and are the worst of all for the health of your heart. They crop up most commonly in hard margarines and to a lesser extent in the soft forms, too. Margarine manufacturers have recently taken steps to reduce the amount of trans fats in their products, but watch out for them in pre-packed snack foods. There is some evidence that trans fats are also linked to an increased risk of breast cancer.

Conjugated linoleic acid

Conjugated linoleic acid (CLA) was first discovered just over 20 years ago by Professor Mike Pariza at the University of Wisconsin in the USA. At that time, researchers in America were concerned that fried hamburgers might be a potential cause of cancer. Pariza found that CLA, a natural fat in beef, had powerful anti-cancer properties. But his startling research also showed that only the meat of free-range cattle, raised on natural grasslands, contained CLA. As well as its anti-cancer properties, this valuable fat stimulates the human body's conversion of stored fats into energy. This is just one more good reason for choosing organic beef.

Monounsaturated fats

Monounsaturated fats are much better for your heart and can even help to reduce the amount of cholesterol in your bloodstream. The richest sources are olives, olive oil, avocados, peanuts and peanut oil. These fats, too, appear to have no role in the formation of cancer.

FATS

Polyunsaturated fats

These vegetable oils contain a mixture of Omega-6 (linoleic acid) and Omega-3 fatty acids (alpha-linolenic acid) and what matters is the balance between them. The healthiest oils are those with more Omega-3 relative to Omega-6. Those with lots of Omega-6 and very little Omega-3 put you in double jeopardy because Omega-6s are thought to be carcinogenic and they also nullify the heart-protection benefits of Omega-3.

The best oils are olive, rapeseed, walnut and flaxseed, all of which have very low amounts of saturated fatty acids, substantial monounsaturates and a good balance between the Omega-3 and Omega-6 fatty acids.

Coconut and palm oils are best avoided as they contain large amounts of saturated fats, little monounsaturated fat and virtually no Omega-3 at all. When you are buying foods that have been canned in oil, steer clear of products labelled 'vegetable oil'; they're almost certain to contain unhealthy coconut or palm oils.

Who needs less?

Most women need to reduce their overall consumption of fats to protect their heart and circulation and minimise their cancer risk. The average woman should reduce her intake of saturated and trans fats and use more of the natural, unrefined as well as, where possible, cold-pressed sources of monounsaturated fats and the best of the polyunsaturated oils.

ESSENTIAL FATTY ACIDS

What do they do?

The essential fatty acids (EFAs) are vital for the growth and development of the brain and nervous system. They are also important for the function and health of every cell of the body and are part of the mechanism that controls cholesterol, helping to move it around the body, break it down and excrete it, so preventing blocked arteries, high blood pressure, strokes and heart attacks. Without EFAs you would lose much of your protection against inflammatory diseases and your body's pain-control mechanism would be reduced. And last, but not least, the EFAs help to relieve eczema and asthma, too.

Of the EFAs, the truly essential highly unsaturated fatty acids (HUFAs) are Omega-3 and Omega-6. Unlike other fats that can be manufactured within the body, we need to get these from our food, though they can, in theory, be made by humans.

How much do I need?

There are no intelligible recommended requirements.

Where do I get them?

Omega-3 is found in many green leafy vegetables, seeds and grains as well as in fish. Omega-6 is found in vegetables, fruits, nuts, grains and seeds as well as oily fish and fish oils. The EFAs in fish oils are absolutely vital for brain development and function but many of us do not eat as much fish as our parents or grandparents did. Vegetarians and vegans can use flaxseeds and flaxseed oil instead, but they aren't as beneficial, which is why being a strict vegetarian or vegan may not be in the best interests of developing babies, growing children and adolescents.

Other fatty acids from vegetable oils, some green leafy vegetables, wheatgerm, nuts and seeds, wholegrain cereals and some fruits, have extremely important functions and although they all fall within the group of EFAs, they're not so essential. It's important to get them, though, for if your diet is deficient in the HUFAs, they may be critical to your overall health and wellbeing.

Who needs extra?

Vegetarians, vegans, people on very low-fat diets, or those suffering from anorexia or chronic bowel disorders should top up their diet with EFA-rich foods or, at the very least, take a fish-oil, or flaxseed oil supplement. Three portions of oily fish per week are a minimum, especially for pregnant women and nursing mothers.

Supplements

Capsules of fish oils can be added to food or drinks. Adults should take 1–2g daily. Children with dyslexia, ADHD, or any of the autistic spectrum disorders can also benefit from a supplement and should take 500mg twice daily.

BEST FOOD SOURCES

APPROXIMATE PERCENTAGE OF DAILY ADULT NEEDS IN AN AVERAGE PORTION

SALMON, HERRINGS, MACKEREL, TROUT, FRESH TUNA, SARDINES 80–90%

MUSSELS, OYSTERS, COCKLES, WHELKS, WINKLES, CLAMS, SCALLOPS, SCAMPI 80%

LOBSTER, CRAB, PRAWNS, SHRIMPS, LANGOUSTINES, CRAYFISH 80%

SUNFLOWER, SAFFLOWER, SESAME, FLAXSEED OILS 40% per teaspoon
EXTRA-VIRGIN OLIVE OIL 30% per teaspoon

RAPESEED, WALNUT, HAZELNUT, PEANUT OILS 20% per teaspoon

DEFICIENCY SYMPTOMS   Rough dry skin • Eczema • Night blindness • Learning difficulties

THE NUTRIENTS

The word 'nutrients' is always being bandied about. Food manufacturers are all too keen on trumpeting the fact that they've added nutrients like vitamin C, iron, B vitamins and so on to their foods. They flash the information across the packaging in large print and you'll find it on bottles of drink, cups of dried soup powder and a host of other food products. Despite what you may think, these foods play little or no part in contributing to the overall nutrition of you and your family.

In complete contrast, the additives that they don't want you to know about, like fat, salt, sugar, trans fats, colourings, flavourings and preservatives, appear in the smallest print size they can legally get away with. And that information is often obscured by sell-by dates, price labels or the use of difficult-to-read colours.

The nutrients are the fine detail of what you eat. The first to look at are the vitamins. Ever since the Polish chemist Kasimir Funk coined the name 'vitamins' in 1911, a maze of conflicting advice has arisen around them. At their simplest, vitamins are naturally occurring substances in foods that are essential for the maintenance of good health. Without them the body's chemistry just doesn't work. The simple example which everyone knows concerns vitamin C. If you don't get enough of it you get scurvy, which is why, once this was understood in the eighteenth century, the ships of the British navy carried barrels of limes to protect the crew – and hence the name 'limeys' that the Americans called the British.

Minerals are the other essential group of nutrients. We need some of them, like calcium and iron, in quite large quantities and others, like iodine and selenium, in minute amounts But need them we most definitely do.

The final group of nutrients are the phytochemicals which include some vitamins, some minerals and a host of other natural plant chemicals known as antioxidants that are powerful protective substances. These antioxidants fight off the damaging effects of free radicals that are produced naturally in the body by its own chemical processes and that get into the body through polluted air, water and food. Just as your iron garden gate goes rusty because of free radicals in the atmosphere, and painting it acts as a barrier and stops the chemicals attacking the iron, so antioxidants in food do the same job for every cell in your body. For full details of these amazing phytochemicals see pages 82–3.

To supplement or not to supplement?

So, does anybody need nutrient supplements? Alarmingly, since many people in the Western world are over-fed but under-nourished the answer is 'yes'. I analyse the diets of hundreds of people every year. They come from every walk of life, from grave-diggers to geography teachers, fashion models to footballers' wives and from 8- to 80-year-olds. Regardless of money, power or position, almost without exception they have one thing in common: their diets lack at least one or more of the essential nutrients. In addition, severe illness, convalescence and old age can all reduce the amount of vitamins the body can absorb and periods of excessive stress, physical activity or even pregnancy can create extra demands.

It's also true that we almost certainly need more of some nutrients than the recommended daily intakes. Folic acid is a prime example. Twice the recommended dose is needed by all of us to protect from heart disease as well as during pregnancy to protect babies from spina bifida. American studies from Harvard University show that consistent intake of folic acid over 15 years can reduce the risk of bowel cancer by 75 per cent. High intakes of vitamin C, around 500mg per day, are known to have an important role in protecting human cells against cancer and help people with early signs of diseased arteries by removing life-threatening fat deposits.

Of course it's always best to get your nutrients from food but there are people for whom this is medically difficult. People with bowel disease, conditions affecting the mouth and throat, on restricted diets due to liver or kidney disease, or with allergies or food intolerance may all find it impossible to eat sufficient of the right foods to get the nutrients they require without supplementation.

VITAMIN A

All the vitamins are essential for life **" but vitamin A is definitely one of the most important.**

What does it do?

This vitamin is crucial for the body's natural defences against viruses and bacteria. Another key function is the protection of the mucous membranes – the lining of the mouth, nose, throat and lungs; without vitamin A, these dry out and cannot perform their vital functions.

Cancer protection is another important benefit and vitamin A is useful, too, for people with chronic respiratory illness like asthma and bronchitis. It's also essential for good night vision, colour perception, prevention of cataracts and to protect against blindness. Millions of children in the developing world who are at risk of blindness could be spared if they took a cheap daily vitamin A supplement.

Vitamin A also plays a key role in growth and bone development and is required by men and women for fertility and reproduction. There is also some evidence that it plays a part in supporting the mechanisms governing taste and balance, and finally, it is key to the growth and maintenance of healthy glowing skin that keeps its elasticity.

How much do I need?

The average RDA is 700–1300mcg, depending on circumstances.

Where do I get it?

The body gets its vitamin A directly from foods containing it and indirectly through its ability to convert beta-carotene into vitamin A. Beta-carotene is the yellow pigment found in foods like carrots, apricots, sweet potatoes and most dark green leafy vegetables, especially spinach.

Because vitamin A is fat-soluble the main sources of it are foods that also contain some

DON'T LOSE OUT As well as very low-fat diets reducing people's overall consumption of vitamin A, the current popularity of special foods like margarines and yoghurts aimed at reducing cholesterol levels is also worrying as these encourage the elimination of vitamin A. Anti-cholesterol drugs, antacid indigestion remedies and a deficiency of the mineral zinc (see pages 64–5) can also be a cause of reduced levels of vitamin A circulating in your body's bloodstream.

fats and oils. The trend towards very low-fat diets is extremely worrying as this not only reduces people's overall consumption of vitamin A but also means that the small amounts that are being eaten are not necessarily being absorbed.

Who needs extra?

People with skin problems like acne, eczema, psoriasis, scarring, burns or dry skin and those taking cholesterol-lowering drugs, on very low-fat diets or suffering from any of the inflammatory bowel problems.

Supplements

Vitamin A is toxic in high doses so never exceed 750mcg per day without medical advice. Be careful when taking other supplements to read the labels as many fish-oil and fish-liver preparations may have high levels of vitamin A.

APPROXIMATE PERCENTAGE OF
DAILY ADULT NEEDS IN AN
AVERAGE PORTION

LIVER (DON'T EAT IF YOU'RE PREGNANT) 2000%

SWEET POTATOES 170%

CARROTS (OLD) 100%

SPINACH 90%

BUTTER 65%

PARMESAN CHEESE 40%

CHEDDAR CHEESE 35%

EGGS (2) 25%

DRIED APRICOTS 5%

DON'T GO TO EXTREMES The body stores surplus amounts of vitamin A in fatty tissues like the liver but excessive stores can be extremely toxic. For this reason, never exceed the recommended dose when you are taking any pills that contain vitamin A and don't eat foods that are extremely rich sources, like liver, more than a couple of times a week. Pregnant women should avoid vitamin A supplements and liver completely. Headaches, nausea, peeling itchy skin, hair loss and bone deformities can be the result if you overdose on this vitamin..

DID YOU KNOW THAT?
Even though there are substantial amounts of vitamin A in foods like liver, oily fish, butter, cheese, carrots, vegetables and even milk, many people fail to get the minimum daily requirement and so put their general health at risk. This is especially true of young women who follow extreme weight-loss diets. I've seen many in my practice who are so obsessed with being thin that they can tell you the fat content of virtually every product on the supermarket shelves and yet have no idea what vitamin A is, does or where to find it.

DEFICIENCY SYMPTOMS Night blindness • Scaly skin • Infections • Inflamed mucous membranes

VITAMIN B1

"Why was it that during the Second World War, in Japanese PoW camps, the Japanese officers and guards became ill while their prisoners didn't?" **The answer lies in the fact that vitamin B1 is found in the residues that are left when wholegrain rice is polished to make it into white rice. While the PoWs were fed on cheap brown rice, their masters ate the much more expensive white rice. The Japanese quickly realised what was happening and gave the PoWs the white rice instead, after which the POWs developed vitamin B1 deficiency and beriberi.**

What does it do?

First identified by two doctors, Jansen and Donath, way back in 1926, vitamin B1, also known as thiamin, is a member of the vitamin B complex and, like all the vitamins in this group, it is water-soluble. It is a coenzyme needed to convert carbohydrates into the energy that's used by the muscles and needed by the nervous system to enable nerve impulses to travel between the brain and the spinal cord.

Early symptoms of even a slight deficiency may be fatigue, nausea, poor appetite, digestive upsets, muscle weakness, memory loss, poor concentration, depression and irritability. If the deficiency is not rectified by supplements or improved diet, constipation, painful calves, pins and needles, burning sensations in the feet and general debility will follow.

When the deficiency is severe, the result can be the fatal disease beriberi. This is rare in the Western world but is still quite common in places where the staple diet is polished white rice. Beriberi affects the nervous system and mental ability, and also causes muscle weakness, severe water-retention and heart and circulatory problems.

How much do I need?

Although the RDA is only 1.4mg, certain people may need considerably more. If you are pregnant, breastfeeding, are about to have or have just had surgery, or are suffering from any prolonged bouts of stress, you will need around 4mg daily.

DON'T LOSE OUT The most common cause of severe vitamin B1 deficiency in the West is alcohol; excessive amounts prevent absorption of this nutrient. Smoking has a similar effect as do the carbonates and citrates that are used as additives in canned drinks and in many processed foods. Long-term use of antacid remedies and large amounts of coffee or tea can also lower the amount of vitamin B1 that your body can absorb.

On the other hand, eating foods that are rich in vitamin C – fruits and vegetables for example – at the same time as eating sources of vitamin B1 can improve absorption and, like most B vitamins, B1 works best when combined with other members of the group.

Where do I get it?

Fish roes, especially cod, most meats but particularly pork, and legumes like peas and beans are all good sources. Nuts and wholegrain cereals provide modest amounts.

Who needs extra?

Anyone on a high-carbohydrate diet, especially athletes, regular exercisers and people with physically active jobs, would benefit from a supplement of 10mg daily, while supplements of up to 50mg a day may help to improve memory and reduce sugar cravings, especially those associated with Pre-Menstrual Syndrome (PMS). There's even evidence to show that up to a maximum dose of 50mg per day might slow the progression of Alzheimer's Disease. Conditions directly affecting the nervous system, such as multiple sclerosis, trigeminal neuralgia, peripheral neuritis and Bell's Palsey may also benefit from up to a maximum dose of 50mg per day.

Supplements

These are readily available. For a maintenance dose take 2mg daily.

BEST FOOD SOURCES

APPROXIMATE PERCENTAGE OF DAILY ADULT NEEDS IN AN AVERAGE PORTION

ROAST PORK 110%

COD'S ROE 100%

FRESH PEAS 50%

PEANUTS 40%

WHEATGERM 30%

BRAZIL NUTS 25%

WHOLEMEAL BREAD (2 SLICES) 20%

PORRIDGE OR OATMEAL 5%

DID YOU KNOW THAT? A combination of poor diet and over-cooking can lead to mild deficiency, for vitamin B1 is easily destroyed by too much cooking – it leaches into the cooking water and then usually gets thrown away – and by sulphur dioxide, which is widely used as a preservative in food processing. Alkaline products like baking powder also break vitamin B1 down.

DEFICIENCY SYMPTOMS Fatigue • Muscle wasting • Pins and needles • Personality changes

"If you've got cracks at the corners of your mouth and a sore red tongue," **then you're probably deficient in vitamin B2.**

What does it do?

Vitamin B2, otherwise known as riboflavin, is involved in the processes that convert your food into the energy that every cell in your body has to have in order to function. It's also important for normal growth and development in babies and children and helps to keep everyone's mucous linings of the lungs, mouth and digestive system in good working order. Your nervous system also needs vitamin B2 for protection and to transmit vital nerve messages. Healthy nails, skin and hair also require adequate amounts of vitamin B2 and it's also thought to be necessary for good vision, fertility and preventing stress.

How much do I need?

The RDA is 1.3mg; 1.4mg during pregnancy; 1.6mg if you're breastfeeding.

Where do I get it?

In principle it's best to get vitamin B2 from your food but processed foods tend to be short of it so try to eat plenty of good fresh produce. For the most efficient absorption it's best to have vitamin B2 together with some of the other B vitamins: in nature the best food sources also contain a spread of the vitamin B complex.

Who needs extra?

People who need extra vitamin B2 are pregnant or breastfeeding women, heavy drinkers, anyone who has a chronic illness or has recently had surgery, people with physically

DON'T LOSE OUT There are some medicines that interfere with the amount of vitamin B2 your body absorbs, especially the tricyclic antidepressants, antimalarials and some chemotherapy treatments. If you're taking any of these type of drugs, speak to your doctor about taking extra vitamin B2. The same is true for all smokers, for women on the pill or on HRT, or if you drink large amounts of alcohol since that, also, interferes with absorption.

BEST FOOD SOURCES

APPROXIMATE PERCENTAGE OF DAILY ADULT NEEDS IN AN AVERAGE PORTION

FRIED LAMB'S LIVER 650%
YEAST EXTRACT (1 TSP) 80%
VEGETABLE PÂTÉ 80%
MUESLI 55%
GREEK SHEEP'S YOGHURT 50%
EGGS (1 LARGE) 30%
ALMONDS 30%
SOFT GOAT CHEESE 30%
WHEATGERM 15%

demanding jobs or who play serious sport, anyone with long-term bowel disease and women on hormone replacement therapy (HRT) or the pill.

Vegans are at risk of deficiency and if you are undergoing prolonged periods of stress you are likely to lose a lot of vitamin B2. And obviously, if you're on any form of restricted diet for either health or weight reasons, you probably aren't getting enough either.

Supplements

As your body doesn't store vitamin B2 you shouldn't take more than 2mg daily as a supplement: any surplus is excreted in the urine, which turns a dark yellow colour with large doses. Zinc or iron supplements should be taken at opposite ends of the day to vitamin B2.

DEFICIENCY SYMPTOMS Sore tongue • Cracked lips • Poor concentration • Cataracts • Itchy eyes

"There are two essential enzymes, NAD and NADP, which are required by the body for the conversion of food into energy. **Without niacin these enzymes cannot be produced and the food/energy conversion process is compromised.**

What does it do?

Niacin, vitamin B3 or nicotinic acid is part of the vitamin B complex. It is vital for converting food into energy so the more active you are, the more you need. It's also essential for healthy skin, nerves and digestion.

How much do I need?

The RDA is 16–18mg though ideally aim for around 25mg from food and take 50mg as a supplement when necessary.

Where do I get it?

The body synthesises niacin from the amino acid tryptophan, present in most foods apart from sugars, fats and spirit-based alcoholic drinks. High-protein foods are the best source, while fruits contain very little.

Who needs extra?

Extra amounts of niacin may be needed by older people with poor digestion, those on very low-calorie diets or with eating disorders, diabetics, pregnant or breastfeeding women, anyone who's had part of their stomach or digestive tract removed and people with raised cholesterol. Those with acne, rosacea, tinnitus, chilblains, varicose veins, migraine and depression may all be helped, too.

Supplements

Deficiency symptoms and full-blown pellagra all start improving within a day or two of taking supplements.

DON'T LOSE OUT Absorption of niacin may be reduced by too much alcohol, by long-term antibiotic treatment, by drugs for the treatment of Parkinson's disease, by the contraceptive pill, by smoking and by high levels of physical activity.

DID YOU KNOW THAT? Since maize is the only cereal that does not contain tryptophan, where maize is a staple food, the deficiency disease pellagra – from the Italian 'pella' for skin and 'agra' meaning rough – is common. It is a condition that affects the hands, face and neck.

BEST FOOD SOURCES

APPROXIMATE PERCENTAGE OF DAILY ADULT NEEDS IN AN AVERAGE PORTION

LAMB'S LIVER 170%
ROAST CHICKEN 130%
GRILLED SALMON 120%
SARDINES 65%
PEANUTS 55%
LEAN BEEFSTEAK 50%
MUESLI 50%
WHOLEMEAL BREAD (2 SLICES) 25%

DEFICIENCY SYMPTOMS Sore tongue and mouth • Dry skin • Fatigue • Irritability • Diarrhoea • Giddiness

"You only need 2mg of vitamin B6 a day but in spite of this nutrient being found in a large range of foods, it's quite common for people, especially women, to get less than the recommended amount in their diet. **Yet more importantly, larger intakes than the RDA can result in the reduction, prevention and even cure of a number of health problems.**

What does it do?

Vitamin B6, also known as pyridoxine, is essential for many of the chemical reactions that enable the body to use proteins and amino acids. It has a role in normal brain function, is important for healthy red blood cells and for the body's correct chemical balance. Vitamin B6 also plays a part in the system responsible for the excretion of water from the body and the mechanism that produces energy from food. It protects against some types of anaemia and helps in the control of stress.

Thanks to its effect on hormone balance, its best known function is in the relief of Pre-Menstrual Syndrome (PMS). It eases fluid retention, prevents mood swings and can dramatically improve depression and reduce episodes of aggressive behaviour in the days leading up to a period.

Another condition that responds well to B6 therapy is Carpal Tunnel Syndrome. This type of Repetitive Strain Injury (RSI) problem (it can also occur spontaneously during pregnancy) affects the nerves of the hand as they pass through the tissues of the wrist and can cause severe burning, tingling and loss of sensation in the fingers. Doctors often recommend surgery but I would suggest trying at least a one-month course of vitamin B6 first.

How much do I need?

The RDA is 1.3–2mg, depending on circumstances.

Where do I get it?

Liver, poultry, oily fish like herrings, bananas and peanuts are all good sources.

Who needs extra?

Your body can't store vitamin B6 and it's excreted the same day so it's essential to ensure you have it regularly. Anyone on a high-protein diet, vegans, vegetarians, the elderly, women taking the pill or HRT, women with premenstrual and menopausal symptoms, alcoholics and people with very low calorie

DON'T GO TO EXTREMES Excessive amounts of vitamin B6 can cause neurological problems including numbness of the hands and feet, clumsiness and general inflammation of the nerves. If this happens, stop taking the supplement immediately. These side effects have been reported at doses as low as 50mg a day, but in general 250mg daily is safe.

intakes for any reason, needs a B6 supplement. This is also true if you're taking penicillin, immuno-suppressants or if you smoke.

Supplements

The safe upper limit is 250mg daily. I recommend starting at a dose of 50–100mg a day, which is fine for the majority of people.

DID YOU KNOW THAT? Research has shown that many people who suffer chronic depression have low levels of vitamin B6 circulating in their blood and just as Naturopaths have long recommended this supplement for PMS, my colleagues and I would certainly advise it for anyone with long-term depression. The whole of the central and peripheral nervous system needs adequate supplies of the B vitamins and this group of nutrients is also helpful for the relief of chronic fatigue and Tired All The Time syndrome. In these instances a B complex tablet, which includes B6, is an invaluable part of holistic treatment.

There is also anecdotal evidence from alternative practitioners that vitamin B6 may help infertility, weight loss, morning sickness, migraine and excessive milk production in nursing mothers – but during pregnancy and breastfeeding do not take more than 25mg a day or you risk overdosing your baby.

BEST FOOD SOURCES

APPROXIMATE PERCENTAGE OF DAILY ADULT NEEDS IN AN AVERAGE PORTION

CALVES' LIVER 90%

GRILLED HERRING 60%

BAKED POTATO WITH SKIN 50%

TURKEY 50%

WHEATGERM 35%

BANANA 15%

RAW CAULIFLOWER 15%

FRESH PEANUTS 10%

WHOLEMEAL BREAD (2 SLICES) 10%

DEFICIENCY SYMPTOMS PMS • Irritability • Depression • Sore tongue

"Enough vitamin B12 is stored in your liver to last around two years but unless you continually replace what you're using, the reserve runs out, your bone marrow doesn't make enough healthy blood cells and the consequence is anaemia." **A varied diet is your best guarantee of getting this essential nutrient.**

What does it do?

Vitamin B12 is part of the vitamin B complex and is essential to prevent pernicious anaemia.

In order for the body to utilise vitamin B12 a substance called 'intrinsic factor', produced by the lining of the stomach, is also required. Failure to produce enough 'intrinsic factor' used to be fatal until it was successfully treated

with injections of liquidised raw liver – the richest source of B12, Nowadays the vitamin itself can be injected.

Vitamin B12 is also vital for the production of a fatty substance called myelin, which forms a protective sheath covering all the nerves in the body and is needed for the rapid transmission of nerve impulses. Deficiency of B12 reduces the amount of myelin and the result can be serious neurological problems.

A further function of B12 is that it works with folic acid and so is important for the normal growth of babies during pregnancy.

How much do I need?

Although the UK RDA is low at 1mcg (the American RDA is 2.4–2.8mcg), it's sensible to aim for 2mcg for children aged under 12, 3mcg for over-12s and 5mcg for adults.

Where do I get it?

It is easy to get the necessary vitamin B12 from meat, fish, poultry, eggs, cheese and all animal-based foods. It is absent from virtually all plant foods except yeast extracts and fermented soya products, though it is often added to fortified

DON'T LOSE OUT The contraceptive pill, sleeping pills, some anti-diabetic drugs and excessive amounts of alcohol can all reduce absorption of vitamin B12.

breakfast cereals. For this reason vegetarians and especially vegans should always take a daily supplement of vitamin B12.

Who needs extra?

Vegans, vegetarians (see above), anyone who's lost blood through trauma or surgery, anyone taking sleeping pills, contraceptives, cholesterol-lowering drugs, or oral diabetic drugs and alcoholics all need extra. It's possible that extra B12 may help protect diabetics from nerve damage and it's certainly a useful supplement for anyone suffering from chronic fatigue.

Supplements

As B12 is best absorbed in the presence of other vitamins it's more effective as part of a multi-vitamin and mineral supplement than taken on its own, unless prescribed by your health practitioner.

BEST FOOD SOURCES

APPROXIMATE PERCENTAGE OF DAILY ADULT NEEDS IN AN AVERAGE PORTION

LIVER 800%

DUCK 555%

GRILLED PLAICE 260%

SCRAMBLED EGGS (2) 250%

ROAST BEEF SANDWICH 150%

SOYA CHEESE 125%

VEGETARIAN CHEDDAR CHEESE 60%

CAMEMBERT CHEESE 45%

YEAST EXTRACT (1 TSP) 5%

DEFICIENCY SYMPTOMS Fatigue • Palor • Poor memory and concentration • Mood swings • Breathlessness

FOLIC ACID

"Is folic acid the ultimate functional food component for disease prevention?" **This was the question asked by Mark Lucock, Lecturer in Human Nutrition at the University of Newcastle in Australia, writing in the British Medical Journal on 24 January 2004. Antioxidants, vitamin C, cholesterol-lowering margarines, red wine, green tea, tomatoes and soya beans – these are all the great buzz words in current nutritional research, but they all pale into insignificance when compared with the simple B vitamin, folic acid.**

What does it do?

Folic acid is found in a wide variety of foods and is best known for its ability to prevent spina bifida in newborn babies. It's the first three months of pregnancy that are crucial in the development of the baby's spine and that is when having adequate folic acid is so important to an expectant mother.

Folic acid is also well known for the part it plays in the body's production of healthy red blood cells, without which we become anaemic. As long ago as 1931, yeast extracts were used to prevent anaemia of late pregnancy in Indian women, though folic acid wasn't identified as the key factor until many years later.

The latest research also shows that folic acid plays a key role in the prevention of heart disease. In 1997, an analysis of 4000 patients in 27 studies demonstrated the link between low levels of folic acid in the diet leading to raised blood levels of homocysteine. High levels of this naturally occurring chemical are known to increase the risk of fatal heart attacks and diseases of the brain, such as Alzheimer's Disease, and of the arteries. Raised blood levels of homocysteine also become more common in post-menopausal women or in women whose periods have stopped for some other reason, so it's extremely important for any woman in this category to make sure that she eats a regular selection of folic-acid rich foods.

And last but not least, there are also known links between folic-acid deficiency and leukaemia, and some types of bowel cancer.

How much do I need?

The average adult needs 200mcg of folic acid daily. Double that amount is essential during the early stages of pregnancy.

Where do I get it?

Despite the fact that folic acid is found in a wide variety of foods, few people manage to get the amount they need each day from their diet.

DON'T LOSE OUT You should be aware that alcohol, the contraceptive pill, aspirin, medicines for Type II diabetes (see page 54) and anti-inflammatory drugs can all interfere with absorption of folic acid and that folic acid itself can interfere with medicine taken for epilepsy; epileptics should consult their doctor before taking folic acid supplements.

It's obvious that it's important for the whole population to increase its overall intake of folic acid and it's particularly important for senior citizens. Indeed, there's now much talk of adding folic acid to bread-making flour, as has already been done in the USA. But take care. It's more than 2500 years since Hippocrates wrote, 'Let food be thy medicine and medicine be thy food', and I don't think he was talking about pills or functional foods such as cholesterol-lowering margarines and yoghurts.

Essential though it may be to sometimes use low-dose supplements to avoid folic-acid deficiencies, it's even more essential that everybody gets folic acid in their food, because with it they will also consume all the accompanying nutrients that nature intended us to eat.

Supplements

Supplements of folic acid are available and, indeed, for anyone suffering from anaemia, a supplement of 200mcg a day can soon help to improve the condition and will help overcome their symptoms of severe tiredness.

It's not advisable though to take large amounts of folic acid – more than 500mcg daily – for long periods without discussing this with your general practitioner, since at these levels it may mask the symptoms of pernicious anaemia.

Take folic acid supplements together with food as this improves absorption.

BEST FOOD SOURCES

APPROXIMATE PERCENTAGE OF DAILY ADULT NEEDS IN AN AVERAGE PORTION

CHICKEN LIVER 400%
OX LIVER 200%
LAMB 120%
BEETROOT JUICE 120%
BRUSSELS SPROUTS 100%
BLACK-EYE BEANS 100%
BREAKFAST CEREALS 55%
BEETROOT 50%
SPINACH 30%
PEANUTS, UNSALTED 25%

DEFICIENCY SYMPTOMS Excessive tiredness • Heart disease

VITAMIN C

"The results of a double-blind experiment published in the journal Advances in Therapy clearly show that an increase in daily vitamin C levels " **– provided by the non-acidic ester-c – not only gives the body added protection against colds but also leads to speedier recovery as well as a reduction in the uncomfortable symptoms such as sneezing, coughing and a runny nose.**

What does it do?

Vitamin C, or ascorbic acid, is a water-soluble vitamin and is probably the best known of all the vitamins. One of its key benefits is the way in which it increases the body's natural resistance to infection, especially coughs and colds and flu. It is also a powerful antioxidant, protecting every cell in your body from the damage, like cancer, caused by free radicals, as well as fighting off cold sores and stimulating wound healing after accidents and surgery.

Finally, together with vitamin E (see pages 46–7), it helps to avoid cataract problems and is essential for smokers whose bodies need much more vitamin C.

How much do I need?

It's clear from all the evidence that the body cannot store large amounts of vitamin C so you really do need to get it on a daily basis. The recommended daily intake is 40–70mg but nutrition experts believe that's nowhere near enough to promote the best possible health. US Professor Gladys Block, one of the world's leading experts on health and nutrition, says that she aims to get at least 250mg each day.

Where do I get it?

Vitamin C is famously linked with citrus fruits, particularly limes. In the days of sailing ships, a lack of vitamin C led to the killer disease, scurvy, among the sailors. Once the link between vitamin C and citrus fruits was

DON'T GO TO EXTREMES Regular supplements of 1g or more a day can cause diarrhoea and can increase the risk of kidney stones. Taking 1–2g daily for up to a fortnight when you have a special need is fine, otherwise for long-term use don't exceed 500–1000mg daily.

understood, ships carried barrels of limes for the sailors to eat.

Though vitamin C is the easiest by far of all the nutrients to get in your diet – it's found in virtually every variety of fruit and vegetable – most people barely consume enough each day. You'll get your daily allowance from a glass of orange juice, a kiwi fruit or 90g strawberries. Blackcurrants, papaya, green peppers and all green leafy vegetables are also excellent sources, but for most people a daily supplement is the cheapest and best health insurance they can buy.

Who needs extra?

For people who need an immunity boost, for example before surgery, for anaemics to improve their iron absorption, for speeding wound healing, for athletes, and for anyone in their sixties or routinely taking soluble aspirin to protect their heart, 500–1000mg daily is the optimum level.

It's also important for women taking the pill and for those on long-term antibiotics or steroid drugs to increase their intake of vitamin C both from food and supplements.

Supplements

Available in various forms – soluble, effervescent, chewable, tablets or capsules – either containing straight ascorbic acid or the slightly more expensive but non-acidic ester-c, which is more suitable for anyone with a history of chronic indigestion, hiatus hernia or stomach ulcers.

BEST FOOD SOURCES

APPROXIMATE PERCENTAGE OF DAILY ADULT NEEDS IN AN AVERAGE PORTION

COOKED BLACKCURRANTS 215%
ORANGES 140%
STRAWBERRIES 130%
RAW GREEN PEPPERS 100%
COOKED BROCCOLI 65%
KIWI FRUIT 60%
HOME-MADE COLESLAW 50%

DID YOU KNOW THAT? Vitamin C is best absorbed when eaten with good sources of bioflavanoids. These are a large group of naturally occurring chemicals found in many fruits and vegetables – especially the most brightly coloured ones – and they prevent vitamin C from being destroyed by oxidation. In citrus fruits, for example, bioflavanoids are present in the pith. Absorption of vitamin C is helped even more if you also eat foods containing calcium, for example cheese, yoghurt, milk, nuts and seeds, tofu and canned sardines, and magnesium, found in wholegrain cereals, wholemeal and rye breads and again in nuts and seeds.

DEFICIENCY SYMPTOMS Scurvy • Repeated infections

"Vitamin D deficiency is a serious problem in the UK and the USA **but rather less so in those parts of Europe where people consume much larger quantities of oily fish.**

What does it do?

Vitamin D actually works more like a hormone than a regular vitamin and is the vital key to strong and healthy bones as without it our bodies can't absorb the calcium in our food. The body manufactures its own vitamin D when skin is exposed to ultraviolet light from the sun. The vitamin D formed in this way is stored in the skin, slowly released into the blood and then converted into a hormone-like chemical in the liver and kidneys. This form of vitamin D is especially necessary. If you don't get enough sunshine on your skin – 10–15 minutes a day on arms, legs and face without sun block (early morning or late afternoon sun is perfectly safe) is recommended – and you're not eating sufficient of the vitamin D-rich foods, then you certainly won't maintain strong bones or teeth.

How much do I need?

Generally, 5mcg a day is recommended but 10mcg is a much more sensible target to aim for, especially if you're over 60 and your diet does not include good sources of vitamin D.

Where do I get it?

Few foods contain vitamin D but this fat-soluble nutrient is abundant in oily fish. There are modest amounts in eggs and it is added to margarines. There is no vitamin D in any fruit, vegetables and other plant foods.

Who needs extra?

Those at special risk of having vitamin D deficiency are the elderly, vegetarians, vegans, breastfeeding and pregnant women, and anyone who spends little time outdoors during the summer. The Asian community is often at risk due to their traditional clothing, diet and lifestyle. Anybody in these groups or with a family history or diagnosis of osteoporosis must take a vitamin D supplement.

Supplements

Be careful when using supplements: vitamin D at ten times the daily need can be very toxic to children and 25 times is dangerous for adults. Don't give more than a teaspoon of cod-liver oil to young children each day, or exceed this amount during pregnancy.

DID YOU KNOW THAT? Dark-skinned people need much longer exposure to the sun in order for their body to manufacture significant amounts of vitamin D.

KEY STAGES OF LIFE In childhood, a lack of vitamin D prevents the bones from hardening and causes rickets, a condition that leads to bone deformity, bow legs and disability. A lack of vitamin D in adults results in osteomalacia – softening of the bones. It doesn't matter how much calcium you get from your diet or from supplements; without vitamin D, the end result will almost certainly be osteoporosis, causing loss of height and a greatly increased risk of fractures, especially of the hip and spine.

Vitamin D is also an essential nutrient for women during pregnancy and breastfeeding since the baby depends on its mother's milk to get its own supplies.

BEST FOOD SOURCES

APPROXIMATE PERCENTAGE OF DAILY ADULT NEEDS IN AN AVERAGE PORTION

HERRINGS 240%
FRESH GRILLED SARDINES 150%
SMOKED MACKEREL 120%
GRILLED TROUT 115%
CANNED SARDINES IN TOMATO SAUCE 110%
COD-LIVER OIL (1 TSP) 105%
BOILED EGGS (2) 20%

DEFICIENCY SYMPTOMS Chronic muscle aches and pains • Bone disorders

"Until fairly recently the role of vitamin E was poorly understood. Animal studies had shown that removing this nutrient from the diet caused infertility but there was no comparable human evidence." **It's now understood what a powerful protective role this vitamin has. Epidemiological studies have revealed startling links between vitamin E and the reduced incidence of heart and circulatory disease and some forms of cancer in populations who maintain a consistently high intake.**

What does it do?

Vitamin E is one of the most powerful natural antioxidants and is essential for protecting the body from the damage done by free radicals. It's especially important for cell walls, skin, muscles, nerves, blood vessels and the heart. Some long-term studies have shown that its heart-protective benefits are greater when high intakes of vitamin E come from food rather than just supplements. This is probably because foods that are rich in vitamin E also tend to be those with high levels of other natural antioxidants.

Vitamin E can also protect against some forms of cancer, especially of the lung and, together with vitamin C, may be useful in the treatment of cataracts. Vitamin E is also believed to be important for fertility; high doses have been shown to increase the number of sperm in men with a low sperm count.

How much do I need?

Although this fat-soluble vitamin is found in a wide selection of foods, many people don't get the optimum 10mg a day intake from their normal diets. Generally the body builds up its

DON'T LOSE OUT Taking the contraceptive pill, environmental pollution and the action of the unhealthy trans fats in many margarines can all interfere with vitamin E levels. Cholesterol-lowering drugs can also reduce the body's levels of vitamin E as can excessive iron or copper intakes. For this reason, if you are taking mineral supplements that include iron and copper, you should always wait at least four hours before taking a vitamin E supplement.

own stores of fat-soluble vitamins but vitamin E is an exception; that's why it's especially important to get adequate amounts on a regular basis.

Where do I get it?

There is some vitamin E in all nuts, seeds and vegetable oils, while the richest sources are wheatgerm oil, wheatgerm, hazelnuts, sunflower seeds and avocados.

Supplements

High doses may cause headaches so start with 50mg a day and work up over a two-week period to 200mg. Do not take at the same time as iron supplements as these reduce the availability of vitamin E.

DID YOU KNOW THAT? The body's absorption of vitamin E is increased by vitamin C and the mineral selenium, which means that eating vitamin C-rich foods together with those containing vitamin E helps ensure maximum absorption. Interestingly, many of the nuts and seeds that are rich in vitamin E are also good sources of selenium.

DON'T GO TO EXTREMES High doses of vitamin E – more than 200mg – should not be taken by anyone with high blood pressure or heart disease without advice from their medical practitioner.

BEST FOOD SOURCES

APPROXIMATE PERCENTAGE OF DAILY ADULT NEEDS IN AN AVERAGE PORTION

WHEATGERM OIL 140%
HAZELNUTS 125%
SUNFLOWER SEEDS 90%
BAKED SWEET POTATO 80%
WHEATGERM 55%
RAPESEED OIL 55%
AVOCADO 45%
BLACKBERRIES 35%
TOMATO PURÉE 10%

DEFICIENCY SYMPTOMS Infertility • Loss of libido • Poor stamina • Varicose veins • Piles • Thread veins

> "Optimum levels of biotin come from the gut where bacteria can manufacture up to five times the amount supplied by the diet." **Unfortunately, this 'home-made' biotin is easily lost when gut bacteria are destroyed by antibiotics, sulphonamides or alcohol.**

What does it do?

Most people know that vitamin B is a complex of different vitamins but not many people understand the importance of this one member of the group, biotin, sometimes called vitamin H. This vital nutrient is a coenzyme without which many of the body's essential processes would not be possible.

It plays a key role, along with the other B vitamins, in the breakdown of fats, proteins and carbohydrates, helping to convert them into usable energy. It's also important in the creation of the essential fatty acids (see pages 24–5) that are required for many bodily functions but especially for the protection of nerves and skin as well as the growth of healthy hair.

How much do I need?

100mcg a day should be sufficient for most people's needs, but if you're over 50, then take 150mcg daily. It is not hard to get this from food but more than half will easily be manufactured by the good bacteria in the gut.

Where do I get it?

Biotin is widely distributed in nuts and seeds. There are significant quantities in offal and in whole eggs.

Who needs extra?

Although breast milk contains the essentials needed to establish a healthy colony of gut bacteria (see Don't Lose Out), there's little biotin in it. Breastfed babies who suffer severe

DON'T LOSE OUT It's generally believed that because biotin is so widespread in our food, deficiencies of this vitamin are rare. The orthodox view is that any deficiency normally only occurs in patients being artificially fed by infusion or in people who consume a large number of raw eggs. That is because artificial feeds don't contain biotin and raw egg white contains a substance called avidin, which prevents the body absorbing biotin.

But unfortunately, the average amount supplied by food is 39mcg for men and 26mcg for women, and although this is enough to prevent severe deficiency symptoms, optimum levels are only achieved through what's manufactured by bacteria living in the gut. This can be up to five times the amount supplied by the diet. But it's this 'home-made' biotin which is easily lost when these friendly bacteria are destroyed by antibiotics and sulphonamides, whether prescribed or present in foods like meat, poultry and dairy products, or when they're severely damaged by alcohol. There's also evidence that smoking reduces the absorption of biotin.

diarrhoea may quickly become deficient in this vitamin and can develop extremely dry scaly skin on their face and scalp.

As well as smokers and people whose friendly gut bacteria have been destroyed, anyone on a very restricted diet for medical or weight-loss reasons, strict vegans or careless vegetarians may need a supplement.

Supplements

These are widely available in capsule and tablet form but a supplement is rarely needed as as biotin is so widely available in common foods.

APPROXIMATE PERCENTAGE OF DAILY ADULT NEEDS IN AN AVERAGE PORTION

CHICKEN LIVER 115%

BOILED EGGS (2) 40%

KIDNEY 35%

MIXED NUTS 30%

UNSALTED PEANUTS 25%

ALMONDS 25%

PEANUT BUTTER 15%

DEFICIENCY SYMPTOMS Delayed blood clotting • Unusually heavy periods • Smooth tongue

"Although vitamin K does occur naturally in some foods it's the activity of the good bacteria in the gut that plays a vital role in the production and absorption of this nutrient."

For this reason a diet containing plenty of complex carbohydrates – the food these bacteria require – and a regular input of probiotic bacteria from live yoghurt is vital.

What does it do?

Vitamin K is essential for the normal clotting of blood and, since mother's milk is a poor source, it may be given to newborn babies to make sure their blood can clot properly.

It also plays a major role in bone building and is vital for protection against osteoporosis.

How much do I need?

There's no RDA in the UK but in the USA the recommended daily allowance is 90mcg for women and 120mcg for men. You should aim for 100mcg daily, preferably obtained from your food.

Where do I get it?

Though vitamin K is widely distributed in food, researchers at Tufts University in the USA found that only 50 per cent of people get enough from their diets.

The best food sources are green vegetables, beans, peas and potatoes, while meat, except liver, contains virtually none. Fish-liver oil and

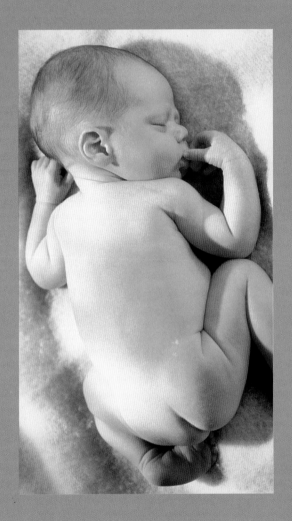

DON'T LOSE OUT Because vitamin K is fat-soluble, long-term use of cholesterol-lowering drugs or functional foods – for example cholesterol-lowering margarines – can deplete levels of vitamin K which the body does not have reserve stores of. This is very rarely a problem as it is abundant in food. Anyone with inflammatory bowel diseases or gallstones may need injections of vitamin K before surgery to prevent hæmorrhage.

safflower and soya-bean oils are reasonable sources and as long as you've got plenty of good bacteria in your gut, you'll make your own.

Who needs extra?

People with chronic inflammatory bowel disease or gallstones, taking prolonged courses of antibiotics or of some of the cholesterol-lowering drugs, or taking high doses of aspirin, as well as women with excessively heavy periods may have problems absorbing this vitamin.

Supplements

I do not advise taking vitamin K supplements except on the specific advice of your own doctor or specialist. It's easy to get it from your food.

BEST FOOD SOURCES

APPROXIMATE PERCENTAGE OF DAILY ADULT NEEDS IN AN AVERAGE PORTION

BROCCOLI 4000%
BRUSSELS SPROUTS 4000%
SPINACH 4000%
DARK GREEN CABBAGE 4000%
LIVER 600%
FRESH PEAS 600%
CARROTS 600%
POTATOES 600%

DEFICIENCY SYMPTOMS Haemorrhage in newborn babies and in adults with gallstones

> "Pantothenic acid is not a name that springs readily to mind when you think about vitamins. You're more likely to see it in cosmetics than on the shelf of the health-food shop."

It is, however, part of the vitamin B complex and is essential for life.

What does it do?

This vitamin is vital for healthy growth and metabolism, plays a key role in your defences against infection, is crucial for supplying energy and is essential for the production of anti-stress hormones.

Because pantothenic acid isn't stored in the body but is found in every single cell, it takes around 12 weeks for tissue levels to fall below the required amount. This is even more likely to happen if your diet consists of processed foods, which may contain less than normal of this nutrient.

How much do I need?

The RDA is 6mg.

DON'T LOSE OUT Pantothenic acid leaches out of vegetables into the cooking water so unless you use the water in soups, stocks or stews, you'll lose the pantothenic acid. Acids such as wine and vinegar, and alkalis such as bicarbonate of soda also reduce the level of pantothenic acid in foods, while around a third is lost when cooking meat. Up to three-quarters disappears during canning but freezing appears to cause little harm.

Where do I get it?

Pantothenic acid is very widely distributed throughout the food chain and is present in large quantities in offal, meat, oily fish, fish roe, nuts, seeds and fresh and dried fruits.

Who needs extra?

Extra pantothenic acid is helpful in situations of prolonged stress, anxiety and tension as it stimulates the body's production of anti-stress hormones. Anyone involved in strenuous physical activity, whether at work or leisure, may need extra supplies.

Supplements

It isn't common for deficiency of this vitamin to occur in isolation; other B vitamins are also likely to be deficient, which is why I would always advise a vitamin B complex supplement. Supplements of pantothenic acid on its own are best taken with professional advice only.

DID YOU KNOW THAT? In animals that are deficient in pantothenic acid the hair turns grey and falls out leaving patches of alopecia. That is why pantothenic acid has been widely used in human hair preparations.

BEST FOOD SOURCES

APPROXIMATE PERCENTAGE OF DAILY ADULT NEEDS IN AN AVERAGE PORTION

CALVES' LIVER 220%

TOFU 60%

FRESH SALMON 50%

TARAMASALATA 50%

BREWER'S YEAST 30%

BEEFSTEAK 30%

AVOCADO 30%

PEANUTS 20%

DEFICIENCY SYMPTOMS Restlessness • Fatigue • Irritability • Burning feet • Mood swings

"Chromium is a comparative newcomer as it's only been recognised as an essential nutrient for about 20 years." **This mineral is very poorly absorbed from food and though marginal intakes in early life may be sufficient for normal body function, the body's stores can be gradually diminished so that by middle age it's common to find mild to moderate deficiencies.**

What does it do?

Chromium – a mineral you only need in tiny amounts – helps control the amount of sugar in your blood and so is part of the body's protection against diabetes. It's involved in the formation of the 'glucose tolerance factor' (GTF) which improves insulin's efficiency.

When the insulin produced by the pancreas and circulating in your bloodstream does not have the effect it should on the control of blood-sugar levels, you develop what is known as insulin resistance. This is what happens in Type II or non-insulin-dependent diabetes (NIDD). In Type I, insulin-dependent diabetes, the patients just stop producing insulin altogether. Triggers for NIDD are a diet that's high in sugars and refined carbohydrates and a lifestyle that excludes exercise, but it's possible that lack of chromium may be another factor.

Chromium also plays an important part in protecting you from heart disease, as well as being a factor in the control of total cholesterol and the balance between good (HDL) and bad (LDL) cholesterols.

How much do I need?

Although there's no official RDA, the American National Research Council suggests an intake of 25–45mcg daily as adequate for adults. Because there's little evidence of overdose risk, there is no upper safe limit recommended in the USA.

Where do I get it?

Brewer's yeast is an excellent source of chromium but it's also found in wholegrain cereals, shellfish, meat, poultry, eggs and in some vegetables.

Who needs extra?

People who are aged over 50, anyone living on a diet consisting predominantly of processed foods, diabetics, people suffering long-term stress and those who are participating in regular amounts of strenuous exercise are all likely to have some degree of chromium deficiency. There is also an increased demand placed on the body during pregnancy and breastfeeding.

DID YOU KNOW THAT? Although chromium is widely found in many foods it's difficult to absorb and only about 0.5 per cent of the amount consumed actually ends up in your body. An average adult contains only 6mg of the mineral. Although this seems a tiny amount, it's critical for good health, vitality and normal life-expectancy.

Supplements

Diabetics, whether using insulin or not, should always consult their doctor before taking chromium supplements as they can interfere with the way your insulin works.

APPROXIMATE PERCENTAGE OF DAILY ADULT NEEDS IN AN AVERAGE PORTION

BEEF 135%

WHOLEMEAL BREAD (2 SLICES) 65%

SWEET PEPPERS 50%

EGGS (2) 50%

OYSTERS (1) 40%

BREWER'S YEAST 35%

MIXED SHELLED NUTS 25%

CHICKEN 20%

DRIED BEANS, COOKED 20%

DEFICIENCY SYMPTOMS Tiredness • Sweet cravings • Irritability • Poor concentration

PHOSPHOROUS

"Phosphorus is one of the most abundant of minerals and is widely distributed in almost all foods. Dietary deficiency is virtually unknown other than in very extreme circumstances." **Tonic preparations containing phosphorus have long been a popular proprietary medicine but almost certainly of very little value, as a piece of cheese or a bowl of mussels will provide just as much and in a more easily absorbed state.**

What does it do?

Phosphorus is an essential mineral and with calcium forms calcium phosphate, vital for teeth and bones. It is also needed for the production of energy, which is released at times of extra physical or mental exertion.

How much do I need?

The RDA for adults is 800mg.

Where do I get it?

All foods except fats and sugars supply some phosphorus but those with calcium and protein too, like meat, fish, eggs, milk and cheese, are the richest sources.

Who needs extra?

Severe inflammatory bowel problems like Crohn's disease, coeliac disease and colitis can reduce absorption of many nutrients, including phosphorus and, of course, anorexia nervosa and other eating disorders present problems too. Alcoholics are yet another group of people who are at risk of having phosphorus deficiency.

Supplements

It is available as tablets, capsules or liquid preparations, usually in the form of calcium phosphate at a normal dose of 1000–1500mg.

DON'T LOSE OUT Although nearly everyone gets enough phosphorus from their food, there are important exceptions. Long-term use of antacid indigestion remedies can cause severe problems with phosphorus levels as those containing aluminium and magnesium combine with the phosphorus and make it impossible for the body to absorb it. Phosphorus is then drawn from bones which weakens them so severely that walking becomes painful and the risk of osteoporosis and fractures is greatly increased.

BEST FOOD SOURCES

APPROXIMATE PERCENTAGE OF DAILY ADULT
NEEDS IN AN AVERAGE PORTION

WHITEBAIT 135%

CALVES' LIVER 90%

SARDINES IN OLIVE OIL 80%

PRAWNS 65%

MUSSELS 60%

TURKEY 45%

EDAM CHEESE 35%

PLAIN LOW-FAT LIVE YOGHURT 35%

KEY STAGES OF LIFE During
pregnancy and breastfeeding most of a
woman's phosphorus is used to supply the
growing foetus and baby but a normally
healthy pregnancy diet supplies more than
adequate amounts. Babies, toddlers, children
and teenagers all need extra amounts to grow
new cells and produce strong bones. By
adulthood there should be at least 450g
stored in the body, most of it combined with
calcium in the bones.

DEFICIENCY SYMPTOMS Fatigue • Stunted growth • Muscle spasms • Delayed fracture healing

"Women of child-bearing age nearly always have low stores of iron and their levels of iron tend to hover around the low end of acceptable." **In men, if their iron stores are low due to poor eating, any significant blood loss can cause problems. Even gradual loss from bleeding gums, haemorrhoids or anywhere in the gut can cause chronic anaemia. Excessive blood loss through injury or surgery can also have quite dramatic effects. Four teaspoons of blood lost through a nosebleed contains 14mg of iron – a day's requirement for a woman and almost twice the amount needed by men.**

What does it do?

Iron is one of the most important of all the nutrients as without it your body can't make haemoglobin – the substance that gives blood its red colour and that transports oxygen via the blood to every single living cell in the body.

As well as the iron circulating in the blood, there is iron stored in the liver and in other organs to make up for day-to-day variations in the amount of iron in the diet. If you are deficient in iron, the result is anaemia – one of the most common nutritional disorders.

How much do I need?

The RDA of iron is 8.7mg for men and 14.8mg for pre-menopausal women, but because iron is poorly absorbed from most foods, this is set at around 10 times the amount you require.

Where do I get it?

Iron from animal sources is better absorbed than iron from any other foodstuffs and all

iron is better absorbed in the presence of vitamin C, so a glass of fresh orange juice with breakfast and plenty of fresh fruits, vegetables and salads throughout the course of the day

DID YOU KNOW THAT? If you are elderly, you may already be eating a poor diet and if, on top of that, you drink large amounts of strong tea, then beware. The tannins in tea make it even more difficult for your body to extract iron from your food.

can make a substantial difference to the levels of iron in the blood.

Wholegrain cereals, peas, beans and cocoa contain plenty of iron but this is poorly absorbed because they also have high levels of phytates which combine with the iron and so reduce the amount you can get. Bran and high-bran cereals act in the same way. And although spinach is a very rich source of iron you'd have to eat a kilo to get as much of the mineral as you would from 100g of beef.

Who needs extra?

Women need twice as much as men to compensate for their monthly blood loss and they need even more during pregnancy to ensure that enough is passed to the baby and to make sure that they have enough stored in preparation for breastfeeding.

Supplements

A variety of iron supplements are available though some, particularly ferrous sulphate, can cause constipation. Natural supplements like ferrous gluconate are less likely to cause problems. There are even some iron-rich mineral waters on the market. These are particularly beneficial as the iron is already dissolved in the water, making it unlikely to cause any digestive upsets.

Do not exceed 15mg per day without professional advice and if you think you may be anaemic, it is important to see your GP to establish the underlying cause.

BEST FOOD SOURCES

APPROXIMATE PERCENTAGE OF DAILY ADULT NEEDS IN AN AVERAGE PORTION

GRILLED LAMB'S LIVER 115%

MUSSELS 100%

PHEASANT 70%

BALTI* VEGETABLE CURRY 45%

NORI SEAWEED 35%

SARDINES IN TOMATO SAUCE 35%

GRILLED RUMP STEAK 30%

DRIED FIGS 30%

* Balti dishes are cooked in iron pans and some of the iron is taken up by the food during the cooking process.

KEY STAGES OF LIFE Unfortunately most women of child-bearing age and 40 per cent of school children do not get enough iron from their food.

DEFICIENCY SYMPTOMS Fatigue • Hair loss • Palor • Headaches • Shortness of breath

"Of all the minerals, potassium is probably the least understood by the general public, yet it is absolutely essential to life itself. **It maintains the balance between acids and alkalis in all the cells and body fluids and even a small upset in this balance can mean the difference between life and death.**

What does it do?

As well as balancing the body's acids and alkalis, potassium plays a key role in the transmission of nerve impulses through the body and in preventing calcium from being lost in the urine. Its other major function is to promote muscle activity and prevent cramp, and it's in this area that most people will have heard about it.

How much do I need?

The average adult needs 3500mg of potassium a day.

Where do I get it?

Potassium is found in all fruits and vegetables, as well as instant coffee and red wine.

Supplements

If you have high blood pressure, irregular heart rhythms or are at risk of a stroke or a heart attack you may need to take extra supplements of potassium – 2000–3000mg per day are adequate for most people. Supplements are also effective in preventing kidney stones in people who excrete excessive amounts of calcium in their urine.

DON'T LOSE OUT Excessive consumption of sodium from salt in any form, too much alcohol, taking water tablets (diuretics) and cortisone medication can all reduce your levels of potassium. Similarly, blood loss, chronic diarrhoea or vomiting, diabetes, kidney disease or prolonged use of laxatives can all cause potassium deficiency and this can be a particular worry in older people as they tend to have lower intakes of most nutrients to begin with.

DID YOU KNOW THAT? Until quite recently the common perception was that cramp is caused by salt lost through sweating. Athletes have always been plagued by cramp and by the fear of getting it at crucial moments and that is why so many athletes used to take salt tablets. Even holidaymakers packed them in their holiday first-aid kits in case they got cramp trying to get off the sun lounger. But it's now understood that not only are salt tablets ineffective in the relief or prevention of cramp, but they also increase the risk of high blood pressure, strokes and heart disease. Moreover, excessive salt intake causes oedema – swelling of the hands, feet and legs due to fluid retention.

Nowadays, footballers and all sorts of other professional athletes pack bananas in their sports bags and you may often see tennis players munching on bananas in the middle of a match. I take much of the credit for the switch from salt tablets to bananas; I used to treat many of the world's leading tennis players and I advised them all to throw away the salt tablets and eat bananas instead. These, I told them, would supply them with easily digestible carbohydrates to give them energy as well as loads of potassium to prevent cramp and to keep their muscles working properly.

BEST FOOD SOURCES

APPROXIMATE PERCENTAGE OF DAILY ADULT NEEDS IN AN AVERAGE PORTION

BAKED POTATOES IN THEIR SKIN 50%
STIR-FRY VEGETABLES (courgette, Chinese cabbage, leek, onion, garlic and spinach) 30%
GRILLED CHICKEN BREAST 30%
DRIED APRICOTS 25%
ALMONDS 25%
READY-TO-EAT PRUNES 20%
DRY ROASTED PEANUTS 20%
TOMATO PURÉE 10%
BANANAS 5%

DEFICIENCY SYMPTOMS Disorientation • Confusion • Depression

"Selenium is a trace mineral, which means the body only needs tiny amounts each day, but a lack of selenium could be catastrophic. There is controversy around the minimum daily requirements, but most experts agree that 70mcg is the minimum that men require." **The average British person only gets around 30mcg, half what they were getting 20 years ago. This has serious implications for their health.**

What does it do?

As well as being a trace mineral, selenium is one of the major antioxidants, protecting against many toxic chemicals by combining with them and aiding their removal from the body. It is also vital for the prevention of heart disease, is part of the body's general defence mechanism and is involved in the function of the natural enzymes that regulate many of our bodily functions, including blood clotting and the protection of DNA – our genetic blueprint.

Selenium deficiency is a major factor in the development of prostate cancer in men, while cancers of the lung and bowel are also thought to be associated with low selenium intake.

How much do I need?

The minimum daily requirement is 70mcg to protect men from prostate cancer. I think that women need the same for heart protection.

Where do I get it?

Generally speaking, organically produced food contains higher levels of selenium than other food. The amount of selenium that ends up in it depends firstly on how much there was in the soil where the food was grown or on which the livestock grazed, and secondly on the amount of processing the food has been subjected to. Canada and North America have high levels of selenium in the soil, while in Europe levels are much lower. In the UK, therefore, selenium intake has dropped since the country switched from eating bread made from Canadian and North American wheat flour to bread made from European wheat flour. What's more, the British diet has become more and more reliant on processed selenium-deficient foods. As a result, virtually everyone in the UK now needs to increase their intake of this vital mineral.

DID YOU KNOW THAT? There is an area of China where deaths from heart disease among young men reached alarming proportions. It was known that the soil in this region contained virtually no selenium and a study began in which half the young men were given a supplement and the other half a placebo. Within six months the difference between life and death was so dramatic that the study was abandoned and all the young men were given a daily selenium supplement.

Who needs extra?

Other people who may need a selenium supplement include smokers, anyone with a family history of heart disease or any form of cancer, people with very poor diets, vegans or vegetarians who don't pay attention to their nutrition, and any man with prostate problems, poor fertility or a history of prostate cancer in the family.

In addition, a supplement may be beneficial if your job involves working with toxic chemicals, toxic fumes or pesticides, for example hairdressing, dry cleaning, film processing and many industrial processes.

Supplements

The mineral is best absorbed in the presence of vitamins A, C and E but do not exceed a daily dose of 200mcg. Selenium is present in most multi-vitamin and mineral pills. Side effects have been observed with total intakes (from food and supplements) above 750mcg.

BEST FOOD SOURCES

APPROXIMATE PERCENTAGE OF DAILY ADULT NEEDS IN AN AVERAGE PORTION

BRAZIL NUTS (PER NUT) 220%

STEAK AND KIDNEY PIE 195%

OILY FISH (HERRING, MACKEREL, KIPPERS) 140%

TUNA CANNED IN OIL 130%

MIXED NUTS & RAISINS 120%

SHRIMPS 70%

WHOLEMEAL BREAD (2 SLICES) 20%

SUNFLOWER SEEDS 10%

MUSHROOMS 10%

DEFICIENCY SYMPTOMS Infertility • Prostate problems • Heart disease • Muscle pain

"Though people may scoff, one of the best known aphrodisiacs of folklore is the oyster, an extremely rich source of zinc. **Casanova reputedly ate up to 70 a day and often enjoyed them in the bath with his latest conquest.**

In addition, zinc is vital for children's growth, wound healing, insulin production and natural resistance to infection. It is also essential for taste and smell and so for the creation of a good appetite. Zinc deficiency may cause anorexia nervosa. Sadly, even in severe cases of anorexia, zinc supplements are seldom advocated by doctors but this simple and inexpensive solution could help these unfortunate people get on the road to recovery.

Brittle nails, especially with white flecks, are nearly always attributed to a lack of calcium. In fact, there's very little calcium in nails and the most common cause is lack of zinc.

What does it do?

Zinc is a greatly ignored trace element. It is essential for healthy sex organs and reproduction and without adequate supplies, men can't produce sufficient sperm and may become infertile. Men's prostate health is also dependent on adequate supplies: a deficiency, especially when combined with selenium deficiency, can lead to enlargement of the prostate and a greater risk of prostate cancer.

How much do I need?

The UK RDA is 7mg for women and 9.5mg for men. I believe it should be more in line with the American RDA of 8–13mg for women and 11mg for men.

Where do I get it?

Meat, shellfish, fish, cheese and eggs are all good sources of zinc. Although wholemeal bread, nuts, wholegrains and some vegetables

DON'T LOSE OUT Taking the contraceptive pill, long-term use of tetracycline, often prescribed for acne, and some antidepressants reduce the body's absorption of zinc. As well as the deficiency symptoms listed, this may cause hyperactivity, retarded growth and damaged hair and nails.

BEST FOOD SOURCES

APPROXIMATE PERCENTAGE OF DAILY ADULT NEEDS IN AN AVERAGE PORTION

CALVES' LIVER 185%
OYSTERS (6) 140%
ROAST BEEF 60%
CRAB 35%
SARDINES 30%
PUMPKIN SEEDS 20%
EGGS (2) 20%
CHEESE 10%

contain reasonable amounts, it's difficult for the body to extract much of it because these foods also contain other chemicals like phytates and oxalic acid, which hinder absorption.

Who needs extra?

As there are no readily available stores in the body to make up for fluctuations in daily consumption, vegetarians and vegans may be seriously short of zinc. This can also be true of children and nursing mothers who both need extra supplies – children for growth and repair of damaged cells and nursing mothers to ensure an adequate amount of zinc in their breast milk.

Supplements

Supplements are available as tablets and also as lozenges where it's combined with vitamin C.

DEFICIENCY SYMPTOMS Acne • PMS • Post-natal depression • Loss of appetite • Slow wound healing

CALCIUM

"The modern obsession with low-fat diets means that many people, especially women and their daughters, have given up eating cheese." **There is also a growing trend to encourage women to believe that they are allergic to dairy products, and there are also the anti-dairy-food extremists who promulgate misleading and scientifically incorrect stories that link dairy foods to cancer. All of this combines to put the calcium status of women in great jeopardy.**

What does it do?

Calcium is vital for bones and teeth and even more important during pregnancy, breastfeeding, childhood and the teens. Older women are at risk of osteoporosis, caused by too little calcium in the diet and poor absorption. Calcium also plays a role in relieving PMS, helps to prevent muscle cramps and is important for heart health, blood clotting and blood pressure.

How much do I need?

The UK RDA of 700–1000mg is far too low and I believe should be closer to the American 1000–1300mg spread.

Where do I get it?

Dairy products contain the most easily absorbed calcium. A glass of milk, a carton of

DID YOU KNOW THAT? One in 12 men will get osteoporosis. Many men now avoid cheese as they believe that the fat content increases their risk of heart disease. Unfortunately, they continue to smoke and eat high-fat convenience foods, especially if they're away from home. The result is their hearts don't benefit, their cholesterol levels don't drop but their bones get weaker.

yoghurt and 60g of cheese provide your daily needs. Also eat plenty of canned sardines – together with the bones – lots of greens and dried fruit, nuts, beans, watercress and parsley. Your body also needs sunlight to make vitamin D (see pages 44–5), without which it can't

DON'T LOSE OUT Some vegetables like spinach and beet greens contain oxalic acid, which prevents the absorption of calcium, while wholegrain cereals, nuts and pulses contain phytic acid, which can also interfere with calcium absorption. For the same reason, sprinkling bran over your breakfast cereal will reduce the calcium you absorb from the milk.

But the worst foods are colas and other fizzy drinks. These contain phosphoric acid, which seriously increases the amount of calcium that the body eliminates.

APPROXIMATE PERCENTAGE OF DAILY ADULT
NEEDS IN AN AVERAGE PORTION

SEMI-SKIMMED MILK 90%

HARD CHEESE 70%

TOFU 70%

CANNED SARDINES 60%

SEAWEED 60%

YOGHURT 35%

FIGS 30%

SESAME SEEDS 15%

ALMONDS 15%

absorb the calcium, so get into the great outdoors.
Oily fish, is the best food source of D.

Who needs extra?

As well as people at certain keys stages of life (see
right) who should watch their diet and lifestyle,
calcium supplements are needed by those
suffering from inflammatory bowel diseases like
Crohn's disease, coeliac disease and colitis; these
interfere with the body's absorption of calcium.

Supplements

The cheapest calcium supplements are made from
calcium carbonate but the body can't get much of
the calcium from these products. It's far more
effective to pay a little more for calcium citrate;
your body can extract twice as much of the
mineral from this.

KEY STAGES OF LIFE Bones need
protecting in childhood, so feed your
youngsters lots of calcium-rich foods and
ensure they do sport and get plenty of fresh
air and sunshine.

Calcium is even more important during
pregnancy and nursing. In their thirties,
women must do regular weight-bearing
exercise as well as eat the right food to
maintain strong bones. Tennis, dancing, keep-
fit, walking or even housework will help.

The menopause is another crucial time and
its symptoms are all too obvious. All, that is,
except the symptoms of osteoporosis. Now's
the time for extra calcium with vitamin D.

DEFICIENCY SYMPTOMS Fractures • Cramp • Muscular aches • Uncontrolled twitching of leg muscles

COPPER

> "Copper is not a mineral that is widely discussed or written about yet it is hugely important even though it's only needed in tiny amounts." **Because it's so widespread throughout the food chain dietary deficiency is rare and even the worst diet will include it as small amounts dissolve out of copper piping and into your drinking and cooking water.**

What does it do?

Copper is an essential trace mineral which the body needs for a wide range of everyday functions. It's crucial for the normal growth and development of babies and children and it is a vital component of many of the enzymes that play a part in the body's most important chemical processes, particularly the formation of healthy blood cells, the building of strong bones and the conversion of food into energy. You also need it for healthy nerve development and function and for the creation of melanin – the pigment that colours skin and hair.

Another major function of copper is that it is one of the vital components in the complex process through which the body creates a group of chemicals called phospholipids. These important chemicals are involved in moving fat around the bloodstream and they eventually become part of the structure of individual cells.

There is a rich concentration of phospho-lipids in all nervous tissue where they form part of the myelin sheath that surrounds and protects every nerve. This sheath works like an insulating cover and stops the electric impulses that travel along the nerves from short-circuiting from one nerve fibre to another. This prevents abnormalities of the nervous system and may be part of the mechanism that protects the body from diseases like multiple sclerosis.

The phospholipids are also part of the mechanism that manufactures the enzymes involved with energy-release (see page 56).

How much do I need?

The UK RDA is 1.2mg but you should aim for between 1.5mg and 2mg a day. Most people would get this from eating a varied and well-balanced diet.

Where do I get it?

Copper is present in many different foods but refined cereals, milk, dairy products and eggs contain very little.

DON'T LOSE OUT Alcohol or drug abuse, kidney disease, chronic diarrhoea, long periods of stress, surgery to remove part of the digestive tract or any of the wasting diseases can result in copper deficiency.

In addition, too much uncooked bran, large doses of vitamin C and zinc supplements can all interfere with the absorption of copper, which may then lead to lowered immunity, osteoporosis and an increase in the amount of bad cholesterol in the bloodstream.

Who needs extra?

People on a restricted diet, on repeated low-calorie weight loss diets, with chronic bowel disease, anorexia, bulimia, or any illness that results in poor nutrient absorption may easily become deficient in copper.

Supplements

Most multi-vitamin and mineral pills contain small amounts of copper but you should only take it as a single supplement with professional advice as it can cause toxic side effects at quite small doses.

APPROXIMATE PERCENTAGE OF DAILY ADULT NEEDS IN AN AVERAGE PORTION

LAMB'S LIVER 750%
LOBSTER 80%
TOFU 65%
CASHEW NUTS 50%
SHRIMPS 50%
PEANUTS 30%

KEY STAGES OF LIFE

More copper in the diet is needed during pregnancy and breastfeeding. In the later stages of pregnancy copper passes through the placenta and is stored in the baby's liver. This is because mother's milk does not provide enough and is to make sure that the baby has sufficient to last until weaning. Cow's milk contains even less copper than breast milk so never give it to a baby, though formula milks are fortified. Copper deficiency symptoms in a baby can be diarrhoea, anaemia, bone fractures and failure to grow and gain weight.

DID YOU KNOW THAT?

As copper is a common constituent of many agricultural fungicides and is frequently used on salad crops, you must wash all fresh produce thoroughly before eating. This is extremely important for children as even the supposedly safe legal limit for fungicide residues of 2mg of copper in 100g of food, may be hazardous to a small child.

DEFICIENCY SYMPTOMS Babies: fractures, diarrhoea and anaemia • Adults: fatigue, anaemia and skin problems

MANGANESE

"Manganese is a vitally important essential mineral and it's surprising that general awareness of its importance is so low. It's stored in the pituitary gland, the liver, pancreas, kidneys and bone, and is an essential component in the function of many of the body's enzymes." **One of these enzymes is Superoxide Dismutase (SOD). It destroys the free radicals that attack the heart and cause some cancers.**

What does it do?

Although you only need this mineral in tiny amounts, without it your body can't utilise protein and its ability to manufacture the sex hormones will be reduced. Manganese is also part of the mechanism that builds strong bones, so it lowers the risk of osteoporosis and it also contributes to the creation of thyroid hormones that control our whole metabolism.

In addition, manganese plays a part in blood-sugar chemistry and is needed for the formation and protection of healthy nerve tissue. It also speeds the growth of collagen, which is important for the healing of wounds, and it boosts the immune system.

How much do I need?

There is no official recommended daily allowance for manganese but the minimum requirement is 1.5mg per day, which is lower than the American requirement of 1.6–2.6mg per day. Ideally you should aim for 2.5–5mg and it should all come from your food. Although it should be widely distributed through the foods in your shopping basket, many people do not eat the simple healthy foods that are the best sources.

DON'T LOSE OUT If you're taking large doses of calcium, magnesium or phosphorous, your body's ability to absorb manganese may decline. Similarly, antibiotics, oral contraceptives and excessive alcohol will lower the levels of manganese in your blood.

Where do I get it?

Spinach, wholegrain cereals, nuts and tropical fruits like pineapple are all excellent sources, as well as tea; one cup provides more than a quarter of the daily need.

Who needs extra?

Apart from the essential functions, getting more manganese into your diet is healthy for everyone, and has special benefits for some. For example, it helps control blood-sugar levels for diabetics and can reduce the frequency of epileptic attacks.

Serious athletes, people recovering from severe illness and women who are pregnant or breastfeeding also need extra manganese in their diets, as do people suffering from diabetes or heart disease, both of which can lead to low manganese levels.

Supplements

Not usually available as a single supplement, manganese is normally present in good multi-vitamin and mineral preparations.

BEST FOOD SOURCES

APPROXIMATE PERCENTAGE OF DAILY ADULT NEEDS IN AN AVERAGE PORTION

HAZELNUTS 165%

BLACKBERRIES 140%

PINEAPPLE 100%

OKRA 90%

GRAPE JUICE 60%

WHOLEMEAL BREAD (2 SLICES) 40%

TEA 25%

DEFICIENCY SYMPTOMS Memory loss • Rashes • Unexplained joint pains • Muscle spasms

"Magnesium performs many different functions in the body and deficiencies may be linked to heart disease. **In less industrialised countries magnesium intake is higher because of the absence of processed foods and the rate of heart disease is much lower. Many things affect heart health but magnesium could be one of the factors in the Western epidemic of heart disease that needs to be explored.**

What does it do?

Magnesium is essential for cell structure and for the body's use of calcium and potassium, which make it important for bone growth and heart health. There is evidence from the USA that there are lower levels of magnesium in the heart muscle of patients who are dying of heart disease. Magnesium is also necessary for the transmission of nerve impulses, which is why magnesium deficiency can often affect the heart rhythm.

In addition, it is also good for teeth, playing a part in the process that manufactures protective enamel.

How much do I need?

The RDA is 300mg but American clinical nutritionists advise 450mg.

Where do I get it?

Magnesium is available in virtually all foods with the exception of spirits, fats, white sugar and heavily processed convenience foods. Although wholegrain cereals contain large amounts of the mineral they also contain phytic acid, which interferes with its absorption, so they need to be eaten in fairly generous amounts.

DON'T LOSE OUT You should be aware that if you consume excessive amounts of alcohol, you risk reducing your body's ability to absorb magnesium.

KEY STAGES OF LIFE Women who are pregnant or breastfeeding should aim for more than the US-recommended 450mg a day. It is also important that children and teenagers get enough magnesium-rich foods in their diet as building strong bones at this stage will help protect them against osteoporosis in the future.

Who needs extra?

Since magnesium is widely available in foods, serious deficiencies are rare, but people on very low-calorie diets, those who have been seriously burned, have had other severe injuries, have undergone surgery or have a chronic debilitating disease all need extra magnesium. Similarly, people suffering from digestive problems such as prolonged bouts of diarrhoea, coeliac disease or diabetes should also increase their food-based intake of magnesium.

Supplements

Magnesium on its own should not be taken as a supplement without professional advice.

BEST FOOD SOURCES

APPROXIMATE PERCENTAGE OF DAILY ADULT NEEDS IN AN AVERAGE PORTION

SOYA MINCE 135%

CASHEW NUTS 45%

ALMONDS 45%

WHOLEGRAIN CEREAL 45%

SHRIMPS 40%

MUESLI 35%

OKRA 25%

RYE CRISPBREAD 20%

DID YOU KNOW THAT? Sixty per cent of the magnesium in vegetables ends up in the water when you boil them so if you use the cooking water to make sauces, gravies and soups you'll get the magnesium back. Other cooking methods don't cause such a reduction in the magnesium content but the processing of many convenience foods results in very low magnesium levels. Similarly, while wholegrain cereals, nuts and seeds are well supplied, magnesium is lost when grain is milled to make white flour; as a result, wholemeal bread contains four times more magnesium than white bread.

DEFICIENCY SYMPTOMS Appetite loss • Insomnia • Irregular heart beat • Fatigue

SODIUM

"It's not surprising that sodium in the form of salt was used as money in many cultures as without it humans can't survive. But in the case of this particular mineral, less is very definitely more." **According to Professor Graham MacGregor of CASH – Consensus Action on Salt and Hypertension – in the UK alone, most of the 100,000 people who die each year from strokes and heart disease could have been saved if they had halved their salt intake.**

What does it do?

Sodium is one of the absolutely essential minerals and its main function is to keep a constant level of water in the body tissues and to control the balance between acid and alkali. It also plays a key role in muscle function and in enabling each individual cell to absorb other essential nutrients.

How much do I need?

Your body only needs about 1g of salt a day and the recommended safe amount is a maximum of 5g, though a report from the Institute of Medicine of the American National Academies of Science advises a maximum intake of 1500mg of sodium a day for adults – the equivalent of 3.8g of salt. The average consumption per head per day in the UK is a staggering 12g and is no better in northern Europe or North America.

Where do I get it?

Sodium occurs naturally in many foods so it's virtually impossible to be deficient in it. Unfortunately, it's rather too easy to get it to

DON'T GO TO EXTREMES With global warming and the gradual increase in periods of hot weather, some people seem to think they should be taking extra salt to compensate for the extra sweating. Don't. Just drink more water.

excess. Many children eat more salt a day than the safe amount for adults and 4-year-old children are already showing changes in their veins and arteries similar to those found in the early stages of high blood pressure. That's because many of the high-salt foods are aimed at the children's market – a bowl of cornflakes contains as much salt as a bowl of seawater.

Avoiding the salt in foods is not so easy, though. Many labels list sodium content rather than salt but you can convert this number into grams of salt if you multiply by 2.5. As a rule of thumb, any food that has more than 0.5g of sodium per serving or per 100g is high in salt and should be avoided.

Supplements

Supplements containing sodium are only required in extreme situations and should only be taken on medical advice. Anyone on a very low-salt diet for medical reasons should consult their doctor before increasing their salt consumption.

WORST FOOD SOURCES

This list shows you which foods to avoid – the higher the score, the higher the salt content. To reduce your salt intake, use less convenience food, don't add salt when you cook and always read the food nutritional content labels.

APPROXIMATE PERCENTAGE OF DAILY ADULT NEEDS IN AN AVERAGE PORTION

COOKED BREAKFAST OF FRIED EGGS, BACON, BREAD AND BAKED BEANS 120%

PREPARED CHILLED LASAGNE 90%

BURGER WITH FRIES 80%

HOT DOG 70%

BACON SANDWICH 70%

READY-MADE CHICKEN TIKKA SAUCE 70%

INSTANT SOUPS 60%

DRY ROASTED PEANUTS 30%

SALT AND VINEGAR CRISPS 25%

DEFICIENCY SYMPTOMS Cramp • Headaches • Swelling of the hands and feet • Mental confusion

IODINE

> "Thyroid disorders are one of the most frequently undiagnosed health problems affecting women."

A lack of iodine in the diet can seriously impair the workings of the thyroid gland and many women just don't get enough from their diets.

What does it do?

Iodine is an essential element that is needed in tiny amounts. The body extracts it from food and stores it in the thyroid where it used for the manufacture of the thyroid hormone.

Once its job is done, the remaining iodine is filtered by the kidneys and removed in the urine. If you are losing more iodine than you're getting out of your food, the thyroid gland grows in size to try and capture more of the iodine circulating in your blood. As a result a swelling appears at the front of the neck, where the thyroid gland is situated, causing the medical condition 'goitre'.

How much do I need?

The RDA is 150mcg but few of the diets I analyse contain even 100mcg, and they often contain much less.

Where do I get it?

Fish, shellfish and seaweeds are the only major sources of iodine and the amounts in other foods depend on the iodine content of the soil in which crops are grown or on which animals graze. In Britain goitre used to be known as 'Derbyshire neck' because the Derbyshire soil is severely deficient in iodine and goitre was very common throughout that county.

Some table salt has added iodine though as people become more aware of the dangers of excessive salt this has become a less valuable source. If you use sea salt it will contain some iodine but unfortunately a lot is lost during the drying process. During the winter months milk can be a good source of iodine since most commercial cattle-feed is enriched with iodine to prevent stillbirth and thyroid problems. Much of this added iodine ends up in cow's milk but once the cattle are turned out to graze, the level falls substantially, especially where there is little naturally occurring iodine present in the soil.

Who needs extra?

Anyone who eats very little fish or seafood, or has eliminated dairy products should consider taking a supplement.

DON'T LOSE OUT Both vitamin A and selenium are important for the body's efficient absorption of iodine and if there is not enough of these nutrients in your diet, you may be making too little thyroid hormone.

Certain vegetables such as raw cabbage, spinach, turnips, kale, and some drugs such as lithium antidepressants and medication for diabetes can also interfere with the body's uptake.

Supplements

Only take iodine supplements on the advice of a professional practitioner.

KEY STAGES OF LIFE Iodine is very important during pregnancy for even if the thyroid enlarges in an attempt to produce more hormone, there may still not be enough for the mother and her developing baby. This can result in poor brain development and serious health problems for the child.

DON'T GO TO EXTREMES Too much iodine can overstimulate the thyroid and cause palpitations, anxiety, insomnia and weight loss. For this reason great care should be taken before using kelp supplements as they can contain high levels of iodine, which are seldom analysed or quantified on the package.

BEST FOOD SOURCES

APPROXIMATE PERCENTAGE OF DAILY ADULT NEEDS IN AN AVERAGE PORTION

DRY, RAW KOMBU SEAWEED 88,000%

DRY, RAW WAKAME SEAWEED 3,500%

HADDOCK 300%

MACKEREL 180%

COCKLES 100%

FULL-FAT MILK (WINTER) 80%

LOBSTER 70%

FISH PÂTÉ 60%

EGGS (2) 35%

FULL-FAT MILK (SUMMER) 10%

DEFICIENCY SYMPTOMS Goitre • Lethargy • Weight gain • Cold extremities • Poor concentration

FIBRE

"Most people call dietary fibre 'roughage' but I prefer to think of it as 'smoothage'" **because getting enough of the right type in your daily diet is essential for the smooth passage of digested food through the large bowel. Even those with wheat intolerance can safely use corn, barley, oats, rye and probably spelt flour.**

What does it do?

There are two different types of fibre – insoluble and soluble. Neither is digested by the gastric juices in the stomach but goes straight through into the large bowel. Most is broken down and fermented by the friendly bacteria that live here and the by-products of this fermentation are very important as they protect the bowel lining and also play a role in boosting your natural immunity.

Any insoluble fibre remaining soaks up water from the bowel and swells, thus providing the bulk needed for a healthy stool and to prevent constipation. So lack of insoluble fibre is the most common cause of chronic constipation, and this condition is even worse in people who have a low consumption of liquids. Related problems include piles, bowel cancer, varicose veins, gallstones, diverticulitis, appendicitis and even hiatus hernia.

Soluble fibre is believed to perform the vital role of helping your body get rid of cholesterol, so protecting you from clogged-up arteries, high blood pressure, strokes and heart disease. It is also thought to help reduce the risk of diabetes and obesity.

How much do I need?

Unfortunately the average amount of fibre contained in the average Western diet is only 12g per day – far below the minimum requirement of 18g.

Where do I get it?

You'll find dietary fibre in most plants, whether fruits, seeds, roots, leaves or stems.

DID YOU KNOW THAT? Naturopaths have always advocated a diet rich in all the foods supplying good quantities of soluble and insoluble fibre. In the late 1960s Dr Dennis Burkitt and gastric surgeon Neil Painter began prescribing high-fibre diets for the treatment of diverticulitis. At that time most patients with this painful and debilitating bowel problem had surgery, which provided only temporary relief. The results of the high-fibre diet were so dramatic that within a few years many doctors started recommending bran to patients with bowel problems. As it turns out, this isn't the answer. Bran can cause flatulence, pain and bloating, as well as being a possible trigger of Irritable Bowel Syndrome. It also reduces your absorption of minerals like calcium, iron and zinc. So throw out the bran and bran tablets and just make sure you consume plenty of high-fibre foods.

Insoluble fibre makes up the bulk of cereals like wheat, corn, rice, oats, rye and barley. Wholemeal bread, for example, has three and a half times more fibre than white bread and if you ditch your breakfast cornflakes and have a wholegrain or oat-based cereal instead, you'll get all the benefits of 16 times more fibre in your cereal bowl.

Cabbage, beans, peas and lentils are also excellent sources and dried fruits like apricots, dates, raisins and prunes are extremely fibre-rich, hence their reputation for relieving and preventing constipation.

The soluble fibre pectin, found in many fruits like apples, pears and berries, is also a valuable form of fibre.

Who needs extra?

Anyone with raised cholesterol, heart disease, chronic constipation, diabetes, and a diet low in wholegrain cereals and root vegetables.

BEST FOOD SOURCES

APPROXIMATE PERCENTAGE OF DAILY ADULT NEEDS IN AN AVERAGE PORTION

LENTILS 65%
DRIED APRICOTS 60%
CHICKPEAS 55%
CHAPATTIS 40%
PRUNES 35%
MUESLI 30%
WHOLEMEAL BREAD (2 SLICES) 30%
PORRIDGE OR OATMEAL 30%
PEANUTS 20%

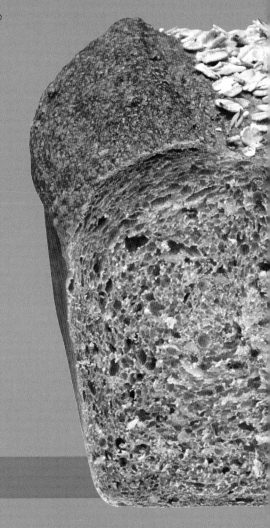

DEFICIENCY SYMPTOMS Constipation • Bloating • IBS

"When American scientists were ordered to stop a large study on Hormone Replacement Therapy because some of the participants were developing serious illnesses like breast cancer, heart disease and strokes, thousands of women rushed to their doctors wanting to know if they should stop taking their HRT pills." **Many of them panicked as they were certain that stopping HRT meant an increased risk of osteoporosis, heart disease and rapid ageing of the skin. But there was no need for panic. The phytoestrogens offer an excellent risk-free alternative.**

What do they do?

Phytoestrogens are hormone-like substances found in plants. Most of them are isoflavones. These natural chemicals function as hormone regulators though they have extremely weak activity compared to synthetic hormones.

All the studies show that where foods containing phytoestrogens are a regular part of the daily diet – for instance in the Far East – women in their middle years suffer fewer menopausal symptoms, much less osteoporosis, a lower incidence of breast cancer and are at a much reduced risk of heart disease.

The benefits of phytoestrogens are cumulative and the earlier the appropriate foods are included in your regular eating, the greater the protection you'll have against the hormone-linked diseases of later years.

But it's never too late. Even if you already have osteoporosis, your bones will benefit from phytoestrogens and if you're suffering from hot flushes, these will improve too.

DID YOU KNOW THAT? As a Naturopath who's spent 40 years advocating the use of safe and natural remedies wherever possible, I've never been a great fan of HRT. It carries known risks and though widely promoted for the prevention of osteoporosis and heart disease after the menopause, I am convinced that for most women the benefits are not justified by the risks.

There's growing scientific evidence that phytoestrogens are a superb alternative and one exciting study has been done with extracts of red clover. Johannes Huber, Professor of Gynaecology at the University of Vienna, worked with 110 post-menopausal women who were not taking HRT but were suffering menopausal symptoms. Over a three-month period, 81 per cent of the patients reported a significant reduction in their symptoms. The results were as good as those achieved with synthetic hormones but of course without any undesirable side effects for, unlike HRT, phytoestrogens don't alter the body's own levels of circulating hormones. This means there is no increased risk of breast cancer, making the phytoestrogens suitable for women who've got breast cancer, have had it or are at risk of getting it.

Where do I get them?

They're present in small quantities in virtually all fruits and vegetables but they occur in much more significant amounts in linseeds, flaxseeds, beans, lentils, chickpeas, wholegrain cereals, nuts and all other seeds. By far the richest food source however is the soya bean and all soya-based products, like soya milk, soya yoghurt, soya cheese and tofu. Soy sauce and manufactured textured vegetable protein are not reliable sources. You'll also find them in some unexpected places – celery, rhubarb, fennel, hops, asparagus and garlic.

Who needs extra?

Any women with period or fertility problems. Before, during and after the menopause. Men with prostate problems.

Supplements

There are now many products on the market which contain concentrated extracts of phytoestrogens. These are mostly made from soya beans, red clover or Mexican yams. These supplements can be extremely effective in the relief of menopausal symptoms and are also valuable as an alternative to female hormone therapy for men with prostate problems. However, regular consumption of all the foods rich in phytoestrogens has a much more profound and protective benefit than waiting until things go wrong and then taking the pills.

BEST FOOD SOURCES

SOYA BEANS
TOFU
SOYA MILK
FLAXSEEDS
ALL DRIED BEANS
LENTILS
NUTS
SEEDS

PHYTOCHEMICALS

"In recent years it's become increasingly evident that certain national diets are healthier than others. Compared with the British or Americans, the French have less heart disease, Greek men live longer, Japanese women have less breast cancer and osteoporosis and the Japanese don't even have a word for hot flushes." **Initially, scientists thought these health benefits came from the extra vitamins and minerals in the diets of the French, Greek and Japanese, but when studies were done in which people on a typical British or American diet were given vitamin and mineral supplements, the results were disappointing.**

The riddle was solved at the Human Nutrition Research Center on Aging at Tufts University in Boston. Here they've been studying antioxidants for some years but Dr. Rob Prior and his colleagues decided to look at the antioxidant properties of whole foods rather than at the antioxidant properties of the individual vitamins and minerals they contain. They discovered that eating the whole foods with the highest levels of antioxidants helps determine how long, how healthy and how free from disease and premature ageing our lives will be. Antioxidants are a group of naturally occurring chemicals that are found in all plant foods. Together with a wide range of other compounds these plant chemicals are known collectively as phytochemicals.

What do they do?

In their natural state, plants contain over 4000 different antioxidant chemicals which protect you against many life-threatening conditions like heart disease, arterial damage and some forms of cancer, as well as protecting your skin against ageing.

How much do I need?

The Tufts researchers discovered that the protective value of antioxidants could be measured in Oxygen Radical Absorption Capacity units – ORACs. The highest protection is achieved when the daily diet provides 5000 ORACs. In the UK and the USA people hardly achieve even 1500 ORAC units a day.

DID YOU KNOW THAT? I have said it before but, according to research by the American Institute for Cancer Research, I am right – food is better than pills. Not only did scientists there discover that eating a mixture of tomatoes and broccoli was more protective against prostate tumour than either food alone, but they also discovered that the combination was much more protective than the isolated phytochemicals extracted from tomatoes and broccoli.

Where do I get them?

These miracle foods are nothing more than simple, everyday, inexpensive fruits and vegetables. Colour is a good guide as the highest ORAC scores are found in deeply coloured produce. Dark green, deep red, purple, blue, yellow and bright orange are the colours to look for. Dark green and bright orange, for example, are an indication of the presence of beta-carotene.

As always in nature, it's the interaction between chemicals in plants that produces this magical benefit so you have to eat the plant foods themselves – you can't get the benefits from a pill. In fact, in February 2004, the international journal Chest showed an increased risk of pneumonia in smokers taking beta-carotene supplements and other studies have shown that supplements of beta-carotene and vitamin E may put people such as smokers at greater risk of cancer.

BEST FOOD SOURCES

APPROXIMATE PERCENTAGE OF DAILY ADULT
NEEDS IN AN AVERAGE PORTION

PRUNES 115%

BLUEBERRIES 50%

STRAWBERRIES 50%

SPINACH 30%

BRUSSELS SPROUTS 30%

PLUMS 30%

BAKED BEANS 20%

GARLIC 20%

FOODS FOR LIFE

As man evolved, and with him a mixed diet, people survived and developed through the millennia. A hundred years ago we didn't know about vitamins, minerals and proteins, yet we thrived and prospered. So why then is everyone now obsessed with the topic of nutrition? It is because, in the 21st century we're reaping a bitter harvest of disease. The prospects for our children and our children's children look bleak.

The way most people eat today undoubtedly places them at higher risk of developing cancer, heart problems and chronic disease and these problems are occurring earlier than ever in the UK, much of northern Europe and throughout the USA. Prostate cancer is seen in younger men, there are growing rates of heart disease in young women, we are seeing an epidemic of osteoporosis, and Type II diabetes (see page 54), traditionally a disease of the later middle years, is now developing in children before they even reach their teens.

But man is nothing if not inventive, and the tide is beginning to turn. Growing numbers of the public are rejecting factory-made food, plastic meals and the burger-and-chips-with-everything mentality. There is no doubt that commercial expediency has forced mass retailers and caterers to at least pay lip-service to the healthy eating messages. Burger chains now offer a token salad bar, breakfast cereal manufacturers are making small reductions in the salt content of their products, and supermarkets are all introducing 'special' healthy eating ranges – but shouldn't the majority of food products on sale be healthy?

Making better food choices

There's now more interest in better ways of eating. Health-food shops, ethnic and vegetarian restaurants, and organic farms, are booming, and we can all benefit. But to do so we must make better choices.

Tragically, making these choices has proved to be an extremely difficult task. In spite of talk of 'food pyramids', 'healthy eating plates', 'five-a-day' campaigns and endless urging by every Western government, our food habits are not changing fast enough and if anything, the march of the fast-food industry is making them worse.

What we need is not only healthy food, but a better balance of the food on our plates. According to the latest research commissioned by the American Institute for Cancer Research (AICR), 72 per cent of American meals are dangerously out of balance. Alarmingly, the worst offenders were in the 18–34 age group, whereas senior citizens were significantly more likely to eat a healthily proportioned meal.

A perfect plate requires one-third complex carbohydrates, one-third fruits and vegetables and a maximum of one-third of animal-based foods. The AICR survey revealed that most Americans tend to get two-thirds of their meal from animal products and only one-third from plant-based foods. The US Department of Agriculture says that a third of the total vegetable consumption of the average American comes from frozen potatoes – mostly eaten as French fries – crisps and iceberg lettuce.

Melanie Polk, director of Nutrition Education at AICR, believes that poultry, fish, dairy and even red meat, have a place on any plate but it's imperative that Americans adjust their eating. 'Every time we sit down to a meal, we are presented with a fresh opportunity to bolster our bodies' natural defences but today, the overwhelming majority of us routinely squander that opportunity.'

The benefits of the Foods for Life

Don't squander *your* opportunities. All the evidence now points irrefutably to the fact that diets which contain the widest variety of the Foods for Life on the following pages offer the lowest risk of chronic disease and cancer. The protective benefits come from the combination of nutrients that these foods contain and any diet which consists of only a narrow selection of plant-based foods eliminates the possibility of these combinations.

If you choose to turn to vegetarianism – and many, especially the young, are making this choice – you can be extremely healthy. In fact, your health is likely to be a great deal better because you are not eating saturated animal fats. In my experience the least healthy vegetarians are those who give up meat in order to avoid cruelty to animals. Whilst I applaud their principles, I worry that many of these vegetarians have little interest in health or nutrition. That's all well and good for the adults, but they should not inflict the cruelty of ill health on their children. So if you choose vegetarianism, you must learn to do it properly. The nutrients that may be lacking from a vegetarian diet are the essential fatty acids from oily fish, and vitamins D and B12, but this is easily overcome with the right foods and, if necessary, with simple supplements.

Whether you are vegetarian or not, if you want the best possible food for life, you need knowledge, so use the information that follows and the recipes in Chapter 4 to create your own nutritious, delicious and optimally healthy plates.

MEAT & POULTRY

Meat of any sort, whether it's beef, pork, lamb, poultry or game, is extremely nutritious. It's an excellent source of protein, a rich provider of the most easily absorbed iron and an effective provider of B vitamins and other minerals.

In the days when all types of meat were a very expensive luxury, the Western approach to its use was closer to that of Far Eastern and other Asian cuisine – small quantities were used to add extra protein and flavour to what were basically vegetable dishes. As the West got richer, people ate meat in ever-increasing quantities until the ideal became a very large piece of meat on your plate with a spoonful or two of vegetables.

The problems of intensive farming

Even this wasn't too bad from the health point of view before the days of intensive farming, but now meat is produced on an enormous industrial scale and profits are increased by the use of antibiotics, growth hormones, very high-energy concentrated artificial feeds and inactive animals. The animals gain weight at such a rate that even lean cuts of meat have fat molecules embedded between the protein fibres where they don't show.

To make matters worse, only free-range grass-fed cattle produce meat containing conjugated linoleic acid (see page 23); the meat that is used in the manufacture of meat products like sausages, pies, pasties and bottom-end-of-the-market burgers is simply unspeakable.

In the USA, UK and most of northern Europe we eat far too much meat. If you want the minimum risk, maximum benefit and almost most importantly of all, the ultimate eating pleasure, then you should eat meat less often and buy the best-quality organic produce you can afford.

Beef

Beef can be cooked and preserved in countless ways. It can be roasted, stewed, braised, fried, pickled, air-dried, sun-dried or salted as well as preserved in the form of salamis and other similar products.

Beef contains trace elements like iodine, manganese, zinc, selenium, nickel and chromium, and a substantial 28g of protein per 100g. Nutritionally speaking, you get almost the same nutrients in the most expensive fillet steak as in the cheapest stewing steak; it just takes longer to cook the cheaper cuts.

There appears to be a significant link between very high consumption of beef and bowel and prostate cancer, and if large amounts of beef fat are eaten, then the risk of high cholesterol, raised blood pressure and heart disease goes up considerably, too. All of this evidence is just another reason for choosing the best organic beef you can afford and following the World Health Organization and Harvard School of Public Health advice to either eat beef only a few times a month or to eat it more frequently but only in very small quantities.

Pork

The Chinese domesticated pigs 7000 years ago and Christopher Columbus took them from the Canary Islands to North America in 1493. In France they claim to use every part of the pig except its squeak, while there are religious prohibitions against eating pork in both Judaism and Islam, probably due to the health risk of tapeworm infection in the very hot climate of the Middle East. That said, it's still best to eat pork extremely well done.

Pork is an extremely good source of B vitamins, iron and protein and modern breeds are so low in fat that they contain little more than chicken, as long as you don't eat the crackling. Lean chops or roast leg of pork contain very modest amounts of fat but keep away from pork belly, which is over a third fat by weight. All pork contains high levels of cholesterol and both ham and bacon contain high levels of salt and preservative chemicals called nitrites. Stick to organic varieties and you'll get the lowest level of both.

Game and game birds

Game has always been popular in Britain and Europe and it's making a comeback in the USA, too, where it is probably the oldest tradition in the whole American food culture.

According to John Ash and Sid Goldstein's book *American Game Cooking*, the farmed game of America is the perfect compromise. The animals are raised without hormones, antibiotics or steroids and are inspected for quality, health and lack of parasites. They range over huge areas without restraint and their year-round availability means that they are always on sale. Much of the game sold in Britain and other parts of Europe is

Lamb

Lamb is an excellent source of protein, easily absorbed iron and zinc, and B vitamins. Of all the farmed animals, lamb is the least likely to have been fed antibiotics and the most likely to have grazed on open pastures. Considered lighter and more easily digestible than beef, the amount of fat lamb contains depends on how it's prepared and cooked. Roast leg of lamb has the least fat, as long as you don't eat any of the fat that's on the meat, whereas grilled chops have the most – and if you eat the fat on your chop you're likely to get a staggering third of its weight in fat. North African and southern Mediterranean methods of cooking lamb are often the most delicious and the healthiest. So next time you fancy some lamb, remember that a Moroccan tagine, a Turkish shish kebab or a Greek braised lamb shank are all low in fat and wonderful to eat.

wild, but some game animals like venison are now being farmed there, too.

The best way to cook all young game birds is to roast them with a rasher of bacon on the breast in a hot oven. Older birds are best casseroled but you should take care not to overcook any sort of game bird.

As well as pheasant, partridge and grouse, there is the small but delicately flavoured quail. Allow two per person and roast with herbs, grill or barbecue. Pigeons roast well, too. The tastiest part is the breast, which can often be found smoked and thinly sliced. American squab are slightly larger than wild pigeon and are delicious de-boned and either sautéed or grilled with fresh thyme.

Rabbit is a perfect health food – delicious and virtually fat-free. Joints can be grilled or sautéed but rabbit stew is the traditional and best method of cooking.

Venison is more likely to be farmed than wild, but it is growing in popularity. When properly dressed and hung, the flavour and texture are superb and the health benefits are extremely important. Containing only one-third of the calories and half the fat of beef and even less than chicken, venison is truly a healthy option and food for life.

Prime cuts should be cooked very hot and just long enough to serve them medium-rare. Otherwise, marinate before cooking. Red wine, oil and herbs are common marinades in Europe and the UK; buttermilk is an American favourite. English-style slow-cooked venison hotpot with lots of vegetables or American hunter's campfire-style cooked in coffee and cider vinegar, are both wonderful dishes.

POULTRY

CHICKEN

Chicken and turkey are now so cheap that they are everyday foods for most people, but the cost we pay for this cheapness is a lack of flavour and texture, a higher saturated fat content and the risk of consuming chemical residues such as antibiotics and growth-promoting hormones. It is far better to spend more money on free-range organic poultry and to eat it less frequently.

Chicken meat contains much less fat than other red meats and as most of its fat is contained in the skin, it's easily removed. As well as protein, chicken provides easily absorbed iron and zinc – twice as much in the dark meat as in the breast. It's an excellent food for pregnancy and the breast contains twice the amount of vitamin B6, so it's helpful for women with Pre-Menstrual Syndrome.

Roast on a rack so the fat drains into the bottom of the pan, and cook the potatoes in a separate dish in a little olive oil. Tempting though it is, don't eat the skin.

DUCK

Duck, too, is an excellent source of protein, iron, zinc and nearly all the B vitamins. If you eat the crispy skin you get three times as much fat as if you only eat the meat. Served with a traditional apple sauce, duck not only tastes wonderful, but the pectins in the apples help the body eliminate much of the cholesterol in the duck.

GOOSE

Goose has long been domesticated. Neolithic man was the earliest to domesticate it and the Romans even regarded geese as sacred, though they also thought goose liver was a great delicacy. French foie gras is considered by chefs and gourmets to be one of the world's most highly prized foods, though those of you who know how the geese are force-fed in order to produce this fatty, degenerate and enormously enlarged liver might not agree.

Goose is enormously rich in iron and zinc and is a good source of phosphorus and potassium. You can get more than a day's dose of vitamin B12 in 100g of goose meat.

Goose is also enormously fatty, containing almost as much fat as it does protein, but the fat can easily be reduced with this simple cooking method. Place the bird on a rack over a large pan of water. Cover the bird with foil, making sure that the edges of the foil are inside the pan. Heat on top of the stove until the water boils and leave the goose to steam for half an hour. By that time much of the fat will have escaped from the skin and fallen into the water. Discard the fat-laden water, then roast on a rack as normal, deducting half an hour from the cooking time. When it's cooked, don't eat the skin.

TURKEY

The modern farmed turkey is a pale and insipid descendant of its wild ancestor in North America. But if you can find a free-range organic bird, you will be well rewarded. Unlike other poultry, turkey is extremely low in fat, containing only 2.7g per 100g. It's rich in protein and supplies some well-absorbed iron and zinc, though there's more in the dark meat than in the white.

Unless great care is taken, turkey's low fat content tends to make it a dry, flavourless bird when cooked. Generally speaking, the larger the bird, the less it dries out and the better the flavour. Leftover turkey is delicious cold and can also be used in curries and hashes. You can even enjoy some of the skin as a crispy treat.

FISH

Many home cooks are afraid of fish. They haven't grown up seeing their mothers buy and prepare it so they don't know what to do with it unless it comes pre-packed and ready to put into a frying pan, boiling water or the microwave oven.

My own fishmonger puts forward the 'theory of the exploding fish'. He tells me that many times a week a potential customer asks him, 'If I buy this fish, will it be all right till I get it home?' – home seldom being more than a 10-minute walk away. He asks if they think it will explode in the bag! This goes to show that our lack of knowledge about fish is astounding and we need to be far more clued-up. And we should all be eating far more fish than we do.

Why eat fish?

Fish are an exceptional source of protein and minerals and sea fish are particularly valuable for their high iodine content. The B vitamins are found in all types of fish and the oily fish are valuable sources of vitamins A, D and E as well as Omega-3 – essential fatty acids without the health hazards of saturated fat.

In Victorian times the average Londoner consumed 7kg of herrings a year and an average of four oysters a week, these being foods for the poor, just like the cockles and whelks, which they also ate in huge quantities. Protein, vital vitamins and minerals, all cheap and abundant. Lack of vitamin D and atmospheric pollution, which blotted out the sun's rays, caused a major scourge of the bone disease, rickets, in the first portion of the twentieth century – vitamin D is essential for

SHELLFISH

Shellfish are divided into crustaceans – crabs, lobsters, prawns, shrimps, crayfish, langoustine – and molluscs – mussels, oysters, cockles, whelks, winkles, clams and scallops. All of them are good sources of protein and other nutrients but molluscs contain much more iron, vitamin A and zinc than crustaceans. You may be surprised to know, for example, that oysters, cockles, whelks and winkles contain as much iron as fillet steak.

Our bodies make cholesterol from saturated fat and there's virtually none of that in shellfish. In fact, far from being bad for your heart, regular consumption of shellfish actually lowers the amount of the dangerous LDL fats (see page 54) in the blood. However, it is certainly true that some shellfish contain quite a lot of cholesterol – but this will only be a problem if you have one of the inherited fat metabolism diseases or a very high cholesterol level.

One other good reason for eating shellfish is its high selenium content (see pages 62–3).

Avoiding contamination

Contamination with toxic residues and heavy metals is a worry. If you're buying farmed fish, choose organic and avoid all but occasional treats of tuna, swordfish and marlin. The health benefits of all other oily fish far outweigh the extremely small risks they pose. All canned tuna is now routinely monitored for mercury contamination.

White fish

These are all very similar from a nutritional standpoint, whether sea fish like cod, haddock, whiting, monkfish, sea bream, red and grey mullet, snapper, plaice, sole and halibut, or freshwater fish like pike, perch, catfish, bream or carp. They all contain virtually no fat, few calories and plenty of protein as well as the B vitamins. They don't, however, contain much iron and though halibut, which is slightly oily, may contribute a little vitamin A, the white fish do not generally supply fat-soluble vitamins. The livers of cod and halibut are very rich in vitamins A, D and E, but these aren't eaten, only used for the production of oil. The roe of white fish is an

calcium metabolism. By then most Britons preferred the flavours of white fish. Though rickets abounded in the wider community, Jewish children in London's East End seldom got this crippling disease – their immigrant parents had brought their taste for pickled, salted and fresh herrings with them from Eastern Europe.

DID YOU KNOW THAT?

• Fish and shellfish are a fairly common cause of severe food allergy. If you've had one bad reaction, be extremely careful not to eat them a second time.

• Some fish are rich in a group of chemicals called purines, which can severely aggravate the painful symptoms of gout. Sufferers of gout should therefore avoid cod and herring roe, caviar, taramasalata, anchovies, whitebait, herrings, sardines, salmon, sprats, mackerel, scallops and mussels. If you suffer from any other forms of arthritis, however, you will find oily fish extremely helpful as they have a potent anti-inflammatory action, which can relieve joint and muscle pains.

excellent source of B vitamins and as good a source of iron as some meat, but fish roe contains cholesterol so may not be suitable for people with inherited disorders of fat metabolism or very high cholesterol levels.

Oily fish

Oily fish like mackerel, salmon, trout, tuna, herrings, anchovy, sardine, whitebait, sprats and eels, contain high levels of eicosapentanoeic acid, one of the Omega-3 family. All Omega-3 fats are essential for healthy cells, brain development, cognitive function and general good health. These essential fatty acids (see pages 24–5) can help atherosclerosis, arthritis, rheumatoid arthritis, cyclic breast pain, behavioural and learning problems, eczema and psoriasis.

As well as offering vitamin D, sprats, whitebait and canned sardines are also excellent sources of calcium as you can eat the bones. Canned tuna contains much less vitamin D and essential fatty acid than the fresh fish as its oil is removed before canning and is sold separately. These oily fish are rich in minerals too – sprats contain as much iron as beef, sardines as much as lamb and 100g of fresh herring and of canned salmon give you more than a week's worth of vitamin D. Avoid fish canned in vegetable oil as this blend may contain a lot of saturated fat. Only buy fish that has been canned in olive, sunflower, safflower or soya-bean oil.

AT THE FISH COUNTER

When buying fish check, that the eyes are bright and shiny, not dull, that the skin still has lots of scales on and that the gills are still red. Fish should always have the fresh smell of the sea – apart from skate which is best eaten when it has a faint smell of ammonia. Look for bright clear spots on plaice and well-defined markings on other fish.

The best ways to cook fish are baking, steaming, grilling or pan-frying in shallow oil, as all these methods minimise the loss of nutrients. Boiling fish results in considerable loss of minerals, especially iodine of which, apart from kelp, fish is the most important source. But as long as you use the cooking water to make sauce for your fish dish, you won't lose out.

When you are buying shellfish check that they feel heavy for their size. All molluscs should be closed and all shellfish should be eaten on the day you buy them. Above all, buy your shellfish from a supplier whose reputation you can rely on.

Watch out for additives in processed fish. Colourings, preservatives and antioxidants are commonly used in the coating of fish fingers, as are brown and yellow dyes in kippers and smoked haddock respectively. Growing public concern about additives means that more manufacturers are producing products without them so undyed kippers and haddock are now widely available.

To me it's very sad that as we become more aware of the dangers of certain fats in our diet, so there is a fear of dairy products. I grow increasingly concerned that many people, especially young women, interpret a low-fat diet as being a no-fat diet and for this reason they exclude most dairy foods from their regular food intake. Sadly this is not always done for health reasons, much more in the pursuit of thinness. However, dairy products play an essential role in our diets and should not be overlooked.

Milk

Milk is a valuable source of essential nutrients, especially during pregnancy, breastfeeding, and for children and adolescents. It's a cheap and easily consumed rich source of calcium – especially vital for teenage girls and women as it helps build strong bones that are less likely to suffer from osteoporosis in later life – as well as a source of protein, zinc and riboflavin (vitamin B2). Just a half a litre will supply

more than half the calcium and riboflavin needed during pregnancy or breastfeeding, a day's dose of vitamin B12, 30 per cent of the protein and 15 per cent of the energy for an average day.

Unfortunately there are some drawbacks to this apparent wonder food. Naturopaths have long believed that cow's milk may be a trigger for infantile eczema, as well as for catarrh, excessive mucous and chestiness in both children and adults, while research at the British College of Osteopathic Medicine in London has found that breastfeeding mothers who consume a lot of cow's milk tend to have babies who are more prone to eczema, chronic catarrh and colic. Sometimes, too, the symptoms of rheumatoid arthritis may be aggravated by cow's milk and it can also aggravate sinus problems.

Lactose intolerance is another common problem, especially for those whose genetic origins lie in China, Japan, the Far East and India. The intolerance is caused by a lack of the digestive enzyme, lactase, which is essential for the digestion of the milk sugar, lactose. After 40 years in practice, I'm still surprised to discover that just removing cow's milk from a patient's diet can sometimes resolve chronic digestive problems, which the patient may have suffered from for many years. Sheep's or goat's milk as well as cheeses and yoghurts made from these are good alternatives. However, before deciding to remove all dairy products from your diet it's essential to seek professional advice to prevent the risk of calcium deficiency.

For most people though, milk is good news, especially if it's organic. The obsession with its fat content is largely unfounded as even full-fat milk is only 4 per cent fat and if it's organic, a lot of that will be conjugated linoleic acid (see page 23). Organic milk also contains essential fatty acids (see pager 24) but both these beneficial fats are much reduced, if present at all, in milk from intensively reared cattle.

Yoghurt

Yoghurt in some form or other has been made since time immemorial. It's believed that the ancient Bedouin, carrying fresh milk across the desert in goatskin bags, found that the combination of heat, movement and obviously, some bacterial contamination with the right sort of bugs, resulted in a delicious food which kept much better than fresh milk.

As well as being an excellent source of calcium – one 150g carton of yoghurt provides 210mg, which is 25 per cent of the daily requirement – live, or 'bio' yoghurts contain beneficial or probiotic bacteria that play a vital role in the body's defence mechanism. They produce enzymes which are absorbed directly through the gut wall and which boost immunity.

Scientific interest in probiotics was first stimulated by the Russian scientist Metchnikoff who published a book in 1908 entitled *The Prolongation of Life*. It describes his studies of Bulgarian peasants who consumed vast quantities of yoghurt made with *Lactobacillus bulgaricus* and who lived longer than most other Europeans. As a result of Metchnikoff's work, the rest of Europe soon acquired a taste for eating these fermented milk products.

Probiotic bacteria are also essential for good digestion. They synthesize some of the B vitamins – biotin, folic acid and B12 – increase the body's uptake of calcium and magnesium, and regulate bowel function. They're also vital to control the growth of harmful bacteria in the bowel. It's important to have a portion of live yoghurt every day whenever you have to take antibiotics since antibiotics can't tell the difference between good and bad bacteria, but just kill them all. Live yoghurt replaces the good bacteria, helps to prevent diarrhoea and helps the continuation of the synthesis of vitamin B, which avoids the depression that commonly occurs in people who are taking antibiotics.

Most commercial yoghurts, especially those with a long shelf-life, are pasteurised and so contain virtually no live probiotics. Instead they boast a host of chemicals; stabilizers, emulsifiers, artificial flavours, colours, preservatives and large amounts of sugar or artificial sweeteners. For your health's sake choose live or 'bio' natural yoghurts and, if liked, add your own unsweetened puréed fruit.

Cheese

Cheese makes an enormously important contribution as part of a healthy balanced diet. As far as I'm concerned, you can discard all the burgers, sausages, commercial bakery products and high-fat convenience foods, for they seldom bring great culinary joy. Instead, allow yourself to savour the wonders of good cheese; the vast variety of cheeses throughout the world is just too good to ignore and the combination of excellent cheese, delicious bread and a glass of good red wine takes a great deal of beating as food for the mind, body and spirit.

Making cheese must be one of the most ancient of all food-preparation techniques. It's likely that

the earliest shepherds and goatherds were producing soft cheeses from their flocks when these animals were first domesticated around 10,000 BC. It was another 3000 years before cattle were domesticated and cheese was made from cow's milk but by 3000 BC the Sumerians were making 20 different varieties.

Both the ancient Greeks and Romans developed sophisticated cheeses and the Romans transported them to their armies wherever they were, as every legionnaire's daily rations included a portion of cheese. Much of the cheesemaker's art was lost during the Dark Ages and it only survived among a few isolated mountain dwellers, and in abbeys and monasteries.

Today, happily, there is a huge resurgence of interest in farm-made regional cheeses, and small producers are making wonderful quality cheeses from cow, sheep and goat's milk.

It's hard to better a small portion of good cheese as a source of essential protein, calcium for building strong bones and vitamin D to help absorb the calcium, for a selection of B vitamins for the central nervous system, for vitamin A as a cancer protector and for healthy skin, and for a spread of essential minerals. It is also a very useful source of zinc, which is vital for normal male sexual function; although the zinc is not present in enormous quantities in cheese, it is in an easily absorbed bio-available form and 100g of most types of cheese will provide over a quarter of a man's daily requirements.

There are variations in the nutritional value of different cheeses but it's worth knowing that 100g of Cheddar cheese supplies more than a day's dose of calcium, half a day's protein requirement, nearly half the zinc, half the vitamin A, a fifth of the selenium, a quarter of the iodine, three-quarters of the vitamin B12 and a fifth of the folic acid that a woman needs each day.

Unfortunately most cheeses have a high saturated-fat content and this is the type of fat that is known to cause heart disease and cholesterol deposits in the arteries. But in spite of people's worries about saturated fat and cheese, it's interesting how little cheese the British consume compared to the rest of Europe. The average Briton gets through a total of 8.1kg of cheese a year; Australians eat 9.2kg, Canadians 15.3kg, the Dutch 14.8kg and in France – where they have much less heart disease than in Britain – they eat a staggering 22.3kg.

In general, the harder the cheese, the higher the fat content, with the obvious exception of cream cheese, which is the fattiest of all. Stilton, Cheddar, blue cheese and Parmesan are all high in fat, but Camembert, Brie, Edam and feta cheese contain considerably less. There are now many low-fat cheeses made from skimmed milk, which contain around 15g total fat per 100g. Cottage cheese contains only 4g fat per 100g and curd cheese around 11g. Many processed cheeses – though they hardly deserve the name of cheese – are high in fat. They're not as high as Stilton or Cheddar but are worse than Camembert and Brie. Their saving grace is that they are good sources of calcium and protein.

Goat and sheep cheese

Cheese can be made from any animal milk, but goat's and sheep's milk have been the cheesemaker's staple since earliest times. Most goat cheese is eaten very young and soft and has a characteristic taste and smell. As they mature, goat cheeses become slightly firmer, developing a stronger flavour with a definite tang. Sheep's milk makes delicious and usually mild cheese but matures to a much firmer texture. The famous Spanish Manchega is an exceptional variety, hard with a full but still mild flavour. French Roquefort, Italian Pecorino and Greek feta however, are strongly flavoured sheep cheeses.

Both sheep and goat cheeses are lower in fat and lactose than cheese made from cow's milk. People who can't tolerate cow's milk cheeses often find them a suitable alternative.

DID YOU KNOW THAT?

• Many farm-produced cheeses are made from unpasteurised milk, which may be contaminated with bacteria, particularly salmonella and listeria. These cheeses are eaten by millions of people who suffer no ill effects, but anyone with a compromised immune system should avoid them, as should pregnant women, for a listeria infection can prove serious in pregnancy. Similarly, the chronically ill and elderly may be seriously affected by salmonella poisoning, so such people should avoid unpasteurised cheeses as well.

• Cheeses contain a chemical, tyramine, which can be a trigger of migraine attacks, though if you've cut cheese out of your diet and are still getting the migraines, go back to eating the cheese. Soft goat and sheep cheeses, cottage and cream cheese contain very little tyramine and are usually alright for migraine sufferers.

• Some antidepressant drugs can react badly with tyramine. Anyone taking monoamine oxidase inhibitors (MAOIs), should avoid cheese, especially very mature hard cheese. The result of combining the two can cause a dramatic increase in blood pressure and fatalities have resulted.

Vegetables are an indispensable part of healthy eating, truly foods for life. Throughout the world populations with longer life expectancy and a lower incidence of heart disease, high blood pressure and many forms of cancer are those for whom vegetables form a far larger part of their daily food intake than they do in the UK, USA and Northern Europe. Throughout the Mediterranean, the Middle and Far East, and Asia, meals mostly consist of lots of vegetables and little, or even no meat, compared to the meat and two vegetables culture in the UK and USA – where one of the vegetables is probably chips.

Around the world, cancer-research organisations have consistently found that eating more vegetables means less cancer, so we should all aim for a higher consumption of both raw and cooked produce. While all vegetables are healthy and nutritious, some deserve special attention for their abundance of health-giving properties.

Root vegetables

Generally speaking, root vegetables like potatoes, sweet potatoes, yams, carrots, parsnips, swede and turnips are an excellent source of filling carbohydrate. They are also rich in the soluble fibre that is essential for

healthy bowel function, reducing blood cholesterol levels and providing food for the probiotic beneficial bacteria that live in the gut. This group of vegetables are also important providers of vitamins, minerals and specific phytochemicals that protect some of the vital organs.

Potatoes are a wonderful nutritional package containing B vitamins, minerals and vitamin C. In fact, in the UK they account for 50 per cent of the average daily consumption of this essential vitamin. They are not fattening and I despair of diets which exclude them and all other carbohydrate-containing foods. If you only eat them fried, smothered in butter or as a

mayonnaise-oozing potato salad, then it's a different story, but boiled, baked or roasted in a little olive oil, they are nutritious and delicious. Use olive oil and herbs instead of butter and cream to make mashed potatoes, and buy organic so you can eat the nutrient-rich skin when they're boiled or baked. Potato juice mixed with apple, carrot and a little honey is an excellent traditional remedy for stomach ulcers and tea made from raw potato peel is rich in potassium and helps reduce high blood pressure. Sweet potatoes have many of the same values but additionally are a rich source of beta-carotene and the other cancer-protective carotenoids. Eat lots if you're a smoker.

Carrots are so rich in beta-carotene that just one reasonable-sized old carrot provides enough for your body to convert into a whole day's dose of vitamin A. Old doesn't mean one that's been lying around your kitchen for a month; it means not one of the new, very young carrots, which are paler in colour and contain less beta-carotene. Many studies have shown a specific link between a high consumption of carrots and a reduction in the risk of cancer. Carrot purée is an ideal early food for babies and an excellent treatment for all forms of diarrhoea in both children and adults. And it is a fact that eating carrots is good for your skin and eyes – and they do help you see in the dark.

Swede, parsnip and turnip are all extremely healthy even though in many countries swede is regarded as animal feed. They're rich in fibre, vitamin C and minerals, and are surprisingly low in calories. Because of their fibre and carbohydrate content they're filling and nourishing, so are very useful as part of any weight-loss plan.

Beetroot is unique for its high levels of anti-carcinogens and its very high carotenoid content.

It is also an excellent source of folic acid. The natural chemicals that give beetroot its deep red colour are absorbed into the red blood corpuscles and can increase the oxygen-carrying ability of the blood by up to 400 per cent. Beetroot is a traditional treatment used for leukaemia and throughout eastern Europe it is always eaten to build resistance after any serious illness. Don't throw away the green leafy tops as they can be cooked like spinach and are rich in beta-carotene, folic acid, potassium, vitamin C and iron.

Soft vegetables

Soft vegetables like sweet peppers, avocados, sweetcorn, pumpkin, squashes and courgette should be regulars in everybody's shopping basket. They're rich in nutrients and many are best eaten raw to preserve their vitamin content.

Avocados are often on the hate-list of dieters but they should be every woman's best friend. They're a rich source of vitamin E, which is important as a protective antioxidant, but are also valuable for healthy skin and the prevention of wrinkles. They also supply considerable amounts of potassium and large quantities of the extremely healthy monounsaturated fats. These, especially the oleic acid and the other nutrients avocados contain make them one of the most powerful antioxidant foods for protection against cancer, strokes and heart disease. Puréed avocado is good for invalids, ill children and convalescents as it's easily digestible and contains some antibacterial and antifungal chemicals.

Sweet peppers are an important source of nutrients. They're very low in calories but very rich in vitamin C and the red, orange and yellow peppers supply large quantities of beta-carotene, some of which the body converts to vitamin A. All peppers have a wax-like substance on their skins which protects them against oxidation so their vitamin C content remains highly significant even weeks after harvesting. They'll retain even more if you keep them in a cold dark place.

Sweetcorn or maize is a good source of protein, fibre and reasonable amounts of beta-carotene and vitamin E. The sooner you eat it after picking the better as it will contain more sugar than starch then, but this changes quickly so that a two-week old corn on the cob will never taste quite the same. Frozen cobs can sometimes taste better as they're processed extremely quickly, but avoid canned sweetcorn, which is often very high in salt.

Pumpkins, squashes and courgettes are all interesting, nutritious foods. Pumpkin is extremely low in calories and very rich in beta-carotene, while pumpkin seeds contain protein and highly significant amounts of zinc, a mineral that is often deficient in the Western diet. All the yellow-fleshed squashes are good sources of beta-carotene but in courgettes and marrows the beta-carotene is only present in significant amounts in the skin, so they're best cooked and eaten with the skin left on. Courgettes supply valuable amounts of folic acid and potassium.

The allium family

This family is unique in the vegetable kingdom for its health-giving properties. Onions, leeks, garlic, spring onions and shallots are foods which must never be ignored. They are amongst the most protective of all vegetables and have traditionally been used in the treatment of colds, coughs, bronchitis, catarrh and joint problems. Modern science, however, has found a whole new range of medicinal properties to help people with heart and circulatory diseases.

Garlic is the king of this family and was used for its medicinal benefits by the ancient Egyptians, physicians in Persia, Roman legionnaires and right through the Middle Ages. In fact, it has always been the most commonly used medicinal plant throughout the world. It's a powerful antibiotic, antiseptic and antifungal and helps the body to get rid of toxic substances like alcohol and heavy metals. But we now know that garlic also reduces the level of cholesterol in the bloodstream, lowers blood pressure and makes blood less sticky, so minimising the risk of blood clots. Everyone should eat a clove of garlic every single day of their lives.

Leeks have been eaten and used as medicine for 4000 years. They're extremely good for all sorts of throat and voice problems, they supply beta-carotene and potassium, and have the same benefits as garlic though they're rather less potent.

All types of onions – red, white, spring, shallots – have been used traditionally for the treatment of many respiratory problems, as well as rheumatism, arthritis and gout, and traditional Chinese physicians use them as a poultice, for boils. Their extremely high concentration of sulphur compounds is the source of their medicinal properties.

Cruciferous vegetables

This is a large family which includes cabbage and all its relatives. Properly cooked they're all delicious and extremely valuable as they contain powerful anti-carcinogenic chemicals called indoles. These are particularly effective against colon, stomach and mouth cancers and even more so against breast cancer. Rich in vitamin C, A, folic acid and beta-carotene, they're also all important as part of a balanced diet. It's no accident that throughout Europe cabbage is known as 'the medicine of the poor'. As well as all its other nutrients, cabbage leaves contain large amounts of sulphur which makes them an excellent food for anyone with chest infections or skin infections like acne. The iron in dark green cabbage is well absorbed because of the cabbage's high vitamin C content and its significant amounts of folic acid make all members of the cabbage family important for all women of child-bearing age.

Broccoli, Brussels sprouts, kale, cauliflower and the oriental varieties like pak choi and Chinese cabbage all have unique flavours but the same health benefits. And don't ignore sauerkraut, which is a form of pickled cabbage; it is an amazing health-giving food. Its vitamin C and enzymes are well-preserved – 100g will provide almost 20 per cent of the recommended daily allowance – and it also contains potassium and calcium and loads of health-giving bacteria produced during the fermentation process.

Salads

This is another important group of vegetables which can provide valuable amounts of beta-carotene, vitamin C and folic acid. Dark-green and red-coloured lettuce are the best nutritionally and chicory is also a good source, but is best eaten raw. Celery contains generous amounts of folic acid and is also a mild diuretic, helping to prevent fluid retention. Watercress is an exceptionally valuable salad stuff, rich in vitamins A, C and E and some iodine. Most importantly it contains a unique chemical called phenethylisothiocyanate which can neutralise the tobacco-specific lung carcinogen known as NNK. This amazing chemical is only released when watercress is chopped or chewed and if you're a smoker you should eat a large handful every single day.

Ripe tomatoes are the richest source of a carotenoid called lycopene which helps protect against heart disease and cancers of the breast and prostate. They're also very rich in vitamins C and E and beta-carotene and are extremely low in calories. Canned tomatoes lose little of their nutritional value.

PULSES

It doesn't matter whether you're enjoying canned baked beans or a bowl of dhal in an Indian restaurant, you will be reaping the amazing benefits of pulses – one of the most ancient of our staple foods. And they are versatile, too, used in dishes ranging from the chuck-wagon dishes of the Wild West to hot and spicy Mexican dishes and Middle-Eastern falafel.

Pulses are part of the legume family which also includes peas and all the green beans. The entire family is nutritious and inexpensive – in fact it's the cheapest protein food you can buy – and when dried can be stored without any loss of nutrients.

An average steak is around 27 per cent protein, roast chicken 24 per cent, a beefburger 20 per cent, a hot dog 9.5 per cent and beans range from 19 to 26 per cent. Where pulses are a substantial part of the traditional diet, they're eaten with wholegrain cereals to make up for missing amino acids. So lentil dhal is served with rice or chapattis throughout India, while in the Caribbean rice'n'peas – the peas are in fact black-eye beans – provide the perfect combination of pulses and starches.

Beans are an excellent source of calcium, iron, copper, zinc, phosphorus, potassium and magnesium and because of their high potassium and low sodium content they're ideal for anyone with high blood pressure.

They are also a rich source of soluble fibre (see page 78) and B vitamins, vital for a healthy nervous system. Most importantly, they also supply folic acid, which is vital for vegetarians (see page 40).

There are many varieties of beans, all full of the best nutrients with none of the unhealthy ones. They are excellent for diabetics as they are broken down slowly without causing a sudden rise in blood sugar and increased demand for insulin. Eating pulses is also known to reduce the risk of Type II diabetes (see page 54). Natural chemicals in beans block and slow downs the spread of cancerous cells so they are highly cancer-protective. The only bad thing about beans is the wind they generate but you can reduce the flatulence factor by cooking without salt in an uncovered pan. The herb summer savory is known in Germany as 'the bean herb'. It is always added to pulses during cooking as it prevents excessive wind.

Soya beans provide the most consistent levels of complete protein and are a rich source of protective antioxidants, since they contain phytochemicals like phytosterols, saponins and phenolic acids, all of which prevent free radical damage. Consequently, soya-based foods such as tofu, soya milk, soya cheese, soy sauce and miso can protect against heart and circulatory disease as well as cancer. Japanese studies show a 30 per cent reduction in stomach cancer in people eating a daily portion of soya.

Soya also contains hormone-like phyto-estrogens. Both men and women can benefit from these as they help protect against breast, ovarian and cervical cancer, as well as prostate cancer. Soya foods can also help male-pattern baldness. But it's menopausal problems that

Chickpeas are good for fibre, calcium, iron and zinc. These creamy coloured, round beans are popular throughout the Middle East where they're also made into flour. They're the basic ingredient of hummus.

Butter beans provide fibre, potassium and iron. They are large, flat, oval white beans, traditionally added to soups and casseroles, as well as salads.

Black-eye beans have an exceptionally high fibre content and they're rich in folic acid, selenium and other minerals. They are an essential part of Caribbean cooking and are also popular in the southern states of America.

Baked beans in cans are an excellent source of fibre and a reasonable source of iron, selenium, iodine – but watch out for the salt. You can make your own but it's a slow, laborious process.

Aduki beans are good for fibre, magnesium, potassium and zinc. These small sweet-tasting beans are widely used in oriental recipes.

can show the most dramatic and obvious benefits from soya. Long-term consumption of soya is known to dramatically reduce the risks of osteoporosis, hot flushes, mood swings and other menopausal problems. Even adding soya milk, cheese, tofu and beans to the diet and taking medicinal soya extracts can help diminish the unpleasant symptoms which many women suffer. Soya milk and soya cheese are also excellent substitutes for anyone allergic to dairy products while tofu and miso are foods that should appear regularly in the diets of vegetarians and vegans.

Pinto beans are rich in potassium, fibre and folic acid. These long, mottled, oval beans are widely used in Mexico, South America and the USA and contain more fibre than any of the others.

Mung beans are slightly lower in starch but good for folic acid, magnesium and manganese. These tiny green beans are the source of the commonly used beansprouts.

Kidney beans are excellent for fibre, potassium and zinc. The dark-red variety is the most common and is used to make chilli con carne.

FRUITS

Fruits provide essential vitamins, minerals and natural phytochemicals and all those people who live longer and suffer less from strokes, high blood pressure, heart disease and cancers have enjoyed a high consumption of fruit all their lives.

Fruits offer a kaleidoscope of colours and nutrients, each fruit having its own particular value and qualities.

Apples are a good source of vitamin C and the soluble fibre pectin, which helps lower cholesterol. They contain malic and tartaric acids, which are good for digestion. Even the smell of a ripe apple is soothing and cholesterol-lowering.

Pears are an excellent source of pectin so they help prevent and treat constipation. They provide good amounts of potassium, which is beneficial for the heart and for blood pressure, and they're extremely easy to digest so they are a good food for anybody with IBS or other bowel problems.

Berries provide exceptional amounts of vitamin C. The darkest-coloured – blueberries, blackberries, red- and blackcurrants, loganberries, and raspberries – have the most protective phytochemicals. Blackberries contain vitamin E, cranberries the specific antibacterial substances for urinary infections, whilst strawberries are one of the few antiviral foods – also good for arthritis, rheumatism or gout.

Plums are a rich source of potassium and are very low in calories. The darker ones, like damsons, are also rich in anti-cancer chemicals.

Apricots, peaches and nectarines are all delicious and when ripe provide some beta-carotene. The dried fruits do contain more calories but are an exceptionally rich source of minerals and fibre.

Cherries are a real seasonal treat, so wherever you live, eat as many as you can during the short season that they're available. They're a

rich source of vitamin C and bioflavonoids and they also contain the anti-cancer chemical ellagic acid, which inhibits the growth of malignant cells. Sour varieties like the morello are perfect for cooking and dried cherries are mildly diuretic so they are a traditional herbalists' treatment for fluid retention.

Citrus fruits are probably the greatest provider of vitamin C worldwide. They also contain some fibre and potassium and the American National Cancer Institute has advised that eating more citrus fruit and drinking more citrus juice can be a major protector against stomach cancers. Oranges, grapefruits, tangerines, lemons and limes are all excellent and pink grapefruit is an exceptionally good provider of beta-carotene.

Grapes have been used in wine-making for thousands of years and red wine is known to help prevent heart disease. The same phytochemicals are found in grape juice, and both grapes and raisins are rich in fibre, antioxidants, antibacterial and cancer-protective natural substances. They are also a great energy source thanks to their natural fruit sugar content.

Bananas are the original fast food but with the important bonus of being exceptionally healthy. They provide instant energy, slow-release energy, folic acid, vitamin B6 to reduce the symptoms of PMS and considerable amounts of potassium, which prevents cramp. Their combination of ease of digestion, instant energy, cramp prevention and easy availability makes bananas the perfect snack for anyone who is engaged in sport or other physically demanding activities.

Pineapple is unique thanks to the healing enzyme bromelain that it contains. Bromelain has the amazing ability to dissolve blood clots, so fresh pineapples and fresh juice will help resolve bruising and all sorts of sports and physical injuries. The fruit and juice relieve sore throats and tonsillitis, and eaten before any long journey can help to prevent thrombosis.

Mango overflows with nutrients, all in a form your body can easily utilise. Vitamins A, C and E, portassium, iron and fibre are here for the taking.

Kiwi fruits possess great nutritional value, which few people appreciate. Weight for weight they are substantially richer in vitamin C than oranges and contain more fibre than an apple. They're very rich in potassium, which is important for the prevention of high blood pressure, for muscle activity and good digestion. They're also a valuable food for the elderly as, thanks to their high-fibre content and their unique mucilage, they make a gentle and effective laxative.

Figs contain large amounts of beta-carotene, fibre, iron, potassium and ficin, an enzyme which helps protein digestion. Dried figs are a wonderful source of instant energy and of nutrients.

Prunes, or dried plums, are regarded by many people as a bit of a joke and fit only to be used as laxatives, but nothing could be further from the truth. They have the highest ORAC score of any food (see page 82). A hundred grams of prunes contain 5700 ORACs, while the optimum intake for protection against heart and circulatory disease, cancers, and ageing is 5000 per day.

Dates supply significant amounts of iron, making them an excellent food for anaemia or chronic fatigue. Semi-dried and without the sticky syrup, they are perfect for a lunchbox and are a much healthier snack than commercial confectionery. Like other dried fruits they're also an excellent source of fibre.

Everyone nibbles nuts with a drink, but they are usually roasted and salted, which is bad for your heart and pushes up your blood pressure. Freshly shelled nuts and seeds, though are extremely valuable.

Rich in protein, minerals and all vitamins, except vitamin B12, nuts and seeds are nutritionally equal to any meat, but for optimum benefit they need thorough chewing. Because of their high oil content, they go rancid quickly and rancid fats are bad news. They interfere with vitamin E and may cause blood clots and stomach cancer.

Almonds are the richest in calcium and provide zinc, magnesium, potassium and iron. But they also contain oxalic and phytic acids, which reduce absorption, so eat them with vitamin C-rich foods.

Brazil nuts are one of the richest sources of selenium. Five a day will protect you against heart disease and prostate cancer.

Cashew nuts, plain or roasted are rich in heart-protecting monounsaturated fat. They're a good source of potassium, nicotinic acid and folic acid. Cashew-nut butter is highly nutritious.

Chestnuts can be bought with or without their shells, fresh or dried, ground into meal and even canned. Cooked with vegetables, added to soups or used in traditional turkey stuffing, they're delicious and nutritious. Dried and ground into flour they are excellent for people with coeliac disease or any form of gluten intolerance as they are gluten free. Chestnuts are much lower in calories than other nuts because they contain far less fat, but they are also low in protein.

Hazelnuts, cobs and filberts are an excellent source of protein, fibre and magnesium, with iron, zinc and lots of vitamin E – 100g provide nearly a week's worth. They are also very low in salt. They're good eaten on their own, used in cooking or turned into hazelnut butter.

Peanuts started life in South America, but they are really legumes rather than nuts. They're extremely nutritious whether eaten raw or roasted, but are not so healthy when salted. You can eat them straight from the shell or use them in sweet or savoury recipes. They're extremely high in protein, 100g providing nearly half a day's requirements, and comparatively low in fat. They're a good source of fibre, magnesium, iron, zinc, an excellent source of boron, important for the absorption of vitamin D and calcium, and are a valuable source of iodine.

Because peanuts are very slow to break down during digestion, they are excellent for diabetics and for the prevention of Type II diabetes (see page 54). Contrary to what many people believe, far from being fattening and unhealthy, they actually help encourage weight loss. They also contain monounsaturated fats which help the body eliminate cholesterol and are protective against heart disease. Peanut butter has the same benefits but do choose organic, low-salt varieties.

Pecan nuts were once part of the staple diet of the North American Indians and are traditionally used in many American recipes, both sweet and savoury. Use them in salads, stuffings, nut roasts, biscuits and cakes, and not forgetting that all-time American favourite, the

pecan pie. They're a good source of protein, unsaturated fats and reasonable amounts of fibre. They also provide modest amounts of calcium, magnesium, iron and zinc, and lots of vitamin E.

Pine nuts are a great Mediterranean delicacy. Combined with garlic, basil and olive oil, they are used in traditional Italian pesto sauce. They make a very good addition to salad dishes and in the Middle East they're frequently mixed with rice. They're an excellent source of protein and though quite high in fats, they're mostly of the unsaturated kind. Magnesium, iron, zinc, potassium and vitamin E are also present in substantial quantities.

Pumpkin seeds are very nutritious in spite of their 569 calories per 100g; almost a quarter of their weight is protein and they are lower in fats than most other nuts or seeds. They're a good source of fibre and magnesium, an excellent source of iron and zinc, and also contain a little vitamin A. These make much healthier nibbles than the usual salted nuts, and because of their high zinc content – essential for fertile sperm as well as being a specifically protective substance for the prostate gland – they're valuable for men. A handful a day is good health insurance.

Sesame seeds have been popular for centuries in the Middle East and the Far East, where they have a reputation as an aphrodisiac. This may well be due to their vitamin E and iron content. They're an exceptional source of calcium and a very good source of protein and magnesium, too, as well as being rich in B vitamins, especially niacin and folic acid. Sprinkled on top of or added to cakes and especially wholemeal bread, they add lots of nutrients and a distinctive nutty flavour, or eat them in the form of tahini, widely available in health-food shops, delis and good food shops. They're also an essential ingredient in Asian cooking, where they're added to stir-fries, while sesame-seed oil is excellent both for salads and wok cooking.

Sunflower seeds are extremely nutritious as well as tasting good. They provide large amounts of protein, B vitamins, iron, zinc, potassium and selenium, and are one of the best sources of vitamin E. Sprinkle onto savoury meat or vegetable dishes, add them to salads or include them in bread, cakes and desserts.

Walnuts have been a nutritious delicacy for many centuries. Wet walnuts, eaten immediately after picking and before the shells have dried out, are a great delicacy. But whether eaten as they are, freshly shelled, or chopped into cakes or biscuits, or pickled or pressed into oil, walnuts are healthy. Low in saturated fat, high in poly- and monounsaturates, they provide protein, a little zinc, vitamin E and useful quantities of folic acid. Walnuts are also very low in sodium.

CEREALS

Cereal is the name given to the seeds of a group of plants from the grass family. The most important cereals grown in the world are barley, maize, millet, oats, rice, rye and wheat. Their nutritional value is much the same for all of them, and their main constituents are energy-producing starches.

Unrefined cereals are richer in fibre, B vitamins and minerals. With the exception of yellow maize none of them provides beta-carotene. They also lack vitamins C and B12. In spite of being a staple food for many, they need to be eaten with vegetables and protein.

Some contain phytic acid which interferes with absorption of iron, calcium and zinc. This is less important when they are cooked, but eating uncooked bran may cause nutritional deficiencies.

Barley (wholegrain or pot barley, sometimes called Scotch barley) provides the highest level of nutrients, but the more commonly used pearl barley has lost up to 60 per cent of its vitamin B1. Pot barley can be ground into barley meal and used in bread-making, though its low gluten content produces heavy loaves. Pearl barley, like white flour, is nutritionally much poorer. Barley is sadly underused; it makes a cheap, filling and highly nutritious addition to soups, stews and casseroles thanks to its high mineral and fibre content.

Maize is a cheap and reliable provider of food energy. Wholegrain in the form of ground maize and popcorn provide the nutrients, but grits are made from milled corn and are nutritionally deficient. Maize flour contains no gluten so can be used by people with coeliac disease (see also Sweetcorn, page 100).

Millet doesn't contain gluten and so is another cereal that coeliacs can eat. Its nutritional value is the same as other cereals but because it's high in protein and low in starch, it's easily digested and much less likely to produce wind and bloating. Because millet is never highly refined it retains all of its essential nutrients and is an excellent source of the silicon that is needed for the formation of collagen and for healthy hair, skin, teeth, eyes and nails. Add it whole for extra vitamins and minerals to all soups, meat and vegetable dishes, or use millet flour for baking. This valuable cereal should be used much more frequently than it is.

Oats provide 12g of protein per 100g. They also contain healthy oils, some vitamin E, lots of B vitamins and highly significant quantities of calcium, potassium and magnesium.

From ancient kitchen medicine and traditional herbal remedies to the most up-to-date scientific research, oats have proved themselves invaluable as food and medicine. The soluble fibre in this cereal can reduce cholesterol levels by up to 20 per cent. Their slow-release energy can help regulate blood-sugar levels and protect against diabetes. Oats also help prevent gallstones and can cure the most chronic constipation, and because they don't contain phytic acid, they won't reduce the body's absorption of minerals. They should be an everyday part of your diet in the form of porridge, muesli or other oat-based cereals.

Rice has been the dietary staple of the East for centuries, where it is a wonderful basis for good nutrition. It's low in fat and provides protein and most of the B vitamins, but not vitamins A, C or B12. It is gluten-free, so is suitable for coeliacs. Brown rice is rich in nutrients but white rice loses most of the vitamins, especially thiamin. Plain boiled brown rice is an excellent treatment for diarrhoea and mixed with stewed apple will help settle an upset stomach and lower blood pressure.

Rye's nutritional value is similar to wheat, with two important exceptions. It contains considerably more fibre and much less gluten. The lack of gluten means that bread made from 100 per cent rye flour tends to be heavier than wheat breads. If you're not a coeliac but do have gluten sensitivity you will almost certainly be able to tolerate rye. Most rye breads are a mixture of rye and wheat flours but pumpernickel and black bread should be made exclusively from rye. If you have gluten problems, check the labels carefully. It's quite common for rye breads to be coloured with caramel to make them darker, so you can't judge by the colour alone.

Wheat offers protein and is a great source of energy, B vitamins and minerals. It is a vitally important staple food in the Western diet, with most of it ending up as flour and then bread. Although bread consumption is declining, it still accounts for a quarter of all the protein in the northern European diet whereas 100 years ago it made up three-quarters. Any regime which excludes bread and other carbohydrates is a nutritional disaster; regardless of how heavily these unhealthy eating plans are promoted, ignore them. You should eat at least four slices of bread a day.

Bulgar, burghul or cracked wheat is often used in the Middle East instead of rice. It's made by soaking wholewheat grains in water, then putting them into a very hot oven until they crack. These delicious, nutritious and nutty-flavoured grains are a great addition to any salads, but are particularly good as the Lebanese recipe, tabbouleh. This is made from soaked, dried cracked wheat, mixed with onions, mint, parsley, lemon juice and extra-virgin olive oil.

Couscous is one of the most popular dishes of North Africa. It's prepared from the inner part of the wheat grain, otherwise known as semolina. It's normally cooked by steaming in a couscoussier, though you can improvise by lining the top of an ordinary steamer with a piece of muslin. It can be used to make sweet or savoury dishes.

Semolina is produced by extracting the coarse particles of the wheat endosperm and in India and the Middle East is used to make wonderful sweet desserts, often flavoured with rosewater or other perfumed extracts. In Italy, semolina is the basic ingredient for gnocchi, prepared with milk, semolina, egg, Parmesan and nutmeg – a rich combination of essential nutrients.

THE SEVEN AGES OF LIFE

Around the world, there are populations that are renowned for their vitality, good health and longevity. As well as maintaining strength and mobility, the men in these communities seem to have the ability to father children well into what most people in Western civilisation would consider old age. The Cretans, Bulgarians and the Himalayan mountain tribe of the Hunzas are three prime examples who share one common factor: an extremely healthy diet. In this chapter, you'll discover the basic principles of eating healthily for each of the Seven Ages of Life. You'll find which foods are vital for conception, pregnancy, childhood, the teens, adulthood, the golden years – in fact, everything you need to know about eating from the cradle to the grave. Not only will these guidelines help to ensure the best possible passage through life, they'll also give you the maximum protection against infection, disease and the attrition of living in the twenty-first century.

But before you go on to read about the Seven Ages of Life, look at the Vitality Eating Plan that I give on pages 112-13. It should be your mainstay whatever your age.

THE VITALITY

Glowing health and vitality are everyone's birthright. They will give you bags of energy, a positive outlook on life and serenity of mind. They will bring you both physical and mental vigour. They will make you look good because you feel good. They will give you a clear skin, bright eyes and glossy hair. They will keep you free from all the many problems that we are conditioned to expect as we go through the Seven Ages of Life – from acne to brittle bones, from morning sickness to postnatal depression, from PMS to menopausal problems and from memory loss to loss of libido.

From the fertilised egg to old age, health is determined by nutrition. Of course other factors are important too; smoking, alcohol or drug abuse, environmental pollution, accidents and state of mind, all play their part. But regardless of these, poor nutrition means poor health while optimum nutrition gives you the best protection from the hostile world that surrounds us.

This straightforward Vitality Eating Plan shows how you can secure your birthright of good health for yourself and your family. How you can fortify yourself against physical strain and mental stress. How you can beef up your natural resistance to infection and disease. How you can kiss goodbye to the traditional woes of womanhood. How you can protect yourself against today's crop of disabling or life-threatening diseases – arthritis, osteoporosis, cancer and heart disease. And how you can keep your good looks for life – without resorting to the beauty parlour or the plastic surgeon.

This plan doesn't call for expensive pills or potions. It doesn't involve complicated diet sheets, expensive meal substitutes or the latest food-fad regime. It's a positive guide to vitality eating, based on the essential nutritional food you'll learn to include in your weekly shopping basket. And these are everyday foods that you can buy at any supermarket, corner shop or street-market stall. Wonderful foods that can cost very little yet, in terms of your health, are worth their weight in gold.

EATING PLAN

10 simple rules for vitality eating

1 Have a mixed diet of as many different foods as possible.

2 Eat regular meals and make sure that you have the time to enjoy and digest them.

3 Eat plenty of fresh fruit, salads and vegetables, particularly the green leafy and yellow ones.

4 Cultivate a taste for wholegrain cereals.

5 Get most of your protein from fish, poultry, pulses, and less from meat, which should be as lean as possible.

6 Have regular, but modest amounts of eggs, low-fat cheeses and other dairy products.

7 Use plenty of fresh seeds and fresh, unsalted nuts, together with dried fruits. Add them to your meals and eat them as nourishing snacks.

8 Drink plenty of fruit and vegetable juices, lots of water and only sensible quantities of tea, coffee and alcohol.

9 Bread, pasta, rice and potatoes are very healthy. Have plenty of them, but watch what you do to them. Lashings of butter, cream sauces and French fries are not part of this plan.

10 Make sure that at least one-third of your daily food starts out as fresh, raw produce. For the other two-thirds, get into the kitchen. There is nothing as vital as home cooked food made from wholesome and nourishing ingredients. It is also a lot less expensive than takeaways, canned foods and TV dinners.

There is no need to feel guilty about the odd treat. As long as you are sticking to the spirit of the Vitality Eating Plan, you shouldn't become a food freak. There is nothing more boring than someone who takes their own food to a party, wrapped up in a brown paper bag. When your friends all go out for a meal, join in, enjoy whatever you eat and have a good time. A little of what you fancy does you good. There's nothing wrong the occasional chocolate eclair, doughnut or burger and chips, as long as they are not your staple diet.

Preconception

We all know that food is essential for our existence. What most of us fail to understand is the difference between what we need to eat to stay alive and avoid serious illnesses, and what we need to eat to be super-healthy. If you are thinking about starting a family, then it's time to get super-healthy. It's also time to take stock of your own, and your partner's, eating habits.

The impact of poor diet on the reproductive system is dramatic. While there is a vast market for commercially produced, nutritionally enhanced feedstuffs, designed to provide an optimum diet for animal breeding stocks, tragically, the medical establishments in most Western countries have not shown much interest in applying knowledge about food and the part it plays in preconception to the human race.

Up to 5 per cent of human births result in abnormal babies and there is overwhelming evidence that this number could be dramatically reduced by an improved diet for the mother or the use of vitamin and mineral supplementation. Although there is little evidence of gross malnutrition in the general population in the West, sub-clinical malnutrition – very small nutritional deficiencies that have wide-ranging effects – is now recognised by the scientific community as a matter for serious concern. The nutritional state of women and their sexual partners in the three months before conception is the key to having a healthy baby.

DID YOU KNOW THAT? Curmonsky, chef to Napoleon, said, 'Properly speaking, there are no aphrodisiacs capable of endowing those blind to life with sight. But for those with poor eyesight in this matter, there are substances which act as magnifying lenses'.

To magnify your chances of conception, and a good pregnancy, the only lens you need is one to read the labels on the foods that you feed to you and your other half.

Danger foods

There are some 'danger foods' which you should avoid and some which should be taken in moderation if you are pregnant, trying to conceive or think there is the possibility of your being pregnant.

■ SOFT UNPASTEURISED CHEESES, UNPASTEURISED MILK, RAW OR UNDERCOOKED EGGS OR ANY FOOD PAST ITS SELL-BY DATE. This reduces the risk of bacterial infections like salmonella and listeria, which can damage the foetus.

■ PROCESSED MEAT PRODUCTS AND UNDERCOOKED HAMBURGERS. These can contain the bacterium E.coli VTEC, which lives in the intestines of cattle. In addition, carcasses are often contaminated in the slaughterhouse. There have been a number of outbreaks of infection by E.coli VTEC in the UK and there have been major problems in the USA during the last 15 years. It can cause serious kidney failure, which puts the life of the developing baby at grave risk. If you're cooking a steak, the intense heat on the outside of the meat is enough to kill the bacteria, even if the middle is rare. When infected meat is chopped or minced to make burgers the bacteria is distributed throughout the meat. Hamburgers should never be eaten until they're thoroughly cooked right through, the juices run clear and there is not the slightest trace of pink in the middle of the burger.

■ UNDERCOOKED POULTRY, to avoid the risk of salmonella infection.

■ LIVER, LIVER SAUSAGE AND LIVER PÂTÉ contain extremely high levels of vitamin A, which may cause birth defects.

Foods to be taken in moderation

■ TEA AND COFFEE (Voltaire called coffee the beverage of eunuchs; he may have had a point!) When you drink tea and coffee at, or soon after meals, they inhibit your body's absorption of your food's nutrients – including vital zinc.

■ ALCOHOL is not healthy for sperm or eggs, so do not drink any more than an occasional glass of decent wine.

■ ALL FOOD WHICH HAS BEEN HIGHLY REFINED, PROCESSED, DENATURED, OR OTHERWISE 'MUCKED ABOUT WITH'. This is always less nutritious than fresh produce.

TOP 10 FOODS FOR CONCEPTION

AVOCADOS Usually high on the weight watchers list of forbidden fruits, this is a must for all women, especially those trying to become pregnant.

BEEF AND LAMB These provide essential iron for the extra demands of pregnancy and vitamin B12 to protect from anaemia.

BUCKWHEAT This contains a chemical called rutin which has a powerful effect on the circulation, strengthening the tiny superficial vessels and helping in the control of blood pressure.

CABBAGE Dark green cabbage, kale, spring greens, collard greens, Brussels sprouts and broccoli all provide vital folic acid.

CARROTS Eat at least one large carrot a day to give you your vitamin A.

KIWI FRUIT As well as being an excellent source of vitamin C, they provide some vitamin E, which is needed for fertility.

OILY FISH Herrings, sardines, mackerel, pilchards, wild salmon or organic farmed salmon should be eaten at least three times a week. Fresh tuna, swordfish, and marlin are best avoided.

ORGANIC-FREE RANGE EGGS AND POULTRY It's essential to eat organic at this time of your life.

PUMPKIN SEEDS These provide vitamin E and fibre as well as being an extremely rich source of zinc – vital in preventing chronic fatigue and loss of appetite.

SOYA BEANS The beans and soya products like tofu, soya milk, yoghurt and cheese are all good sources of phytoestrogens.

THREE MONTH COUNTDOWN TO CONCEPTION

Three months is the optimum amount of time to prepare for conception. For any couple trying to conceive here is a simple summary of the information you'll need to make things go smoothly. Photocopy this page and stick it to the fridge door as a daily reminder that the next twelve weeks could be the most important in your lives.

Three months to go

■ **ALCOHOL** Although an occasional alcoholic drink for women isn't a problem, 40 per cent of low fertility in men may be the result of even a modest consumption of alcohol. Three months' abstinence will raise sperm counts enough for fertilisation in half the men with fertility problems. Keeping off the booze also improves sperm motility.

■ **SMOKING** Stop before you even think of trying for a baby. It's easier now than once you are pregnant.

■ **VITAMINS** Take a daily antioxidant vitamin supplement and 200mcg of folic acid, eat two avocados a week, and plenty of olive oil and sunflower and sesame seeds for vitamin E.

■ **OBESITY** If you're overweight, now's the time for that healthy, well-balanced, exercise and weight-loss programme. Obesity upsets the testosterone/oestrogen balance and may cause infertility.

■ **MEN AND TIGHT PANTS** Men should throw away their Y-fronts and tight jeans now and wear boxer shorts and loose-fitting trousers instead.

■ **ZINC** Start eating plenty of shellfish and a generous handful of pumpkin seeds each day for extra zinc. Sperm is rich in zinc, each ejaculation containing 5mg – half the daily requirement for a man – so you'll need to keep your supplies to a healthy level. Zinc also increases the protection of the sperm against free radical damage. For women, zinc is important to prevent fatigue and to maintain a good appetite.

■ **ESSENTIAL FATTY ACIDS** Throughout this three-month period women must eat at least three portions of oily fish each week for the essential fatty acids they provide. Avoid canned tuna, which is a poor source and which may also be contaminated with heavy metal and toxic chemical residues, as are swordfish and marlin. Fresh or canned sardines, wild or organic farmed salmon, herrings, mackerel, whitebait and anchovies are all suitable.

■ **CAFFEINE** Cut down on all caffeine and caffeine-containing cola drinks. Have a couple of cups a day if you must, but otherwise drink green tea, herbal teas or modest quantities of Indian tea.

- **EAT ORGANIC** Avoid all meat or poultry that may have been fed on growth hormones and eggs and dairy products that may have come from animals fed on growth hormones. This is one time when you should choose organic products as much as you can.

- **EXERCISE** Ease back on your exercise. Sensible activity is a great aid to fertility, as it encourages general fitness, but excessive or obsessive exercise can reduce sperm counts.

- **CHEMICALS** Avoid contact with chemical solvents and garden or agricultural insecticides or pesticides. If possible use organic products.

Two months to go

- **VITAMIN C** You should both increase your vitamin C intake to 500mg per day. As well as reducing the risk of sperm clumping, it increases your natural resistance to infection – neither of you wants to get ill now. Use the non-acidic form, ester-c, to avoid any chance of digestive discomfort.

- **BIOFLAVONOIDS** Eat two oranges or have a large glass of fresh orange juice and two kiwi fruits every day for bioflavonoids as well as vitamin C.

- **BETA-CAROTENES** Eat at least two portions a day of beta-carotene-rich foods – carrots, broccoli, apricots, spinach and other orange or dark green leafy vegetables or fruits.

- **WATER** Drink 'mineral' or 'natural spring' water to avoid the hormones that are in domestic water supplies. Some environmentalists believe this to be one of the main causes of a 50 per cent decline in sperm counts over the last 30 years.

One month to go

- **VITAMIN C** Increase your vitamin C intake to 1000mg daily.

- **FOLIC ACID** Make sure you're taking a supplement every day.

- **VITAMIN E** Now is the time for a daily supplement to help prevent varicose veins and stretch marks.

- **PRUNES** should now be a regular on your daily menu. Not only are they the richest food source of protective antioxidants – 5 a day provides more than 5000 ORAC units, which is a whole day's ideal consumption – they also prevent the constipation that is so common during pregnancy.

- **GARLIC** Eat at least one whole clove of garlic daily or take a whole garlic extract tablet. This powerful member of the onion family protects you from bacterial, viral and fungal infections and also makes the blood less sticky so that when you do get pregnant it reduces the risk of blood clots.

DIETING = FAILURE TO CONCEIVE?

Studies of women attending fertility clinics show that 50 per cent of them had been dieting to lose weight. Resulting nutritional deficiencies upset the hormone systems which then prevented conception.

A study in London compared calorie intakes and babies' birth-weights in a group of affluent middle-class women and much poorer working-class mothers. The average calorie intake of the poor mothers was 1689 per day, and the average birth-weight of their babies was 3026g. The richer mothers consumed 2044 calories a day and the average birth-weight of their babies was 3313g.

Many of the working-class babies were well below the 2500g danger level, at which point the risk of abnormalities increases dramatically. Perhaps because of the significant economic differences between the two groups, the working-class mothers spent their food money very badly, buying more takeaway meals and convenience foods and less in the way of fresh fruit and vegetables and good carbohydrates than the richer group.

ARE YOU FIT FOR FATHERHOOD?

According to the Old Testament, an angel of God appeared to the wife of Manoah and said, 'You are barren and have no child. But from now on take great care. Take no wine or strong drink and eat nothing unclean. For you will conceive and bear a son.' And, in due course, as we know, the mighty Samson arrived.

Today, the angel's list of instructions would be much longer and would certainly include some pertinent advice for Manoah, too. Although every would-be pregnant woman is bombarded with guidance on how to modify her lifestyle, eat the correct food and cut out smoking and drinking in order to ensure healthy and speedy conception, it's just as important for her partner to accept his part of the responsibility.

Dangers to your sperm

The life story of the sperm is a fascinating one. It takes about twelve weeks for it to develop from first cell to maturity and during that time it's very sensitive to any damage from outside sources. There are three main dangers to watch out for:

■ **SMOKING** There is growing evidence that smoking can reduce the level of male hormones, interfere with sperm development – sperm need large amounts of vitamin C and smoking destroys it – and even cause genetic changes which could lead to the birth of a malformed child. A German study has shown definite links between congenital defects and fathers who are smokers.

■ **ALCOHOL** Animal studies have shown that alcohol, too, can severely damage sperm and can lead to genetic abnormalities. If you're planning to become a father you should make sure you have no more than two or three drinks a week in the three months leading up to conception.

■ **METAL** Sperm can be damaged by a wide range of substances which contain metal. These may be found in the food cupboard and around the home. Out-of-date canned foods, especially cans of acidic fruits, can be a source of lead, as can old water pipes and old paint, so avoid stripping old paintwork. You shouldn't use shampoo containing selenium or deodorants

> ❝Vitamin C is particularly important as it prevents sperm from clumping and becoming less motile.❞

or anti-perspirants which include aluminium. Similarly, avoid aluminium saucepans, kettles and pressure cookers, and milk-substitute powders containing aluminium salts.

What to eat

Sperm cells, just like cells in any other part of your body, are totally reliant on the nutrients they're supplied with to keep them functioning efficiently.

■ A healthy, balanced diet will give you an adequate intake of all the essential vitamins, minerals and trace elements.

■ Wherever possible, choose organically grown produce; it hasn't undergone any processes that might rob it of its full nutritional value and won't contain hormones, antibiotics or other chemicals.

■ Vitamin C is particularly important as it prevents sperm from clumping (sticking together) and becoming less motile. Eat some citrus fruit and have a glass of fresh fruit juice every day as well as a generous intake of all other fresh produce. Give yourself extra insurance by taking a good multi-vitamin and mineral pill.

DID YOU KNOW THAT?

Just as we all feel a bit lazy when we're sitting in the sun, so the sperm cells get less active when they're too hot. And over-heated testicles mean less sperm, too. So avoid wearing Y-fronts and other tight underpants or jeans, and don't take a hot bath, especially just before intercourse, as this will affect the ability of the sperm to swim up the vagina and fertilise the egg.

Pregnancy and

The folklore of pregnancy is a minefield of myth and magic and a catalogue of 'dos and don'ts'. The first step on the road to a safe, happy and successful pregnancy is to ignore conflicting advice from well-meaning friends and relatives as well as all the old wives' tales. Rely on your own common sense and make sure that you understand as much about this wonderful event as possible. Don't be afraid to ask your midwife, doctor or consultant about things that worry you.

Of course, there are problems and risks, and you may not feel 100 per cent for every single day of the nine months. But you can swing the odds in your favour. You can combat the morning sickness, reduce the tiredness, avoid the excessive weight gain and see that your growing baby is getting the best possible nourishment, while at the same time protecting your own future health. You can even do something about the seemingly inevitable indigestion, constipation, varicose veins and piles. It's a simple question of how, what and when you eat, of getting the right balance of rest and exercise and of having a positive outlook and bags of confidence.

SMOKING AND PREGNANCY If you didn't manage to give up smoking while trying to conceive you really must do it now. Apart from the damage which it does to you, it can do serious harm to your growing baby. As well as restricting its growth rate and resulting in a lower-weight baby, babies born to smokers are likely to have smaller lungs and are much more likely to suffer from asthma and other chest problems.

DID YOU KNOW THAT?

One of the strangest things women may experience during pregnancy is pica. This is the medical term for unnatural cravings that drive people to eat substances which are not foods. It can also happen in young children and in some psychiatric illnesses. Earth, clay, coal, wood and chalk are the commonly chosen items.

This strange abnormality is a sensory malfunction which seems to be linked to iron deficiency rather than to any social or behavioural disturbances. The symptoms can be reversed by giving iron supplements.

The onset of pica should be taken seriously as a sign of potential anaemia during pregnancy, which can translate into anaemia for the baby. Although iron stores in the bodies of anaemic babies can be increased by supplements, brain stores don't respond in the same way and this can have long-term effects on behaviour and IQ. These effects begin during pregnancy and can affect the baby after birth and during its development. A lack of iron in the mother's blood also means reduced oxygen-carrying capacity which may also affect growth and development of the foetus.

Another consequence of pica is the risk of lead poisoning, especially if soil is one of the 'foods'.

Motherhood

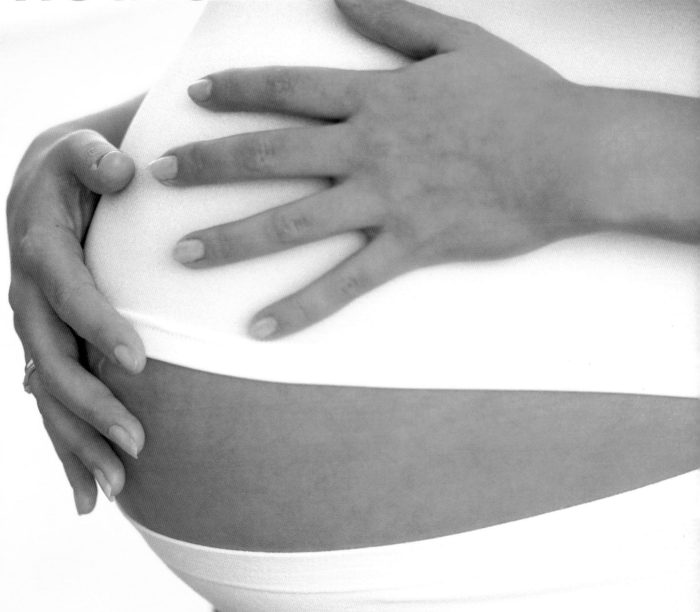

"When you're pregnant you're not eating for two but you are eating for one and nourishing one and a bit."

EATING FOR PREGNANCY

You are what you eat, and your baby is what you eat, too. When you're pregnant you're not eating for two but you are eating for one and nourishing one and a bit, so you have extra nutritional needs. This means that you must take care of yourself because your baby will get as much nourishment as it can at your expense.

On the other hand, don't become a food freak, don't get obsessed by diet and don't worry about every bite you take. What you need is a simple commonsense approach. This will ensure that you have a healthy pregnancy, a healthy baby, the energy to look after your baby once it's born and the certainty of returning to your pre-pregnancy weight with as little fuss as possible – though this will inevitably take longer if you're breastfeeding (see page 134).

How many calories?

The average calorie requirement for women between the ages of 19 and 50 is 1940 per day, give or take a little depending on how physically active you are. You only need 200 calories a day extra if you're pregnant – and that's only in the last three months. It's important that you get your calories from a good mixture of different foods. During pregnancy your total food

intake should increase by around 20 per cent but your body's need for folic acid, vitamins B and C, calcium, zinc and magnesium go up by far more than that. Vegetarians, and particularly vegans, may be at risk of vitamin B12 deficiency during pregnancy and any woman who's been trying to lose weight by drastic dieting could be missing out on the whole range of essential nutrients. If you're in either of these groups talk to your doctor about a vitamin and mineral supplement.

Daily requirements during pregnancy

To guarantee a healthy balance of nutrients and plenty of the good soluble fibre, aim for a minimum of five portions each day of fresh fruit, salad and vegetables – approximately 500g in weight, not counting potatoes.

You also need around 60g of protein a day. A grilled herring, for example, supplies 24g, three walnuts provide 2g, four tablespoons of brown rice provide 4g, a chicken leg provides about 30g, 30g of cheese provide 7g, 170g of cod provides 35g, a two-egg omelette provides 15g, and 115g of cooked lentils provides 19g.

Pregnancy extras

■ **FOR CALCIUM AND VITAMIN D** Sardines (with the bones if canned) and other oily fish (wild or organic farmed salmon, herrings, pilchards, mackerel, and not more than two portions a week of tuna – fresh not canned – swordfish or marlin), milk, yoghurt, cheese, beans, cereals and nuts for the calcium, the sardines and milk for the vitamin D. It's important to understand that your absorption of calcium from food can increase by 65 per cent if there is sufficient vitamin D (see page 44) in your blood. It's almost certain that the official RDA of 5mcg of vitamin D is too low and studies have shown that even women with normal vitamin D levels will absorb more calcium if they take a supplement. As well as the foods listed here, exposure to sunlight will help increase your vitamin D levels.

■ **FOR IRON AND FOLIC ACID** Meat, chickpeas, other green vegetables, dried apricots, dates and raisins.

■ **FOR BETA-CAROTENE AND VITAMIN A** Carrots, spinach, oily fish, eggs, dairy products, dark green and yellow vegetables all provide beta-carotene and vitamin A in safe amounts.

■ **FOR VITAMIN C** Green peppers, citrus fruits, kiwi fruits and most vegetables, even potatoes, are extra sources of vitamin C.

TOP 10 FOODS FOR PREGNANCY

APPLES neutralise the acidity produced by indigestion. They contain pectin, a fibre that keeps the bowels functioning and that lowers cholesterol.

BROCCOLI is a rich source of vitamins A and C. It also provides iron, calcium, potassium and folic acid.

BROWN RICE provides many B vitamins, some fibre, iron, potassium and protein.

CANNED SARDINES (INCLUDING THE BONES) will provide your baby with essential fatty acids for brain development. They're also a good source of calcium to protect your skeleton.

CLOVES are a great aid to digestion. They help to reduce nausea, flatulence and dyspepsia.

GARLIC is not only good for your heart, circulation and blood pressure but also a powerful antibacterial and antifungal to protect against infections.

HERRINGS are a fine source of vitamins A, D and B. They also contain iodine, selenium, phosphorus, potassium, iron and calcium. Most importantly, they supply the Omega-3 fatty acids.

KIWI FRUIT give you twice as much vitamin C as an orange, more fibre than an apple, as much vitamin E as an avocado, and lots of potassium, a lack of which can lead to problems of fatigue and poor digestion.

ONIONS are renowned for being good for the heart and circulation.

WALNUTS are high in protein, B vitamins, calcium, potassium, phosphorus, zinc and iron and essential fatty acids.

Foods to avoid during pregnancy

■ **FATS** There is evidence that the seeds of coronary heart disease are sown in earliest childhood – a high consumption of sugar and saturated fat by nursing mothers means high-fat milk for babies (sugar raises the saturated fat content of breast milk) – and some experts believe the seeds are even sown during pregnancy, so this is a time to avoid foods that are high in animal fats.

It's easy to cut out the fat you can see but much more difficult to cut out the hidden fats so you need to know where these are lurking. They are in sausages, salamis, pâtés, meat pies, pasties, scotch eggs, bacon, ham, burgers and the dreaded doner kebab. Doner kebabs provide around 85 per cent of their calories from fat, while the shish kebab is one of the lowest fat fast foods.

Bakery goods like biscuits, Danish pastries, cream cakes, croissants made with butter, ice cream and crisps may all be rich suppliers of the unhealthy saturated fats.

Beware of traditionally high-fat products which are sold as 'low fat'. They seldom are; they may be 'lower' in fat, but many still supply far too much.

■ **SALT** Watch out for salt (see pages 74–5) as packages often state only the sodium content which is a much lower number. Too much salt can cause fluid retention and raised blood pressure, which is the last thing you want at any time, but especially during pregnancy. Too much salt can also increase the amount of calcium excreted by your body. This can be disastrous during pregnancy, not just for the baby, but because it can also cause an increased risk of osteoporosis in later life.

But you do need a certain amount of sodium, especially during pregnancy. To make sure that you get the small quantity you need, eat fish, eggs, meat, poultry, dairy products, nuts and seeds, which not only contain sodium but are also good sources of potassium, which can counteract some of the harmful effects of excess sodium. Also eat beans, bananas, oranges, potatoes, melon and most other fruits and vegetables. Try not to add salt during cooking and certainly don't sprinkle it over your food.

DON'T GO TO EXTREMES It's surprising how many women go on weight-loss diets during early pregnancy. Do not do this unless you are specifically advised to by your doctor. As long as there's no medical reason against it, all you need is a little extra exercise.

> "Too much salt is disastrous in pregnancy, not just for the baby, but because it can lead to osteoporosis."

Motherhood

■ **CARBONATED DRINKS AND ARTIFICIAL SWEETENERS** You may be trying to watch your calorie intake during pregnancy but it's important to emphasise that low-cal, lite or diet drinks contain significant amounts of artificial sweeteners which your baby would be better off without. Even more importantly, carbonated drinks increase calcium loss from the body and so should be avoided during pregnancy.

■ **FROZEN AND CHILLED FOODS** As well as observing the guidelines on unpasteurised cheeses, raw and undercooked eggs, and undercooked meat and poultry (see page 115), it's important to be extra careful with frozen and chilled foods. You really do need to follow the manufacturer's instructions implicitly and make sure that foods are thoroughly thawed before cooking if the instructions say they should be. Microwaves can be a hazard as few people know the wattage of their particular machine and have probably lost the instruction manual long ago. The microwaving instructions on the food packaging relate to the power of the machine and the length of microwaving time required. Do check and make sure you know the details of your microwave before taking unnecessary risks with your own and your baby's health. Microwaved frozen food which is not thoroughly cooked right to the middle is a serious food-poisoning hazard.

■ **RASPBERRY LEAF TEA** Do not drink raspberry leaf tea during the early stages of pregnancy. It's a great aid during the last ten weeks as it strengthens the long muscles of the uterus and helps with contractions. But that's not what you want to happen in the sixth or seventh month of your pregnancy. When making raspberry leaf tea use one teaspoon of chopped fresh or dried leaf per cup and do not leave to infuse for more than five minutes.

Pregnancy and

THE PROBLEMS OF PREGNANCY

Although, hopefully, pregnancy is a time of joy and expectation, it is also a time of worry and can be marred by a number of pregnancy-related problems.

Morning sickness

Most women can master this misery. Eat a little nourishing snack before bedtime so that your stomach isn't empty while you sleep and keep a top-up store on your bedside table for midnight feasts – for example, oatmeal biscuits, crispbreads, walnuts, raisins, sesame seeds and a bottle of plain mineral water. As soon as you wake up, take the best anti-morning sickness medicine of all – a centimetre of fresh ginger root grated into a mug of boiling water, left for 5 minutes, strained and sweetened with a little honey. Failing that, have a drink of peppermint tea, lime-flower tea with a little fresh ginger grated into it, or weak Indian tea with a little honey and no milk, and a plain unsweetened biscuit. Whichever you choose, it's best if your caring partner brings it to you in bed so that you have it before getting up.

Anaemia and toxaemia

You must cut down the risk of suffering these serious complications of pregnancy. Iron and protein are the key foods. Include at least two portions of green leafy vegetables and three protein foods each day, preferably meat, poultry, oily fish and shellfish. Dates, raisins and dried figs will also provide some iron. Magnesium is another key mineral here, and the richest sources are chickpeas, kidney beans, cashew nuts and mackerel.

Constipation

This is so easy to prevent, and yet causes more discomfort than many of the other problems. Tackle it before you get it by increasing the amount you drink. Have at least 1.5 litres of fluid each day, most of which

should be water. Keep off the fizzy drinks and watch out for the high natural sugar content of even the pure fruit juices; they should be diluted fifty-fifty with water. Make sure you eat at least three high-fibre foods daily; brown rice, wholemeal bread, dried fruits, vegetables, potatoes cooked with their skins, apples, pears, baked beans and porridge are all great sources of natural fibre which help keep everything on the move. Don't sprinkle spoons of bran over your breakfast cereal; bran prevents you from absorbing calcium and iron.

Varicose veins and piles

These are not inevitable; both are linked with constipation so avoiding that protects you from these problems, too. Vitamin E is essential for blood vessels; get it from kiwi fruit, herring, tuna, extra-virgin olive oil, nuts and canned tomatoes. Garlic and onions are also great protectors of your circulatory system. Have two of the above foods daily. Avoid standing, take plenty of walks or other exercise, and if there is a family history of varicose veins, wear good support tights or stockings.

Exhaustion

You will need as much energy as you can muster for the new baby, so lots of sustained-energy foods are vital during these nine months. Complex carbohydrates are the best source of slow-release energy and are much healthier than sugars and refined starches. Brown rice, wholemeal bread, lentils, beans, nuts, good cereals like muesli, porridge or any salt-free unsweetened commercial wholewheat cereal should be your first choices. Eggs, fish, poultry, lean meat and low-fat dairy products supply the protein that you need and if you are vegetarian, you need to eat a good mixture of cereals and pulses.

Acid indigestion

Lots of women have problems with indigestion or heartburn during the last month or so of pregnancy. The bulge gets in the way and puts excessive pressure on the diaphragm which allows the reflux of acid from the stomach to get into the oesophagus causing severe heartburn. For this reason it's more comfortable to avoid large meals and to eat little and often, but make sure that your total food intake doesn't go up. Use plenty of cloves in your cooking, avoid the frying pan, chew your food well, and don't eat on the hoof. If you're expecting more than one baby, the problem may well be worse (see page 129).

High blood pressure

This is the most dreaded of all pregnancy problems because it can result in strokes, heart disease, kidney problems and may also trigger of pre-eclampsia. Salt (see page 74) is your blood pressure's worst enemy, so throw away the salt cellar and use as little as possible in cooking. You must read the labels on all ready-made foods as these account for 75 per cent of the average 12g of salt consumed by people each day. And don't be confused by the fact that most food manufacturers don't list the salt content but give you the amount of sodium instead (see page 75) to make things look more acceptable. The recommended daily allowance of salt from all sources is no more than 4–5g. Also keep your blood pressure in check by following my advice on weight gain, varicose veins, anaemia and constipation. Eat lots of herrings, other oily fish and all the Top 10 Foods for pregnancy, especially the garlic and onions.

Stress

This is another key factor in raised blood-pressure and the emotional upheaval of pregnancy doesn't always help. Relaxation exercises, yoga, meditation and regular physical exercise are great aids to controlling your blood pressure and learning to say 'no', avoiding over-commitment and being organised will all help reduce your stress levels, too.

WEIGHT GAIN DURING PREGNANCY

The easiest thing for you to control during pregnancy is your weight. It is also one of the most important, both for you and the baby. For a start, all the possible discomforts of a normal pregnancy – backache, heartburn, piles, varicose veins, stretch marks and tiredness – will be made worse by overweight and if you are really overweight, then the serious problems of high blood pressure, toxaemia and pre-eclampsia will become more likely.

But your baby is your prime concern. You should aim to gain 9–14kg over the nine months, though the rate at which you gain them will vary. There's very little change during the first ten weeks; the healthy average gain during the second ten to twelve weeks is about 250g, and from then on, it should be about 500g a week.

It's easy to do it right. Gain a maximum of 14kg and have a baby at around the ideal birth weight of 3–4kg. On the other hand, a junk-food diet that adds 22kg to you, may result in an underweight 2kg baby, which will be more at risk.

Certainly avoid any crash diets, especially during the first three months, which is the time for good calories and the vital nutrients which the growing baby needs. And if you find your weight has got to the limit after six months, then the last three months are not the time for panic measures. This is when the baby's brain is developing and that needs protein, especially from oily fish, and calories. If you think you're putting on too much weight, do not try going on any form of restricted diet without advice from your doctor.

To help keep your weight under control, eat at least four of the Top 10 Foods for Pregnancy each day, a varied mixture of the healthy, low-fat, high-nutrient foods mentioned elsewhere in this section of the book, and aim for no more than 2400 calories and your 60g of protein a day (see above).

The special needs of multiple births

Naturally you're going to gain extra weight if you're expecting more than one baby, so it's even more important to try and keep your weight gain under control. Gaining approximately 18kg for twins, 22.5kg for triplets and 31kg for quads, will keep you within the normal range. To help you along, be extra careful about your consumption of fats, sugars and salt, and eat more wholegrain cereals, fruits, vegetables and salads.

Keeping your weight gain under control with more than one baby on the way becomes harder due to the need to increase your daily input of essential nutrients. For example, your need for iron and folic acid goes up dramatically in multiple births – around 570mg of extra iron for yourself and 430mg extra for each of your babies during the nine months of pregnancy. If your iron stores are reasonable and your diet is good, the increased demand may well be met – helped along by the cessation of your monthly periods – but this is unlikely to be sufficient iron saving to cope with multiple births, so in these cases supplementation is usually essential. Don't try doing this for yourself but make sure you get accurate professional advice.

Indigestion

If you're expecting more than one baby, you will get much larger earlier on in pregnancy and this can cause extreme digestive discomfort. Eat smaller meals, but more frequently and don't eat large amounts late at night, as the indigestion and heartburn will keep you awake – and you're going to need all the rest you can get for later on. Don't make the mistake of trying to prop yourself up on pillows in bed to prevent the gastric reflux which causes heartburn. It doesn't work and you end up with a stiff neck and even more backache than in a normal pregnancy. The trick is to raise the head-end of your bed by about 8cm. You can get bed blocks for this purpose or use bricks; the castors on the bed legs will sit in the hollow of the bricks and your bed won't roll across the room during the night.

WHERE DOES THE WEIGHT GO DURING PREGNANCY?

Baby	3.2–3.6kg
Placenta	0.7–0.9kg
Amniotic fluid	0.8–0.9kg
Womb	0.9kg
Breasts	0.9kg
Extra blood	1.4–1.8kg
Fat stores	1.8–2.72kg

"You should aim to gain 9–14kg over the nine months, though the rate at which you gain them will vary."

There's nothing else in life quite like it: the joy of that moment when you first hold your newborn baby in your arms. Suddenly all those long dreary months of waiting seem worthwhile. But as any mother can tell you, motherhood can be tough going, and the first time round, especially so. For a start, you'll be more tired than you ever imagined possible and you'll never get as much sleep as you need.

Even the simplest household chores can suddenly seem overwhelming, a cross word will reduce you to tears, and you'll wonder despairingly how on earth other women ever cope with it. Once your baby is a toddler, you'll get a decent night's sleep at last, but then you'll need it to cope with an active, demanding two-year-old. And the average mother of four- and five-year-olds will thank you with tears in her eyes, if you can arrange just a couple of hours for her away from it all.

The importance of proper meals

When life is so hectic and demanding, preparing proper meals for yourself may seem a chore you can forget about. Instead, you go for the temporary 'lift' provided by a cup of tea or coffee and a couple of sweet biscuits, then later in the day, you make do with food out of a can or the remains of the nursery lunch. What this sort of eating can't and won't do, however, is give you the strength, the nervous resilience and the sheer stamina that Vitality Eating supplies. Study the Vitality Eating Plan on page 113. Don't short-change yourself; your health is vital. Not just for you but for the whole family.

What should you eat?

Your midday meal doesn't have to be a lot of fuss; a baked potato or a wholemeal roll with a piece of cheese, a couple of sticks of celery and an apple, followed by a carton of low-fat yoghurt – stir in a little honey and some nuts. That makes a beautifully balanced meal that will keep you going for hours. Between-meals snacks? Dried fruit – especially apricots – will give you a real energy lift. Eat liver once a week and apart from that, cut down on red meat and spend the money on extra fresh fruit and vegetables, especially cabbages, watercress and spring greens, which will raise your resistance to infection and stress.

Motherhood

TOP 10 FOODS FOR MOTHERHOOD

APRICOTS These are rich in beta-carotene that your body converts into vitamin A. Dried apricots are rich in iron, but wash before eating to remove the sulphur dioxide used as a preservative.

BASIL This has a mild calming action. The old herbalists used it to help restore regular periods, and as a remedy for nervous headaches.

CHEESE A matchbox-sized piece of cheese a day will help replace calcium lost during your pregnancy. Soft cheeses like Brie and Camembert contain less fat than hard cheeses – the exception is cream cheese.

GRAPEFRUIT This is loaded with vitamins A and C; pink grapefruit are even higher in vitamin A.

LIVER This is crammed with vitamin A, B complex, and masses of iron and zinc.

LEAN RED MEAT, SEAFOOD AND PUMPKIN SEEDS for zinc.

SAGE This versatile herb helps get your hormones back on an even keel and can improve milk production.

SESAME SEEDS All seeds are regenerating, vital foods and are especially useful to help you meet the demands of a rushed and busy life.

WATERCRESS This contains a natural antibiotic. It's also rich in beta-carotene that your body converts into vitamin A and iron.

YOGHURT Not only is yoghurt twice as easy to digest as milk, it contains acidophilus bacteria which will re-create a healthy balance of bacteria in your gut.

MOTHER'S MISERY

There are many woes that seem to strike when you're a new mum, but follow my advice, eat the right foods, and you'll soon see the back of them.

Postnatal depression (PND)

This may seem like it's all in the mind, but it's a reality. Of course you need professional therapy for severe PND, but you can help yourself, too. Rest and the right diet can help banish it for good.

First, get more rest at all costs, even if it means a messy house and no clean shirts for your husband or partner. Your diet must include generous amounts of wholegrain cereals – oats, wholewheat, brown rice, rye and barley – for the stress-proofing that their B-complex vitamins will give you. You also need live yoghurt for its calcium and vitamin B-producing probiotic bacteria. All the green leafy vegetables are important for their magnesium – another nutrient badly needed by the stressed nervous system – as well as their iron, folic acid and health-protective phytochemicals. Zinc is another vital nutrient, and it's specially likely to be deficient in mothers who took iron supplements in pregnancy, as the two minerals need to be in balance. Liver, shrimps, beef, cheese, sardines and wholemeal bread all supply zinc, and a handful of pumpkin seeds also contain zinc as well as vitamin E. For an extra shot in the arm, take a daily tablespoon of dried brewer's yeast; blend it with a carton of low-fat yoghurt, a banana and half a glass of orange juice to make a delicious drink that's also a complete meal. Brewer's yeast is loaded with B-vitamins and vital minerals, including zinc.

Another thing you can do to help your PND is to use intensive light therapy. There's good evidence that this – so successful in the treatment of Seasonal Affective Disorder (SAD) or Winter Blues – can also be very helpful for PND.

The antidepressant herb, St. John's Wort, is another valuable aid for mild to moderate depression. It's as effective as conventional antidepressant drugs but without the side effects. Take care though; it should not be taken at the same time as blood-thinning drugs, some types of contraceptive pill, especially the mini pill, or with conventional antidepressants. If you have any doubts, discuss them with your doctor or pharmacist.

Motherhood

Stress

Non-stop demands on your attention can be a particularly exhausting form of stress, which in turn lowers your resistance to infection of any kind. To beef up your immune defences, eat foods rich in vitamins A and C: brightly coloured fruits like oranges, grapefruits – especially the pink ones – peaches, nectarines, blackcurrants and all the wonderful berries. Even frozen, these summer berry fruits are an amazingly rich source of vitamin C and are amongst the best providers of the antioxidant ORAC units (see pages 82–3). Another invaluable piece of advice comes from the famous Swiss Dr Bircher-Benner, who cured illnesses with a diet containing a high proportion of raw foods. He used to tell his patients, 'Eat green leaves every day.' It's advice you couldn't do better than follow to help beat stress. Cabbage, watercress, spring greens, spinach and all kinds of lettuce are richly protective, supplying antibacterial chlorophyll – wonderful, incidentally, for your skin – as well as vitamin A and useful minerals like calcium and magnesium.

Obesity

You may feel that by rights you should be worn to a shadow, yet you may actually be overweight, and listless with it. Eating sweet snacks – the classic coffee and croissant, or tea and a doughnut – that are high in calories, fats and sugar but low in real nutrition and in fibre is one of the commonest causes. Have a healthy snack instead – a piece of fruit, a handful of raisins or a carton of yoghurt with a little honey stirred in. And remember that excess fat and refined carbohydrates put a heavy workload on your digestive system, while lack of fibre can bring it all to a grinding halt. In the short term, poor digestion will stop you ever feeling on peak form. In the long term, it can lead to much more serious health problems such as cancer, arthritis and heart disease. Achieving good digestive health is another reason to ensure that your diet contains a good daily dose of the probiotic beneficial bacteria from live yoghurt and fermented milk drinks.

Fatigue

This is what makes young mothers tense and irritable. It also doesn't leave you feeling very sexy, and you won't have much energy to spend on looking attractive either. At times like these, remember the stores of energy and nutrition packed into the tiny seeds of sesame. In the traditional medicine of the Middle East, sesame seeds have always been associated with enhanced sexual energy and sexual prowess. Eat them in the form of tahini (sesame-seed paste), stocked by every health-food shop and many ethnic grocers, or as hummus, the savoury dip made from tahini and chickpeas. It's delicious with flat wholewheat pitta bread and chunks of raw vegetables and the zinc in the sesame will also do wonders for your skin.

The fragrant herb basil is a wonderful tonic for fatigue. Italians wouldn't make a tomato salad without it. Pesto sauce, made with lots of basil and pine nuts, is an extra-delicious sauce for pasta. You can buy it ready-made or make your own.

Both fatigue and weight problems will respond to active exercise, especially out in the open air. Pram-pushing may give you fresh air and sunshine, but you need something just a little more strenuous 2–3 times a week. Swimming is the ideal exercise for you and your baby will love it too! Make it a family outing that you'll all enjoy.

BREASTFEEDING

Providing breast milk for your baby is a high-energy process and those mothers who are both able, and choose, to breastfeed need a substantial increase in their amount of daily calories. The average woman between the ages of 19 and 50 has a daily calorie need which is a couple of chocolate biscuits short of 2000 calories. In the first month of breastfeeding she'll need 450 more each day, increasing to 570 a day by the third month.

If you breastfeed almost exclusively beyond three to four months, with only the occasional complementary or feed, your calorie requirement remains at an extra 570 a day, dropping to 550 after six months. But if you start weaning at three months and introduce a substantial amount of complementary feeds, you only need an extra 480 calories a day, dropping to 240 after six months.

What to eat

Breastfeeding mothers need food that is rich in vitamins, minerals, proteins and essential fatty acids. If your milk doesn't contain enough, the baby will deplete your own stores, especially your calcium, which will be taken from your bones. You'll need at least an extra 550mg of calcium each day and 350mcg of vitamin A.

In addition, you'll also need more protein from yoghurt, vitamin C and vitamin K from spinach and cabbage, vitamin E from avocados, nuts, seeds and olive oil, and iron to prevent anaemia. If you're taking iron supplements, make sure they're an organic form rather than ferrous sulphate which can compromise your vitamin E uptake. Also get lots of B vitamins by eating brewer's yeast, wholegrain cereals, eggs, offal, leafy green vegetables, dairy products, root vegetables and molasses. This will increase the amount that ends up in your breast milk.

A high sugar intake raises the saturated fat content of breast milk, so you should also be sparing with the chocolates, biscuits, cakes and pastries, and you might like to follow traditional advice and avoid garlic and onions as your baby may not like the taste of them in your milk..

BREAST VERSUS BOTTLE

The decline in breastfeeding is, I'm sure, the result of breasts having become universal objects of sexuality rather than sources of nutrition for babies. In spite of recent efforts to persuade women to return to breastfeeding, many are too embarrassed to do so in public places and some find the whole idea distasteful. This is a tragedy for the babies.

Breast milk is perfect for human babies; cow's milk and formula milk aren't. There is now overwhelming evidence that formula milks can never rival mother's milk and I'm sure there are as yet undiscovered nutrients in mother's milk that aren't currently in any formula milk. For example, it's only in the last few years that a substance called lactoferrin, found in the colostrum that is produced during the first few days of breastfeeding, has been identified as an important immune-boosting factor for the baby.

Certainly breastfeeding conveys immunity to a host of infections directly to the baby. It also lessens the likelihood of anaemia and avoids the introduction of potential allergens to the baby's digestive system, which is unable to cope with them at such an early age. The protection against allergy is even greater if the baby is breastfed for at least 16 weeks.

If there is a family history of food allergies, hay fever, eczema or asthma and especially in both parents, it's worth taking special precautions when breastfeeding. Keep your consumption of wheat, dairy products, eggs and shellfish to a minimum, and avoid altogether any foods which you know are specific allergens. Fish, strawberries and peanuts are common examples.

In addition, breastfed babies have a head start when it comes to getting enough of the essential fatty acids that can make a significant difference to brain development and future intelligence. Breast milk is a uniquely rich source of these special fats. There are now some formula milks that are fortified with essential fatty acids but these can never be quite the same.

Then there's the question of convenience. Breastfeeding avoids all the paraphernalia of bottles, sterilisation and preparing formula milks and eliminates possibilities of bacterial infection. Breast milk is available on demand and breastfeeding is still one of the most powerful influences in mother and baby bonding.

And last, but not least, at a time when childhood obesity is becoming a major talking point and epidemic in the Western world, it's worth noting that a number of studies have shown that breastfeeding can help stem the tide of obesity. Research figures suggest that 28 breastfed babies out of every 1000 will end up as obese children, compared with 45 out of every 1000 who were bottle-fed. The strength of the anti-obesity effect increased with the length of breastfeeding.

"What breastfeeding mothers need is food that is rich in vitamins, minerals, proteins and essential fatty acids."

What to drink

It's vital to increase your fluid intake when breastfeeding but this doesn't have to mean cow's milk. In fact, Naturopaths believe that breastfeeding mothers who drink more than 500ml of cow's milk a day are more likely to have babies with eczema, asthma and colic. Water is fine, as are herb teas, China tea, weak Indian tea and diluted fresh fruit juices. Home-made vegetable soups are a great bonus, too as they give you the liquid you need as well as masses of vitamins and minerals with every swallow. Keep off sweetened or low-calorie fizzy drinks and all alcohol.

Eat organic

Trying to eat as much organic food as possible is important at any time but it becomes a major issue if you're breastfeeding. Studies of breast milk around the world have shown that it contains residues of a whole range of potentially harmful chemicals from DDT to weed killers and chemicals used in the plastics industry. As yet there's no direct evidence that these residues have any harmful effect on babies, but it's better if they're not present. Eating organic produce and washing fruit and vegetables before eating will limit their levels and eating only organic meat, poultry and dairy products will avoid antibiotics and growth hormones passing through into the milk.

The advantages of bottle feeding

Bottle feeding has one advantage, and that is for the mums. Apart from being able to hand the baby over to someone else at feed time, bottle-feeding mums will lose weight and get their pre-pregnancy shape back a lot quicker than the breast-feeders. Bottle-feeders do not need to increase their calorie consumption as breast-feeders do, so they can start to cut down on their intake within two or three weeks of giving birth. Whichever method of feeding your baby you choose, I would advise all new mothers to concentrate on replacing their depleted nutrition stores as soon as possible. To this end, bottle-feeders should eat the same foods as breast-feeders, but keep the calories down.

PROBLEMS OF BREASTFEEDING

Don't give up just because things seem difficult. Although in these days of a highly mobile society it's not always easy to turn to mother or grandmother for help, there are many professionals who can advise you and guide you along the right path. And if breastfeeding proves impossible you must not ever feel guilty, whatever the reason. If you can't breastfeed, accept it and realise that it's not in any way your fault.

Motherhood

From Baby

Feeding children can be a battlefield and just to make parents' life more difficult it's heavily mined and booby-trapped as well. Unfortunately as a parent you're like the home guard ranged against the armies of food manufacturers, the peddlers of soft drinks, sweets and snacks, the giant fast-food industry and vending machines dispensing rubbish instead of food. You may also be fighting the institutional caterers at your child's school, who often have to rely on the cheapest and least nutritious ingredients or food that may be pre-cooked, transported for hundreds of kilometres, then reheated.

Consequently, children's taste buds develop an enormous preference for sweet, salty and fatty foods but a diet high in sugar, salt and fat means health problems later in life:

■ High blood pressure, strokes and circulatory disease (the seeds of heart disease are sown in childhood; every 3 minutes someone dies of premature and preventable heart disease).

■ Gallstones, digestive problems and bowel cancer.

■ Arthritis, back pain and osteoporosis.

■ Hormone-linked problems like acne, painful periods, low sperm counts and reduced fertility.

■ Type II diabetes (see page 54), which used to be called adult-onset diabetes, now frequently occurs in children, condemning them to live with the risks of blindness, kidney and heart problems, circulatory disorders and the loss of limbs.

These long-term effects on a youngster's health are quite terrifying and it's these that every parent should think about before they buy the next bag of crisps, can of cola, burger and chips, or bottle of 'health' drink, which is nothing more than a collection of chemicals, sugar, sweeteners, a touch of vitamin C and a tiny percentage of juice. By allowing our children to develop the habit of eating junk food, we're producing an entire generation that will have to live with the disastrous consequences of our apathy.

As well as the many major diseases, other consequences include a much higher risk of anaemia, lowered resistance to illness, weaker bones and appetite loss.

Overfed yet undernourished

Few children in the affluent West go to bed hungry, but millions are in fact malnourished according to even the most modest nutritional standards. One survey after another, many of them carried out by government agencies, shows an alarming decline in the nutritional content of the food our children eat today.

CONSIDER THESE FACTS:

■ In the USA and UK one in five 4–18 year olds doesn't eat any fruit at all.

■ Up to 50 per cent of children in the UK don't get enough vitamins A, B12, folic acid and vitamins D and E.

■ Many children in the UK go short of calcium, iron, zinc and selenium.

THE RESULTS ARE ALREADY APPARENT:

■ One in 5 children is now clinically obese in the UK and USA.

■ Type II diabetes, which normally occurs in middle age, is now regularly seen in six- and seven-year-old children in the UK and USA.

But that's not all. Asthma, eczema, allergies, hyperactivity, behavioural problems, learning difficulties, eating disorders, M.E. or Chronic Fatigue Syndrome, and even addictions to alcohol, nicotine, caffeine and illegal drugs, are increasingly common health problems affecting children throughout the Western world.

It's no coincidence that the rising toll of these diseases in children has coincided with the steady decline in the quality and nutritional value of the food they eat. A study by the Medical Research Council in England revealed the horrifying truth. The study examined the difference between the food eaten by four-year-olds in 1950 and in the 1990s. To everyone's apparent amazement – but certainly not mine – mothers knew more about healthy eating 40 years ago than they do today. The massive growth of supermarkets, convenience foods, the fast-food industry and the multi-billion pound advertising budgets for junk foods are all part of the reason for this change.

According to American paediatricians and nutrition experts, the same is true in the USA. The American Diabetic Association warns that one in five children is not just overweight, but clinically obese. Not surprising when you consider that sugar consumption has increased 28 per cent in the last 17 years in America, and is especially high amongst children.

Doctor Michael Jacobson, Director of the Center for Science in the Public Interest in Washington DC, has called for better food labelling. 'Sugar consumption has been going through the roof, fuelling soaring obesity rates and other health problems. It's vital that the FDA require labels that would enable consumers to monitor – and reduce – sugar intake.'

But in spite of all the health education initiatives, the phenomenal growth of the organic movement, health-food shops and the sale of vitamin pills, the typical diet of our children gets worse by the day.

READ THE LABEL You can feed your children a hundred times more healthily with home-cooked food than if you use processed food aimed specifically at children. You only have to look at the labels to find that most are full of chemicals, salt, sugar and fat. A survey by the UK Food Standards Agency found that 59 per cent of people say they read food labels but hardly any understand what they mean. But the more you look, the better your grasp of the information will get. And you owe it to your children to get clued up.

From Baby

MAKE FOODIES NOT FADDIES

It's not difficult to make sure your baby grows into a food-loving toddler, a healthy teenager and a well-nourished adult, but you must start early and you must start by feeding him or her good home-cooked food as often as possible. Whenever you can, buy organic food and make sure you wash all fruits and vegetables – even organic ones – before use.

After four months and by six months introduce puréed solids, beginning with baby rice and then any vegetables, followed by fruits. Use the vegetables you're eating, but don't add salt during cooking. If you start with vegetables, baby tastes savoury flavours before sweet, but introduce one at a time. Cook the vegetables until soft, then purée until smooth, adding boiled water if it's too thick. When you start mixing flavours, use a maximum of three ingredients, but however you prepare food for your baby, stick to the KISS principle (see page 190), which means using the freshest produce possible and cooking it simply.

HERE ARE SOME USEFUL WEANING TIPS:

■ Don't try more than one new flavour a day.

■ Try out new foods between meals as a taster so baby doesn't associate foods he or she doesn't like with mealtimes.

■ If some food gets spat out, don't give up; it may take six or more attempts before baby accepts that particular taste.

■ **FROM AROUND SIX MONTHS,** start introducing a little chicken meat, tropical fruits, berries, dairy products, wheat and oats, but I strongly advise against commercial bread and most commercial

" The three best ways I know of introducing children to fruits and vegetables are with soups, juices and smoothies. "

breakfast cereals as both contain enormously high levels of salt – far more than is healthy for your baby. It's worth making your own bread or serving pasta instead, which most little ones love to play with as well as eat. Organic oat-based cereals are excellent, too, but don't forget that they can be very filling so keep the portions small to avoid the risk of excluding other types of healthy food from baby's diet.

■ **AROUND NINE MONTHS** start offering eggs, beans and fish.

■ **FROM THE AGE OF TWO** you can give prawns and other shellfish, but it's best to wait another couple of years before letting them eat mussels, scallops or oysters.

Children shouldn't be given nuts or seeds – and this includes peanuts and peanut butter if there is a family history of allergies – until they're five because of the risk of allergic reactions. But peanuts are in fact legumes – members of the bean family, not real nuts – so unless a close relative like a brother or sister, parent, grandparent, uncle or aunt, or first cousin has had an obvious reaction to them, they can be used from one year onwards.

The pre-school years are your last chance before children get exposed to the world of mass catering, so now's the time to establish proper eating patterns. Slowly introduce them to more adventurous foods – minestrone soup, Welsh rarebit with wedges of lightly sautéed apples, slightly spicy grilled chicken breasts with roast vegetables, which children often prefer to steamed or boiled vegetables. Stuff pitta breads with salad, real cheese and dressing. Start using more garlic, onions, herbs and spices in cooking and always make sure that they have plenty of fresh fruit to nibble on.

BABY FOODS Baby foods are a great convenience but do buy the best quality and make sure they're organic. It's best to save them for travelling, holidays and the desperation days which happen, even in the best organised of families.

WHAT ABOUT MUM? Two or three months of trying to get pregnant, nine months of carrying and nourishing the baby, breastfeeding, sleepless nights, and rushing around after a toddler will have taken their toll on you, the mother. And what with the stress and worry of being a parent, especially if it's your first time, you may well find yourself struggling both mentally and physically. By the time your child gets to the 'terrible twos' you may be wishing you'd never started, but don't despair; this period will pass.

What you need now is plenty of energy but not all from carbohydrates. Save starchy foods for your evening meal to encourage relaxation and better sleep. Mornings should start with protein – eggs, fish, cheese, fresh fruit, yoghurt and one slice of good wholemeal bread. If you're flagging during the day, snack on high-energy foods like halva, tahini, sesame, sunflower and pumpkin seeds, dried fruits and fresh unsalted nuts. Eat more protein for lunch; oily fish is ideal but alternate this with poultry, beans and lots of vegetables and/or salads.

ON TO SCHOOL

Once they get to school they're going to need more calories, lots of B vitamins and plenty of iron to keep them fuelled with energy for body, brain and growth. That means lots of dried fruits, wholemeal bread, oily fish like salmon and sardines, meat and poultry, rice, potatoes and beans, dark green leafy vegetables, cheese, yoghurt, unsalted nuts and seeds. Home-made fishcakes and home-made burgers will be favourites, too, and there's nothing wrong with chips as long as it's just a couple of times a week.

This is a time when you should try sitting down to meals as a family as often as possible. One of the disastrous changes in children's eating habits has been the decline of the family meal. How many people now sit round a table to enjoy a family breakfast, lunch or dinner? Instead, each member of the family – even the children – chooses what he or she wants when they want from the fridge or freezer, zaps it in the microwave and eats it in isolation in front of the TV or the computer screen, which is where the average American child spends four hours a day.

By contrast, in places like the Mediterranean, it's wonderful to still see whole families, from babies to grandparents, sitting round the table talking, shouting, arguing, and enjoying a meal of lovingly prepared food. Tragically this tradition, which helps bind the fabric of our society together, is crumbling away in the face of relentless invasion by the McCulture of the fast-food industry.

But why are family mealtimes important? Apart from the social aspects, a study of over 16,000 boys and girls in the UK, published in the Archives of Family Medicine, found that children aged 9–14 who ate dinner round the family table were more likely to eat fruit and vegetables than those who were left to raid the freezer. And there was less chance of them drinking fizzy drinks or picking fried foods that are high in fat or sweet, sugary snacks. The family meal also inevitably provided many more of the essential nutrients like calcium, iron, folic acid, vitamins B6 and 12, and the antioxidant vitamins C and E.

Eating out

Eating out with your children from the earliest possible age can also help to encourage healthy food choices, but keep away from burger bars and other fast-food outlets. Restaurants are not always child-friendly, though ethnic ones usually score better. In an Italian restaurant what child can resist playing with breadsticks and simple pasta? In a Chinese, Thai or Vietnamese restaurant encourage them to master chopsticks and eat delicious dishes like duck with pancakes, spring rolls or prawns with noodles and vegetables. In an Indian restaurant, let them taste a mild curry or dip into the selection of little pots that come with a vegetarian thali, to say nothing of samosas, chapattis, naan bread and mango chutney.

Cooking with your children

Did you know that there are children today who don't realise that chips are made from potatoes, that bacon comes from a pig and that milk comes from a cow? Delia Smith, Britain's most popular cookery writer, was denounced as patronising when she explained on television how to boil an egg, but how many parents today spend time teaching their children about cooking? It's essential to get your children involved in cooking at home. I know it's messy and time-consuming, but if they help cook it, they'll eat it. And they'll also acquire an interest in food and a knowledge of buying and preparing the raw materials, unlike children who never watch a meal being prepared or help with the cooking. These children are the ones who grow up doomed to a life of takeaways and ready-made meals.

Why is it worth it?

We know that it only takes small changes in the way you shop, cook and feed your children to transform their health and wellbeing. They will see, and more importantly will feel, the difference in a few short weeks. They'll have more energy, they'll sleep better, their concentration and school grades will improve, and they'll be nicer people to have around the house.

What they can't appreciate though is how much of an investment you're making in their long-term health, offering them a chance of freedom from heart disease, brittle bones, obesity, joint disease, rotten teeth, in fact, all the diet-related diseases of Western society. And by encouraging your children to have a healthy interest in food and cooking you can be sure they'll do the same for your grandchildren.

GETTING THEM TO EAT THEIR FRUIT AND VEG

The three best ways I know of introducing children to fruits and vegetables are with soups, juices and smoothies. When children are very small, soups and smoothies should be really smooth and lump-free. You can also increase their dairy intake with home-made ice creams, sorbets and ice lollies made with organic milk and cream, real fruit and pure, preferably freshly squeezed, juices.

From Baby

Don't make meals a battleground

But remember that there's no place in a happy and balanced home for the food police and mealtimes don't need to become a battleground. Fish and chips, hot buttered toast, Danish pastries, ice cream and even a bar of good chocolate are as much part of family eating as a plate of spinach or a bowl of home-made soup. What your children eat and enjoy occasionally doesn't matter a bit. It's how they eat most of the time that puts them on the path to healthy living.

THE VEGETARIAN OPTION About 5 per cent of UK households include a vegetarian and if you're not a vegetarian family, a 14 year-old who suddenly decides to give up meat and fish can be very worrying. But if you help them do it right, they can also be very healthy. You have to make sure they get enough iron, vitamin B12 and protein, which means dark green leafy vegetables, a mixture of good cereals and pulses like rice and beans, or chapattis and dhal. Veggie burgers, tofu, soya beans and Quorn are all good additions, and to guarantee enough of the essential fatty acids try to persuade them to take a fish-oil capsule. It's not good for them to rely exclusively on dairy products as this results in too much fat in the diet, though cutting out dairy products, too, and being a vegan brings a host of other risks.

TOWARDS THE TEENS

As children move towards the teens, increasing numbers of girls, and boys too, develop eating disorders and become obsessed with their weight. If you've fed them sensibly until now and they're reasonably active, the risks of this happening are minimal, but it's important that diet fads and low-fat, low-calorie food should never be a daily topic of conversation at home.

Children of this age – and beyond – like to graze. To help prevent them from putting on excess weight, remember the following:

PORRIDGE OR MUESLI for breakfast gives them a whole morning of slow-release energy.

DON'T PUT JUNK FOODS IN YOUR FRIDGE AND STORE CUPBOARD – if they're not there, your children won't be snacking on crisps, doughnuts, chocolate-chip cookies or chocolate-covered cereals.

KEEP A COLD ROAST CHICKEN IN THE FRIDGE for instant nibbles.

DRIED FRUIT, NUTS AND SUNFLOWER SEEDS provide instant healthy energy at any time of the day.

LEFT TO THEIR OWN DEVICES, THIS AGE GROUP OFTEN ENDS UP EATING UNHEALTHY FINGER FOOD in front of the computer or TV, so that's another reason why you should encourage family mealtimes wherever possible.

The Teens

Your children's grown-up life starts here. Childhood is almost behind them, school no longer seems to stretch ahead forever, and already they may be enjoying a first taste of the independence that will soon be theirs. They may be starting their first job or going on to further serious study. These are years of growth, development and hormonal change, and they demand the best possible nutrition. They are years, too, when your teenage children will need all the energy they can get, to help them enjoy the fun and cope with the stresses of this busy, exciting and active phase of their lives.

To give them the best possible chances in life, you need to look at what your teenagers are eating. Although it's simple in theory, in practice, persuading most of them away from the burger and chips, pizza and milkshake or hot dog and cola habit is really difficult. But this is the time of their lives when you should try to establish and encourage the healthy eating habits that will stay with them for the rest of their lives.

Though I prefer to use the idea of the 'healthy plate' (see page 17), the World Health Organisation uses a food pyramid which suggests that teenagers should aim for six daily servings of starchy foods – rice, wholemeal bread, potatoes, pasta, wholegrain cereals; a minimum of five portions of fruit and vegetables; and two portions each of dairy products and non-dairy proteins – vegetable or animal. In practice, this provides a

KEEP MOVING! Do all you possibly can to make sure your teenager doesn't become a couch potato – sometimes easier said than done, I know, but worth the odd argument. As well as the physical benefits of exercise, the endorphins released by the brain contribute to the feel-good factor and have a positive influence on mood. And tell your teenager that exercise doesn't mean swaying gently in a smoke-filled disco. They should pick an exercise they really enjoy – basketball, running, swimming, tennis, martial arts, football, or simply a brisk walk – and try and build it into their life. Perhaps you can find something you can do together, then both of you will benefit, physically and emotionally.

diet with lots of variety and the wider the selection of foodstuffs, the broader the spectrum of vitamins and minerals. Teenagers should be encouraged to keep their consumption of fried and high sugar foods to a minimum – they should be considered as occasional treats, not as a staple part of the diet.

Three meals a day

Three meals a day are essential, starting with a proper breakfast. If they race for the bus every morning after no more than a half a piece of toast and a snatched hot drink or a can of fizzy drink, then the temptation to boost their mid-morning nose-diving blood-sugar levels with another fizzy drink, or a chocolate bar or packet of crisps will be almost irresistible.

Porridge or oatmeal is a great breakfast and they can make it themselves in just 2–3 minutes. It will give them vital minerals like iron, zinc and calcium, plus nerve-strengthening B-complex vitamins. They should eat it with milk and add a little honey for sweetness. They could also get their oats from muesli. That makes an equally good start to the day since both are excellent sources of slow-release energy that will keep them going until lunchtime.

If lunch is sandwiches, make sure they're made from wholemeal bread; add a hard-boiled egg, cheese, tuna, canned sardines or chicken for protein. And include plenty of chopped parsley or cress, too; they're just the stuff for a glowing, unblemished skin. They should round off their lunch with a carton of yoghurt – steering clear of those that are high in sugar and additives – and a piece of fruit.

Like the adults in the family, they should try to sit down to a sensible, leisurely meal in the evening, since lunch is so often eaten in a rush. It should always include a vegetable such as spinach, celery, carrots, or spring greens, and salad – or at least one raw vegetable – is a must. This need not be more than a couple of scraped carrots cut into chunks, a crisp stick of celery and some slivers of red or yellow peppers. Or they could try that USA favourite – a spinach salad with thinly sliced mushrooms and a creamy, garlicky dressing.

They certainly won't want to be a social outcast, so will regularly find themselves heading for a fast-food outlet with the rest of the gang. There's no reason why they shouldn't, but encourage them to choose a beanburger and milk or juice once in a while as a healthier option, or a salad – these are now widely available. And point out to them that one king-sized cola contains a massive 14 teaspoons of sugar!

The Teens

IT'S SO TROUBLESOME BEING A TEEN

Teens have a lot of problems that are particular to their age, but eating the right foods can go a long way to helping them solve them.

Obesity

If your teenager is overweight and trying to lose it, you should check that they're not cutting down on the foods they need for growth and energy. Point out to them that the key factors in overweight are excess fat and sugar and explain to them that there's an awful lot of fat – and the unhealthy saturated kind too – in most processed foods. Sausages, burgers, salami, meat pies, potato chips, fries, ice-cream, cheesecake and milk shakes are the worst offenders. Sweet fizzy drinks and chocolate really pile on the sugar and many breakfast cereals have added sugar and salt. If their sweet tooth aches, steer them towards a banana, an apple, some dried fruit, or some fresh dates instead, to give an instant energy lift-off.

Anorexia

This is no longer just a girls' problem; around 10 per cent of anorexics are now male. The vital mineral to combat anorexia is zinc, lack of which zaps the taste-buds and destroys the appetite. Good sources are shrimps, liver, lean meat, wheatgerm, sesame and pumpkin seeds, mackerel, cheese, green vegetables and, best of all, oysters.

Stress

Exams, friendship problems, family clashes, first love – all these can induce stress in teenage children. Help them cope by making sure they eat plenty of food that's rich in B-complex vitamins – wholegrain cereals, liver, meat, chicken, fish and leafy green vegetables are all good sources.

Low energy

This is often a problem for teenagers, and girls are especially at risk because of the monthly drain on their vital iron reserves. Make sure they're getting plenty of iron in their diet, not just from liver, but also from egg yolks, spinach, lentils, nuts, seeds, raisins and dates. Drinking tea or coffee at the same time as eating these foods hinders the body's ability to absorb the iron, but luckily, vitamin C has the opposite effect, so offer your teenager a piece of fruit, a salad or an orange juice at the same time.

Skin problems

These should take care of themselves if teenagers watch their fat and sugar intake, and if they're eating wholegrain cereals, they'll get zinc, which is great for the skin. Their best friend, though, is green-coloured food, full of beta-carotene. The body processes this into vitamin A – vital for healthy skin and clear eyes. Green also means chlorophyll, which has a cleansing, nourishing and antibacterial action on the skin. And the cabbage family is a great source of potent antibacterial sulphur compounds. A green food should always be on the menu, even if it's only a sprig of parsley.

DID YOU KNOW THAT? In general, the American recommended dietary allowances – now properly known as Reference Nutrient Intake – for all age groups are somewhat higher than those in Britain, and although the American recommendations exceed the estimated daily requirement by about a third, many youngsters on poor-quality diets fail to reach even these lower British levels. Eating high-calorie, low-nutrient convenience foods pushes out the consumption of healthier foods containing more of the essential nutrients. In fact, American studies have shown that some adolescents get up to 45 per cent of their calories from fat, making them prime candidates for heart disease and strokes in later life.

On the other hand, fanatically health-conscious parents are known to reduce their children's fat consumption so much that they become deficient in energy, which can delay puberty and retard growth and mental development. Professor Vincent Marks at the University of Surrey, England, coined the phrase 'muesli belt malnutrition', an accurate description of this over-zealous attitude to healthy eating.

TOP 10 FOODS FOR TEENS

DATES To satisfy their sweet tooth. They'll supply badly needed iron too, and they're high in potassium.

EGGS These are the original low-calorie convenience food. They are a good source of protein, supplying around 6g a time.

LENTILS These are rich in protein – 100g contain more than 23g of protein – and if they eat vitamin-C rich food at the same meal, that will help in absorbing the lentils' valuable iron and zinc.

ORANGES If they eat a whole fresh orange at the start of a meal that will help them absorb more iron, calcium and other useful minerals from their food.

PORRIDGE OR OATMEAL They couldn't do better than to follow the example of the hardy Scots and start the day with this traditional Scottish breakfast.

PUMPKIN SEEDS These make a great snack. They provide valuable B vitamins, iron, zinc and unsaturated fatty acids.

SPINACH This owes its deep, dark-green colour to its high chlorophyll content. It is also high in beta-carotene.

PARSLEY This is rich in vitamins A and C, as well as iron.

THE GREENS Cabbage, spring greens, Brussels sprouts, kale and collard greens all supply sulphur compounds.

BEEF Most youngster like burgers. If you make your own you know exactly what's in them – huge quantities of protein, iron and B vitamins to fuel the growth this age group needs.

THE SPECIAL NEEDS OF TEENAGE BOYS

Adolescent boys need to eat more food than adult men relative to their weight and size. They need the extra nutrients to support growth and their relatively high levels of physical activity.

Generally speaking, nutritional recommendations for adolescent boys are based specifically on age, but this is not always the best guide. Not only is there a continuous process of growth and development, but the process doesn't always proceed at a regular pace. Growth spurts come at different times between the ages of 12 and 16, and this is when the boys need the most energy. Puberty and sexual maturation also require extra nutrients and these stages also occur at different times in different boys.

How active?

Matters are still further complicated by the huge range of possible activity levels. Some boys may spend most of their lives in front of a computer screen exercising little more than their mouse finger; others may be more physically active, spending some of their time engaged in sport, while yet others may become serious and competitive athletes. These boys have very particular requirements in respect of their nutrition. To achieve peak performance they need a top-quality diet which provides sufficient energy and, surprisingly, a much higher demand for water.

So it makes much more sense to equate these youngsters' food needs with their specific state of development. After all, the dramatic bodily changes which are so obvious across the span of puberty – from the earliest signs of change to the final growth spurt – make it simple to adjust the teenage boy's diet to suit his needs.

To maintain a healthy diet, at least 50 per cent of a teenage boy's calories should come from complex carbohydrates, a maximum of 35 per cent from fats and not more than 15 per cent from protein.

Here are the American recommended nutritional requirements for boys according to age.

NUTRIENT	11–14 YEARS	15–18 YEARS
Energy (kcal)	2300	3200
Protein (g)	34	52
Vitamin A (mcg)	600	900
Vitamin D (mcg)	5	5
Vitamin C (mg)	45	75
B6 (mg)	1.0	1.3
Folic acid (mcg)	300	400
B12 (mcg)	1.8	2.4
Calcium (mg)	1300	1300
Magnesium (mg)	240	410
Iron (mg)	8	11
Zinc (mg)	8	11
Selenium (mcg)	40	55
Iodine (mcg)	120	150

This is a guide to the energy your teenager will burn up doing a variety of different activities.

ACTIVITY	CALORIES BURNED PER HOUR
Ordinary walking	180
Brisk walking	300
Badminton	340
Gymnastics	420
Tennis	480
Rugby/American football	540
Soccer	540
Squash	600
Jogging	630
Cycling	660
Swimming	720

BOYS AND ACNE

Teenage boys don't think much about their skin until they develop acne (see page 157), one of the worst plagues of adolescence. It's caused by an overproduction of oily sebum by the sebaceous glands, and in boys this can be made worse by androgens, the male hormones responsible for sexual maturity.

While many doctors deny that nutrition plays any part in either the cause or treatment of acne, the experience of many teenagers and nutritional therapists is quite the reverse. A diet that is high in fat increases the amount of fatty acids and triglycerides in sebum, and a diet that is high in sugar also increases the formation of triglycerides. It's these two fatty substances that are the irritant factors in sebum. Youngsters who reduce their consumption of chocolates, sweets, canned drinks, fried foods and crisps nearly always see some improvement in their acne.

BRAIN FOOD FOR EXAM TIME

For many teenagers, the school years feel like one exam after the other, and if they go on to higher education, that feeling doesn't go away for another three, four, or even more, years. But did you know that, whether your children are taking school, national or university exams, one of the keys to success is eating the right food at the right time?

What brains need now is constant supplies of sugar and oxygen for optimum performance. Faced with a day of exams, erratic eating will guarantee poor results. Long periods without food, make blood-sugar levels drop, affecting memory and concentration and sometimes producing enormous mood swings. Irritability, bad-temper and headaches follow and if migraine is a problem, an attack is almost inevitable. If that happens halfway through a paper, their chances of success are gone forever. So the first rule of eating for exam success is to make sure that they eat the right sort of food at least every three hours throughout the day.

Why nutrients?

The right food means an adequate and constant supply of vitamins A, B, iron, zinc, essential fatty acids, and carotenoids. As you've already seen on page 138, the nutritional status of many children is alarmingly poor. They are deficient in some nutrients and the majority miss out on others altogether. As an experiment, a Welsh science teacher found that a multi-vitamin pill improved his pupils' intelligence. They took an IQ test at the start and another after eight months. Some were given multi-vitamins while the others took a placebo. Those on the real pill performed almost five times better in the second IQ test than those taking the placebo.

DID YOU KNOW THAT?

Happily many older students at universities appear to have cottoned on to the brain food message already. According to a leading British supermarket group, its sales of brain foods in its shops near major universities soar dramatically in the few weeks before exams. These bright people realise that even a tiny improvement in their exam results could push their degree up a grade and increase their chances of better jobs or research posts.

NUTRIENT-RICH EXAM FOODS

To make sure their exam diet is A+ it should include plenty of:

SHELLFISH for zinc.
OILY FISH for brain-nourishing essential fatty acids.
MEAT AND POULTRY for vitamin B12 and iron.
WHOLEGRAIN CEREALS for B vitamins.
NUTS AND SEEDS for boron.

FRESH FRUITS, VEGETABLES AND SALADS for all the carotenoids and plenty of vitamin C.
LIVER – though not if pregnant – eggs, butter and cream cheese for vitamin A.
DARK GREEN, BRIGHT ORANGE AND RED FRUITS AND VEGETABLES for beta-carotene which the body converts into vitamin A.

SO IF IT'S EXAM DAY, THIS IS HOW THEY SHOULD EAT:

Breakfast

HIGH PROTEIN, LOW FAT, LITTLE CARBOHYDRATE, SO
■ a large glass of fresh orange juice or pineapple juice
a low-fat bio live natural yoghurt with toasted almonds
or pistachios ■ a poached egg with baked beans ■ an
apple or pear

Mid-morning

■ a snack of dried apricots, raisins, dates and plain
fresh nuts

Lunch

■ a mixed salad with cold meat, fish or low-fat cheese
include plenty of watercress and tomatoes ■ add
sesame seeds, sunflower seeds and pumpkin seeds

Mid-afternoon

■ a piece of low-fat cheese or a hard-boiled egg (if
they haven't already had an egg today) ■ an apple, a
pear or a bunch of grapes

Evening meal

NOW IT'S TIME FOR THE CARBOHYDRATES
■ a thick root vegetable casserole made with potatoes,
swede, parsnip, turnip, carrot, onion, celery, shredded
cabbage, and kidney beans, rice or barley, or ■ a
generous portion of pasta or risotto with their favourite
low-fat sauce ■ a delicious carbohydrate-rich rice
pudding – add plenty of nutmeg

During the evening

■ A banana and a few dates or dried apricots
■ During the day they should drink at least 1.5–2 litres
of fluid, mostly water but including weak tea, herb teas,
natural fruit and vegetable juices and not more than
two cups of coffee
■ Sugar is about their worst enemy so they should try
to avoid it in any form – including honey – during the
daytime. Let them save their sugar fix for the evening
and keep it as small as possible
■ If their mental faculties are needed in the evening for
revision, and a rest day follows, they should stick to
cereals and bread for breakfast, the starch meal for
lunch and the high-protein meal for dinner

Nutritionally perfect for extended periods of brain work,
this day's eating provides 2000 calories, lots of protein,
low carbohydrates, low fat, low salt and well over their
day's needs of every single essential nutrient. If you
help them to follow these guidelines, their minds will
be on full alert when they need it most.

For foods that improve memory and concentration,
see page 182.

What to eat when for peak performance

At this stressful time the object of the exercise is to be at peak performance
for the morning and afternoon, by eating high-protein foods to generate
more of the activity hormones, and to unwind in the evening and sleep
well during the night, helped by eating starchy foods to encourage the
release of relaxing, sleep-inducing hormones. And if they've got exams the
next day, it's no good trying to sit up until the small hours and cram. If
they don't know it now, they never will.

EXAM DIET

Young Adults

You're probably on your own now and life is what YOU make it. You've settled into a job, college or university, you've left home and have a place of your own and your own friends and social life. This is also the age of romance, when the man or woman in your life can swallow up most of your time and attention. It can also be the age of broken hearts . . . unless you're already married and trying to get to grips with domestic chores as well as a job.

But married or single, you'll find the days are never long enough for all you want to cram into them. This is a time of life when your diet should be supplying you with handsome insurance against stress of every kind – trials at work, romance gone awry, too many late nights and too many skimpy meals eaten in a rush. Turn to the Vitality Eating Plan on page 113, have a photocopy in the first kitchen you can call your own – and stick to its simple rules.

Eating at home

At this age, especially if you're single and living in a bedsit, cooking can degenerate into endless snacks of bread, cheese and canned soup, so make sure you don't run out of the basics – potatoes, carrots, onions, a good olive oil, lemons, sliced wholemeal bread and garlic. Stock up on salad stuff that will last 2–3 days in the fridge – celery, red and yellow peppers, watercress, a box of cress and spring onions – and always have a supply of eggs, low-fat yoghurt, cheese, milk, nuts and seeds in the fridge too. Make sure you have a fruit bowl with at least some apples, bananas, oranges and grapes and your store cupboard should always contain cans of salmon, tuna, sardines, tomatoes, kidney beans and sugar-free baked beans. Brown rice, pasta, dried herbs and a jar or two of good quality pasta sauce are also essential staples. With these foods in the house, you'll always be able to whip up a healthy square meal of soup, salad, pasta or risotto, no matter how tired you are when you get home in the evening.

And remember, cooking should be a pleasure as well as a necessity. In fact, it can be a wonderful way to unwind at the end of a stressful day. Master a few favourite recipes – there are lots of really simple ones in this book (see pages 192–237) – so you can prepare a decent meal in the evening with minimal cost and effort.

Everybody – male or female – should know how to make a good, nourishing vegetable soup and anyone can follow the minestrone recipe on page 215. And you should also teach yourself how to use nature's herbal seasonings instead of loads of salt and bottled sauces. Thyme, for example, gives a wonderful flavour to stews, fish and chicken and this natural antibiotic will also help protect you against infections. Basil in a salad helps you relax and unwind. Rosemary is good for the memory. And mint is the best of all medicines for combatting indigestion.

Eating at work

Office lunches can be a healthy treat these days. Most supermarkets and sandwich bars sell a range of ready-to-eat salads, so choose the healthy options like carrots, coleslaw, apples, celery, nuts and brown rice. Add a glass of milk or a carton of yoghurt and a piece of fruit, and you'll be ready for whatever taxing task the boss throws at you during the afternoon.

TOP 10 FOODS FOR YOUNG ADULTS

AVOCADOS They're extremely nutritious, highly digestible and wonderfully filling for their calorie count – around 160 calories for half a pear.

BANANAS These are high in potassium for healthy hearts, and they're full of a useful fibre (see page 79) called pectin.

BEANS All the beans from baked to borlotti and kidney to mung are good sources of energy, protein, fibre and phytoestrogens.

BEEF An excellent source of protein, iron, B vitamins and minerals, beef is even healthier when it is organic as it will be free from hormones, antibiotics and other unhealthy additives.

CARROTS A single carrot will supply your vitamin A needs for an entire day.

CAULIFLOWER Cauliflower supplies silicon for strong bones, healthy hair and firm skin.

POTATOES These are good news for the intelligent slimmer. Even a whopper of a baked potato, crispy skin and all, is only around 200 calories.

SUNFLOWER SEEDS Packed with unsaturated fats and protein and with wonderful nutrients.

THYME This has powerful antiviral and antibacterial properties.

TUNA When fresh this contains Omega-3 fats (see page 24), the good fats which have a strongly protective action on the heart. Canned tuna is a poor source of these oils but other canned fish like salmon, sardines, mackerel, pilchards and sardines are excellent.

PROBLEMS OF THE TWENTIES

Whether you are suffering from menstrual miseries, up-and-down emotions, obesity or skin problems, there is plenty you can find in the larder to help you. If you smoke or drink to excess, then stop now. The longer you leave it, the more difficult it becomes.

Menstrual problems

These can be a real drag at this age. Cramps, irritability, tension, nausea and bloating are among the monthly trials which so many women seem to regard as inevitable. But menstrual problems are as much an index of ill health as muddy skin or lank hair, and they

are just as avoidable. It's kitchen therapy to the rescue once more. Eat plenty of wholegrain cereals, nuts and seeds, particularly almonds, oats, sesame and sunflower seeds, as these supply the magnesium, B-complex vitamins, vital vitamin E and iron that help deal with these problems. Bananas are an essential food, rich in vitamin B6, iron and potassium, which helps your kidneys cope with water-retention problems. They're the dieter's friend too – wonderfully filling and nourishing, but still only around 90 calories for an average-size fruit.

Emotional stress

This can be the result of romantic involvements, financial worries, work problems and skimpy fast-food meals. Eat lots of B-complex-rich wholegrain cereals – wholewheat bread, brown rice and oats – to help you cope. They'll supply a rich diet for the nerves and give you extra stamina, too, because of their high calcium, iron and magnesium content. If the jar of instant coffee is always at hand at home or in the office, ration yourself to no more than three cups a day. Too much caffeine can make you very nervous and irritable, though you may not realise why. Instead, try one of the many coffee substitutes found in health-food shops, or use decaffeinated coffee. Apart from being bad for your nerves, excess caffeine will stop your body absorbing half the good minerals you may be feeding it. For maximum uptake of minerals, eat fruit or fresh vitamin-C rich vegetables and salads at the same meal.

Smoking and drinking

If you acquired these habits in your teens – to prove how grown-up you were – get a grip on them now. Any veteran smoker can tell you it gets harder all the time to give up! The same goes for excess drinking. The female liver, in particular, has a fairly low resistance to alcohol, so don't think you can drink with the boys and get away with it. Both smoking and alcohol generate free radical activity, and these dangerous chemicals damage your body's cells, increasing your risk of heart disease, cancer and wrinkles! Instead of a packet of cigarettes, keep a packet of sunflower seeds in your desk drawer to nibble at. They're little powerhouses of good nutrition.

And don't be browbeaten into drinking for social reasons. These days mineral water is seen on the smartest restaurant tables. Instead of alcohol, drink a non-alcoholic 'cooler' of apple or pineapple juice with bubbly mineral water. Or if you want to drink wine, why not choose white and mix it with sparkling water for a refreshing spritzer. At the very least, make sure you drink a glass of water for every glass of wine.

The other alternative is fresh juice, readily available in the growing number of juice bars, plus there's now a wide range of both fruit and vegetable juices in food shops everywhere. Juice is not only delicious, but is a wonderful source of nutrients. Even cans or cartons of tomato juice chilled and spiked with lemon will deliver substantial amounts or lycopene, a carotenoid, which protects against various types of cancer. Best of all though, buy a simple juicer and try the drinks recipes on pages 234–7.

Skin problems

These can be even more agonising in your twenties as this is a time when your appearance is vitally important to you. Don't panic. Try to have one day a week when you eat nothing but fruit or vegetables, to give your whole system a good clean-out. High on your list of foods should be avocados, as research in Israel has shown that they help reconstitute the springy collagen that keeps skin young. Other vital skin-foods are cauliflower, broccoli and cabbage, chlorophyll-rich spinach and watercress, and all brightly coloured fruit, especially peaches, nectarines and apricots. They're loaded with beta-carotene, which is great for your skin.

Obesity

This will respond to a fruit and vegetable 'fast', too. If it's a real problem, keep a food diary. Write down every single thing you eat and drink for a week, then work out how to 'lose' 500 calories daily of either fat or sugar. Force yourself to exercise briskly – enough to get up a bit of a sweat – at least four times a week. Splash out on some ravishing new fitness clothes and commit to going to a regular exercise or dance class with a friend, if that's the sort of thing you enjoy. If not, play your favourite sport or take a brisk 20-minute walk each day. To do you any good, you must walk fast enough to make you a bit short of breath and slightly sweaty. Brisk exercise tunes your metabolism so you burn up fat faster. For a detailed weight-loss plan, see the Seven Day Diet on pages 160–61.

WATCHING YOUR WEIGHT?

You're in your twenties and, especially if you're female, you may be starting to worry about your weight. In fact, chances are that you will have started to worry about it in your teens, what with peer pressure and the images of stick-like celebs that gaze out at you from the pages of the magazines and from TV programmes. You may not be overweight at all but you may well, by now, have tried a number of diets, only to find that they were difficult to stick to and that when you stopped, you quickly regained any weight you had lost. Well, you're not alone. There are millions of people like you, and the diet industry is growing fat at your expense while you grow slim … and fat again.

There's no doubt that, whatever your age, obesity is a major health problem and of all the nutritional disorders that affect the total population, it is the most common in affluent society. As well as being irrefutably and closely linked to premature death, being seriously overweight is an almost certain guarantee that you will suffer from a range of other health problems.

What happens if I'm overweight?

These health problems include degenerative arthritis in any and all of the weight-bearing joints – ankles, knees, hips and lumbar spine. You risk back pain, disc problems, haemorrhoids, high blood pressure, high cholesterol, increased risk of heart disease and stroke, varicose veins, gallstones, foot problems, and increased risk of breathing difficulties and diabetes. Obesity in children is already producing eight- and nine-year-olds with Type II diabetes, the sort that is normally associated with adults in their fifties.

Being seriously overweight has social consequences, too. For many people, it carries a heavy emotional burden and can lead to psychological disturbance. It can result in relationship problems, lack of self-esteem, poor self-image, and all these can combine to reduce your enjoyment of life both in social and employment terms. It also restricts exercise, leading to a gradual decline in overall fitness and a corresponding increase in obesity.

What causes obesity?

Apart from bad eating, your basic metabolic rate (BMR) is a key factor. This is the efficiency with which your resting body burns up food and converts it into fuel. People's BMRs differ; two brothers living in the same home and eating the same food can have totally different body shapes.

Height	Weight	
1.95m	80.4kg	
1.92m	78.2kg	
1.89m	76kg	
1.87m	73.8kg	
1.84m	72kg	
1.81m	70.2kg	MEN
1.78m	68kg	
1.76m	6.2kg	
1.73m	64.4kg	
1.70m	62.2kg	
1.68m	60.4kg	
1.65m	59.1kg	
1.62m	57.7kg	
1.60m	56.4kg	
1.57m	54.7kg	
Height	**Weight**	
1.87m	67.6kg	
1.84m	65.8kg	
1.81m	64kg	
1.78m	62.2kg	WOMEN
1.76m	60.4kg	
1.73m	58.7kg	
1.70m	56.9kg	
1.68m	54.7kg	
1.65m	53.3kg	
1.62m	52.4kg	
1.60m	50.2kg	
1.57m	49kg	
1.55m	47.6kg	

Height without shoes,
Weight without clothes

The body also contains white and brown fats. The brown fat is able to store huge amounts of energy without causing obesity. Those unfortunate people whose bodies have a smaller percentage of brown fat turn their surplus energy into less healthy white fat.

While there are some glandular disorders which cause weight gain, they are comparatively rare and usually treatable. Thyroid disorders are probably the most common. Steroid drugs, oral contraceptives, HRT and insulin used by diabetics may cause weight gain, too.

THE BASIC STEPS FOR WEIGHT LOSS

Of all the multitude of weight-reducing treatments, the only one that really works and keeps the weight off is to permanently change the way you eat. This is what you have to do.

EAT LOTS OF GOOD CARBOHYDRATES like wholemeal bread, brown rice, potatoes – but not fried – root vegetables, beans and pasta for their high energy, slow-release calories and zero-fat content.

EAT FRESH FRUITS, VEGETABLES AND SALADS to provide vitamins, minerals, phytochemicals and fibre. These should constitute around a third of your food. Eat a minimum of five portions a day, excluding potatoes. As a simple guide, a portion is an amount roughly the size of your fist, so one apple, one pear, one peach, about fifteen grapes, two tangerines, two plums, a large carrot or a handful of cabbage count as one portion.

CHOOSE LEANER CUTS OF MEAT and cut down on all visible fat – if you can see it don't eat it.

EAT MORE FISH AND POULTRY WITHOUT THE SKIN and never eat chicken or duck skin – they're oozing with fat.

CHOOSE SEMI-SKIMMED OR SKIMMED MILK and look for lower fat cheeses and yoghurts.

AVOID ALL THICKENED OR CREAMY SAUCES as well as fatty meat sauces. Use low-fat yoghurt or fromage frais instead of cream.

WATCH OUT FOR THE HIDDEN FAT in biscuits, cookies, cakes, desserts, sweets and chocolates, and all processed meat products.

MODEST AMOUNTS OF ALCOHOL are both enjoyable and healthy as they benefit the heart and circulation. Two glasses of wine for women, three for men, OR a couple of small measures of spirits for women, three for men, OR 600ml of beer for women, 900ml for men daily are believed to be safe. Don't save it all up for a drinking binge.

EAT A NOURISHING BREAKFAST CEREAL like porridge or muesli or a wholewheat product without added salt and sugar.

EAT AT LEAST FIVE SLICES A DAY OF WHOLEMEAL BREAD and be very mean with the butter.

AVOID ALL SUGAR if possible.

NEVER MISS BREAKFAST and don't go for long periods without food.

WATCH HOW YOU COOK YOUR FOOD as more often it's what you do to it, rather than the food itself, that piles on the weight. Don't fry, but grill, steam or bake instead. Roast meat or poultry on a rack so it won't soak up the fat.

TRY USING A SMALLER PLATE – it looks as if you've got more in front of you – and take plenty of time over your meals so they're more satisfying.

SEVEN-DAY DIET

Unlike many extreme diets based on pseudo-science and hocus pocus or that recommend unhealthy meal substitutes or worthless pills, my Seven-Day Diet Plan is bursting with nutrients and is full of delicious produce. You won't ever feel hungry but you will be healthy and you will definitely lose weight.

Most diets fail because you give up in despair and disgust at the thought of yet another low-calorie cracker with cottage cheese. My Seven-Day Diet is satisfying and enjoyable and proves that it is possible to eat well and lose weight if you need to.

My week of healthy eating provides you with all you need of most nutrients, but to make sure you don't miss out on any of the essential vitamins or minerals, it's a good idea to take a simple one-a-day vitamin and mineral supplement which you can get from any chemist, health-food shop or supermarket. Women need some extra calcium too.

You must also drink at least 1.5 litres of fluid each day – water, diluted unsweetened fruit juices and some tea, herbal teas and a little coffee. You may have one glass of wine, 250ml beer or one small measure of spirits each in addition to the other fluid.

This is seven days of delicious healthy eating, which I hope you will enjoy. It is not only a diet. It is a guide to help you change the way you eat for the better.

Monday

BREAKFAST

■ Grilled mushrooms and tomatoes on toast ■ Cup of tea or coffee with semi-skimmed milk (have either drink and a glass of unsweetened juice with breakfast every day)

LIGHT MEAL

■ Large portion of coleslaw made with red, white and green cabbage, carrots, sultanas, onion, apple, natural yoghurt, a little olive oil and a tablespoon of cider vinegar ■ Small portion of cottage cheese ■ Piece of fresh fruit

MAIN MEAL

■ Grilled chicken with chervil and raspberry vinegar (page 219) ■ Poached peaches (page 232)

Tuesday

BREAKFAST

■ Porridge made with half water, half skimmed milk ■ Slice of wholemeal toast with a little butter and honey

LIGHT MEAL

■ Broad bean and sorrel soup (page 216)

MAIN MEAL

■ Any grilled fish with a green vegetable ■ Small portion of soft cheese ■ Large stick of celery

Wednesday

BREAKFAST

■ Half a grapefruit ■ 2 poached eggs ■ 2 grilled tomatoes

LIGHT MEAL

■ Sautéed mushrooms on wholemeal toast ■ Salad

MAIN MEAL

■ Grilled lamb chops with most of the fat removed ■ Peas and carrots ■ Portion of dried fruits soaked and served with low-fat natural yoghurt mixed with a pinch of ground cinnamon, grated lemon rind and 1 teaspoon of honey

Thursday

BREAKFAST

■ An orange, an apple and a pear sliced into a bowl with a carton of natural yoghurt and 1 teaspoon of honey

LIGHT MEAL

■ 2 slices of wholemeal bread without butter, sandwiched with a mashed banana, a couple of chopped dates, a squeeze of lemon juice and a sprinkle of any chopped nuts
■ A fresh pear and a few grapes

MAIN MEAL

■ Chicken cooked any way you like, but not fried, with at least two different vegetables ■ Chopped ready-to-eat Californian prunes and apricots soaked in the juice of 1 lemon, 1 orange, 1 tablespoon brandy and ½ teaspoon of sugar

Friday

BREAKFAST

■ 2 boiled eggs ■ 2 slices of wholemeal toast spread very thinly with butter

LIGHT MEAL

■ Soup (left over from Tuesday) ■ Wholemeal roll

MAIN MEAL

■ Grilled turbot on broad bean and fennel mash (page 218) ■ Salad of watercress, orange segments and chicory ■ Piece of soft cheese
■ Portion of grapes

Saturday

BREAKFAST

■ As much fresh fruit as you like

LIGHT MEAL

■ Toast a thick slice of coarse wholemeal bread until lightly browned on both sides. Rub one side with a cut garlic clove, drizzle on a little olive oil and pile with thin slices of fresh tomato

MAIN MEAL

■ Lamb, lentil and carrot casserole (page 225) ■ 2 tangerines in segments with a small carton of fromage frais and 1 teaspoon honey

Sunday

BREAKFAST

■ 2 slices of wholemeal toast with a little butter and honey ■ A glass of fresh orange juice

LIGHT MEAL

■ Linguine with no-cook anchovy dressing (page 223) ■ A piece of fresh fruit

MAIN MEAL

■ Stir-fried warm beef salad (page 229) ■ Half a small melon

BURN UP THOSE CALORIES Remember that weight loss depends on burning up more calories than you consume so exercise is a vital part of this equation. Eating two slices of bread and butter a day less and walking for ten minutes a day more will produce a regular weight loss of 500g a week. Or a brisk 20-minute walk each day will do. It's as simple as that.

By increasing your physical activity by whatever means are appropriate for your own personal health and fitness, your bonus in terms of health is manifold. You don't just lose weight more easily, but you improve your cardiovascular system, too. You also increase your muscular strength and build stamina and maintain mobility. In addition, exercise produces 'feel-good' endorphins in your brain and that's a huge bonus.

SPECIAL FOR MEN

The young adult years are especially critical for men. This is the time of your life when you will be truly independent, perhaps setting up home on your own for the first time, maybe with a partner and perhaps even starting a family. Chances are you will also be busy at work, forging a career, as well as pursuing all your many other interests. In other words, you will be living life to the full, which is all the more reason to make sure you are getting the nutrition you need to keep you going. And proper nutrition, combined with sufficient exercise, will also set you up with good health for your later years, helping to guard against cancer, heart and circulatory disease.

Your nutritional needs are rather different from those of women. As well as needing more calories and protein, you have a greater requirement of some nutrients, particularly iron, magnesium, zinc, selenium, vitamins B1, B2, B6, niacin, vitamin A and vitamin E.

Even judging by British RDAs, which are lower than those in the USA, the nutritional status of British men is seriously alarming and, because they follow British cooking traditions, the same is true for men in Malta and in some areas of Australia and New Zealand. American men fare no better than these and are more likely to be overweight too, but they are also more likely to use supplements to make up any shortfall. Northern Europeans fare little better but southern Europeans are far less likely to have nutritional deficiencies as their diets are more varied and they consume far more fruit and vegetables.

How to get your nutrients

Most of the foods that are important for men's health are not a problem as they tend to be pretty high on men's 'favourite foods' list. Red meat, game and poultry give you iron, protein and B vitamins – but do choose free-range and organic wherever possible to avoid unwanted growth hormones and antibiotics as these may affect virility, potency and, particularly, fertility.

Get your zinc from shellfish, oysters and pumpkin seeds and your selenium from brazil nuts and wholegrain cereals. These minerals will help protect sperm, testicles and the prostate. Liver and dark-green yellow and orange fruits and vegetables will provide you with vitamin A and carotenoids, whilst nuts, seeds, olive oil and avocados are great sources of vitamin E, which you also need for fertility.

DID YOU KNOW THAT?

- An 18-year-old man has an 80 per cent chance of reaching the age of 65, but an 18-year-old woman's chance is 88 per cent
- Life expectancy for men is 72, for women 78
- Testicular cancer is the commonest cancer in men aged 20–40
- 50 per cent of men are overweight
- 15 per cent of men are obese
- Only 20 per cent of men exercise three times a week
- Almost 90 per cent of men never examine their testicles
- In the last 50 years men's sperm count has halved

How much exercise is enough?

In the past it was normal to calculate the energy needs of different occupations according to whether they were sedentary, moderately active or very active. But in our modern society there are very few jobs which could be called 'very active' compared to fifteen or twenty years ago. Even the construction industry, which must be one that requires most expenditure of energy now benefits from electric tools and mechanical handling and lifting equipment, all of which has removed much of the need for heavy labour.

Today, it's mainly the non-work activities that increase energy needs more than the actual job you do. The following charts will help you calculate your own calorie needs.

TESTICULAR CANCER Although this is comparatively rare, it is the most common malignancy in young men and it's on the increase. Early diagnosis means 99 per cent cure but men are not good at self-examination or going to the doctor. As a result, in one-third of patients the cancer has already spread to other parts of the body. Less than one in five men actually check their testicles, yet this is the best way of spotting the earliest changes.

The time to examine your testicles is after a warm bath or shower. The Orchid Cancer Appeal, a major UK charity involved in testicular cancer, gives the following advice: 'Cradle the scrotum in the palm of both hands and use the thumb and fingers to gently squeeze the testicles, one at a time. Learn to differentiate between the main body and the epididymis, which is made up of the collecting tubes at the back of the testicle. Lumps in these tubes are more common and almost invariably benign. Lumps in the body of the testicle are rarer but more important and need to be acted on quickly.'

What you should look for is any change in the consistency of the testicle or any places which feel hard or swollen. They're usually painless.If you find anything, see your doctor immediately. Don't panic but don't die of embarrassment just because you don't like the idea of discussing this type of problem with your doctor. Most lumps are not cancerous and even though you may have pain or discomfort, that doesn't necessarily mean you've got cancer.

ENERGY USED FOR A VARIETY OF DIFFERENT ACTIVITIES

ACTIVITY	APPROX CALORIES USED PER HOUR
Sleep	65
Driving, computer tasks, office work	100
Average walking, badminton, table tennis, moderately active dancing	250
Tennis, ice or roller skating, fast walking, cycling, slow jogging, hockey	300
Aerobics class, dance class, disco dancing, football	400
Skiing, swimming, heavy DIY like planing, sandpapering, sawing, heavy digging, skipping	500
Weightlifting, squash, running, aquarobics	650

SPECIAL FOR WOMEN

If you are a woman, these are the years of your beautiful prime. You'll never have more natural energy than you have now. Your looks have the appeal of maturity as well as the glow of youth and you have grown-up confidence and poise. But sometimes you wish you were Superwoman. The man in your life probably expects you to be a faultless housekeeper, a crack cook and the gorgeous girl he first fell for, all rolled into one. The job gets tougher as you climb the promotion ladder and if you have children, you'll find they need more and more of your time, love and attention as they head for the troublesome teens.

If you're running a home and a job and raising a family, then you'll sometimes wonder how you got yourself into all this. But don't reach for the quick fix of coffee, the stiff drink or the cigarette, and don't fall on the sweet snacks for the quick energy lift that will let you down later as well as aggravate any weight problems you may have. There are much better ways to keep you firing on all cylinders.

How to be superwoman

Above all, don't be tempted to skip meals, have a quick lunch consisting of nothing more than a drink or a chocolate bar, or serve up endless microwaved TV dinners because it's much too much trouble to cook, and you feel tired to death. For these rich, demanding years of your life, only first-class nourishment is good enough; you can't be Superwoman on anything but the best possible food.

Turn to The Vitality Eating Plan on page 113, to remind yourself what good nutrition is all about. Wholegrains, fresh fruits and vegetables, salads, are basics. So are yoghurt, milk, cheese, supplies of fresh nuts – preferably still in their shells – and seeds stored in the fridge. It's also great to have herbs growing and seeds sprouting ready to use for instant flavour and extra nutrients.

If daily shopping is out of the question, go for the vegetables that will happily stay fresh for a few days – potatoes, carrots and onions, stored in a dark, cool place in brown paper bags, and supplies of salad stuffs like sweet peppers, celery, fennel and watercress in the fridge. In a dark corner of your kitchen, devote some space to sprouting seeds – a helping of pure vitality that's organically grown, morning-fresh, additive-free, and cheap with it.

TOP 10 FOODS FOR YOUNG ADULT WOMEN

ALMONDS These are a very concentrated food, rich in protein, good fats, zinc, magnesium, potassium and iron, as well as calcium and some B vitamins.

CABBAGE For skin-protective sulphur and its rich spread of anti-cancer phytochemicals.

CELERY This is a good nerve tonic as it provides some calcium. Its diuretic properties have been known for centuries and you can eat it to get rid of fluid-retention around the time of your period.

CHEESE This is a rich source of protein, calcium and phosphorus, as well as the B vitamins. It also contains lots of vitamin A, together with some vitamin D and E. Feta cheese, Edam, cottage cheese and curd cheese are low in fat.

FLAXSEED OIL Must be non GM and preferably organic. A rich source of essential fatty acids for brain and central nervous function and lignines for hormone regulation.

GRAPES These are easy to digest, and uniquely nourishing and fortifying.

MELON The cantaloupe and ogen are rich sources of vitamin A.

SAGE Is a really powerful healing and antiseptic herb.

SARDINES These are every woman's friend – rich in protein, vitamins D and B12, calcium and easy-to-absorb iron and zinc.

SPROUTED SEEDS The most live, pure and nutritious food that you can grow on your windowsill.

Young Adults

IT'S A GIRL THING

This is a time of life when certain problems strike women. Take action now and save yourself from more difficulties when you hit the middle years.

Beat PMS

You must do something to overcome this draining and depressing problem. It is not uncommon for it to get worse after you have children, and if it does, it will add further to the stresses of that extra hectic period of your life. When it strikes, fight the craving for sugar and chocolate bars and go for sweet fruits like grapes and melon or dried fruit and almonds, instead. Increase your intake of vitamin B6 from eggs, oily fish like salmon and sardines, wholegrain cereals and bananas. This is a time of the month when you will need more zinc and magnesium, too; get them from pumpkin seeds, liver, shellfish, chickpeas, kidney beans and mackerel. Cut down on tea, coffee, alcohol and sugar. Ten days before your period is due, increase the good carbohydrates in your diet and cut down on sugar and animal fats. Be a grazer and don't go without food for more than three hours. This doesn't mean pigging out and gaining five kilos in ten days; eat the same quantity of food but spread it out into more frequent meals. It's also worth taking a supplement of vitamin B6, potassium and magnesium. Many women find that 500–1000mg of evening primrose oil a day is also a great help.

Look after your heart

This is when you should take a real interest in the affairs of your heart. This is a time of growing responsibility – career, husband or partner, children, or all three. You are likely to be under more pressure and to have less time to look after yourself and your diet. This is not the moment to let things slide. Insure your future heart health by eating plenty of high-fibre foods,

lots of oily fish like sardines, and vegetable proteins like millet, buckwheat and beans. You should also eat foods that are rich in vitamins A and C, such as cantaloupe melon, dark green leafy vegetables and as many onions and as much garlic as you can. Use extra-virgin olive oil on salads. Cut down on animal fats, salt and refined carbohydrates, and drink modest amounts of alcohol – a maximum of 14 units a week. One unit is a small glass of wine, a small measure of spirits or 250ml of beer. Don't make the mistake of thinking you can have all 14 units on a Friday night; binge drinking is highly dangerous. And finally, do take some form of regular weight-bearing exercise. If you enjoy them, active sports, exercise classes or working out in the gym are great, otherwise brisk walking will do the trick.

Make your skin bloom

All-round good nutrition is the basis of a good skin. No amount of expensive lotions and potions will compensate for a bad diet. You need lots of vitamin A from carrots, melon, spinach, nectarines, apricots, kiwi fruit and liver; chlorophyll from all green leafy vegetables, and vitamin E from seeds, nuts, cold-pressed seed oils and avocados. Eat millet for extra silicon and don't forget dandelion leaves and celery with its green leaves, both of which improve the elimination of waste products.

Build super-resistance

You do not have the time to get ill right now, so what can you do to boost your resistance to infection and disease? Your staple diet should consist of the essential foods that are extra-rich in vitamin C, zinc, vitamin A, and the B complex. These are grapes, citrus fruits, apricots, blackcurrants, pineapple, broccoli, peppers, onions, oats, wheatgerm, almonds, sprouted seeds, yoghurt, chicken livers (from free-range chickens), eggs, poultry, game and sardines, mackerel and herrings. Stress is a great destroyer of the body's defence mechanisms so check out the stress-busting foods on page 173. If you're suffering from stress you need all the foods mentioned there, plus lots of celery, which is one of nature's great calmers. Drink limeflower tea with some honey in it to help you relax, and try any form of relaxation exercise. Yoga, meditation or self-hypnosis all work well.

Take care of your bones

The menopause may seem a long way off, but what happens now will determine the state of your bones in thirty years' time, so you must start building up your calcium deposits. To do that you need calcium, vitamin D and sunlight. Each day you should eat a selection of at least three of the following foods: sardines – including the bones – spinach, low-fat cheese, yoghurt, seeds, nuts, celery, turnips, cabbage, chickpeas, herring, tuna, eggs, dried fruits, brown rice, buckwheat and 250ml of skimmed milk. You must also get as much daylight as you can. That doesn't mean roasting on the beach for two weeks of the year, but getting out into the fresh air and light for some time each day. In spite of the links between sun and skin cancer you must expose some of your skin – face, hands, arms or legs are fine – to ultraviolet light for at least ten minutes a day whenever possible. This enables the body to

manufacture its own vitamin D (see page 44) without which you cannot absorb calcium. It is vital that you start exercising now as well. Weight-bearing exercise makes the bones stronger, so indulge in some walking or active sport like tennis, squash, badminton, netball, running or jogging. Cycling and swimming will get your heart and lungs working, but won't add to the strength of your skeleton.

The Middle Years

Traditionally this time of life used to be regarded as the time to settle down. Your career path was established, your children were married and had flown the nest, your financial responsibilities were less onerous, and you had more time to enjoy all the leisure pursuits that you couldn't fit in during your hectic younger years.

But all that has changed in the twenty-first century and instead the middle years can still be full of the sorts of pressures that deplete your body's physical and mental resources. For example, many couples choose to start families much later and it's now common for women to have their first child in their mid- to late thirties, or even early forties. As a consequence you may be well into your middle years before your offspring even start their university education and they could be living at home with you until your fifties or early sixties.

You may be coping with a heavy load of responsibilities in your work, helping children on the threshold of their adult lives to deal with their first stumbles on the difficult path of relationships and marriage, or helping them through the stresses and strains of having children of their own. If you have to help with very young grandchildren, you'll need boundless physical and mental energy. And all these challenges come at a time when women may be facing the beginnings of the menopause and men may be finding it increasingly difficult to handle the stresses of complex work and social issues. What you need is to boost your mental energy and combat the stress. Again, kitchen medicine can come to the rescue.

TIME FOR SOME DIY Massage, combined with essential aromatherapy oils is just what you need to help each other along this emotional helter-skelter. Don't be nervous; anyone can do a massage – it's almost impossible to do any harm. Don't use massage if there is obvious inflammation or infection of the skin, don't apply excessive pressure over the spine or other sensitive areas of the body, and do make sure that your partner is not allergic to any of the ingredients that you are using.

All you need is a warm, quiet room and a reasonably firm, but comfortable surface to lie on. Start with the neck and shoulders, applying gentle pressure with the pads of your fingers, your palms and the balls of your thumbs. Work outwards and upwards into the fleshy shoulder muscles and then gently down the back, massaging from the spine outwards. Buttocks, thighs, legs, arms, hands and feet especially appreciate a massage. To combat stress and tension, use relaxing oils like lavender, orange and hops; for exhaustion try stimulating oils like rosemary, eucalyptus and thyme; for insomnia, try lemon balm or basil. Five drops of oil in 20ml of sunflower, grapeseed or even rapeseed oil is all you need.

> "It's now common for women to have their first child in their mid- to late thirties, or even early forties."

BRAIN FOOD FOR MENTAL ENERGY

Is there really such a thing as 'brain food'? The answer most certainly is 'yes'. Food is needed for the development of the brain while a baby grows in the mother's womb; food ensures there is enough energy for brain function for the child, adolescent and teenager; and food is essential to keep the brain active and functioning correctly well into old age. Poor diet doesn't just affect your physical wellbeing. It can also have a disastrous impact on the way you behave, your ability to think, reason and concentrate, your memory and co-ordination – even your mood.

So what does 'brain food' really consist of? Many old wives' tales have more than a grain of truth in them so granny's exhortation to her grandchildren to, 'Eat fish, it's good for your brains' is not far from the mark. Research at the Institute of Brain Chemistry in London has shown a clear link between the amount of oily fish eaten by pregnant women and the development of the foetal brain. Omega-3 fatty acids supplied by the mother through the placenta make up the greatest proportion by far of brain tissue during foetal growth.

Both before and after birth the brain depends on a constant supply of energy, in the form of glucose and oxygen delivered to the brain cells by circulating blood. For optimum brain function the diet must contain foods which provide both instant- and slow-release energy. Instant-release energy comes from the natural sugars in fruits and vegetables and some starchy foods, slower-release energy comes from the complex wholegrain cereals and some vegetables. The slowest of all energy-givers are proteins like meat, fish and eggs. The diet must also be rich in foods containing iron in a form that the body can easily absorb. Meat of all sorts and particularly liver, are rich sources. Other forms of iron are more difficult to absorb but this can be improved by eating foods rich in vitamin C at the same time.

What happens when things go wrong?

Just as certain foods help the brain function, so others cause it to mis-function. What about the irritability and bad temper you feel when you've had too much coffee? Or the way in which excessive amounts of alcohol can turn people into raging monsters? There are other links between food and behaviour which are far more subtle and insidious.

In almost every study of essential nutrients, emotional and mental disorders have been amongst the most prominent results of deficiency.

WHAT TO AVOID

■ Refined carbohydrates – white flour, sugar, confectionery and bakery products. These are severely impoverished in many of the vital substances like fibre, B vitamins, vitamin E and minerals.

■ Tea, coffee, chocolate and alcohol either stop the absorption of, or destroy the vital substances.

■ Too much bran will affect your mineral uptake.

■ Aluminium – Alzheimer's sufferers tend to have higher levels of aluminium in their bodies, though a positive link between aluminium and the disease has not yet been established. Eating acid fruits cooked in aluminium pans may increase the amount of this metal in your body.

Despite a mountain of evidence, there are still many people who ignore the idea of a food-mood connection. This is a tragedy, especially in the light of the extraordinary and pioneering work of Dr Carl Pfeiffer at the Brain Bio Center in New Jersey, one of the foremost institutions in the world for research into psychiatric illness and nutrition. Much of his work focused on the benefits of high-dose vitamins and minerals in the treatment of depression and more serious psychiatric problems like schizophrenia. More recent studies by Dr Alex Richardson at Oxford University, England, have shown that the simple addition of highly concentrated fish-oil extracts to the diet can be beneficial too, even in some patients with schizophrenia. So far these reports are only isolated observations and much more work has to be done in this area, but even without further research, Richardson's work reinforces all the granny stories about fish and brains.

But you don't need a degree in medicine and psychiatry to understand the sinking lethargy that smothers you at the end of a long, hard and much-too-busy day. Breakfast vanished in the rush, there just wasn't time for lunch, and the thought of cooking at the end of the day was just too much. Of course, when you feel low, it's easier and quicker for the doctor to write a prescription for tranquillisers, antidepressants or sleeping pills than to ask about your eating habits or getting you to keep a diet-diary of all your food for a week. But is your lethargy all in the mind? Not at all; it's mostly in what hasn't been put into your mouth.

TOP 10 BRAIN FOODS

Don't become a food freak. Simply get your just desserts of brain food.

SHELLFISH for essential zinc, protein and some essential fatty acids.
FRESH, SMOKED OR CANNED OILY FISH with the exception of canned tuna; they are all rich sources of the vital essential fatty acids the brain needs.
SPROUTED BEANS are, weight for weight, among the richest food sources of brain nutrients.
SEEDS AND NUTS for magnesium and vitamin E.
APRICOTS for instant-release energy from their natural sugars and for beta-carotene.
BEETROOT to help improve the oxygen-carrying capacity of blood.
OATS AND OTHER WHOLEGRAIN CEREALS for slow-release energy.
ROSEMARY for the essential oils which stimulate brain function and improve memory and concentration.

THE STRESS FACTOR

Martin Luther King knew a thing or two about life and he certainly hit the nail on the head when he declared, 'The ultimate measure of a man is not where he stands in moments of comfort and convenience, but where he stands at times of challenge and controversy.'

At moments of comfort and convenience stress is not a problem, but when challenge and controversy stare us in the face, the way in which we react, physically, emotionally and spiritually, is the measure of our success in dealing with stress.

The idea that stress is the exclusive province of the boardroom and the high-powered executive is just not true. No-one is immune from it. It exists on the factory floor, in the typing pool, at the kitchen sink, on the building site and in young and elderly alike. But it is in these middle years that stress

WHAT TO AVOID

■ If you're sensitive to caffeine stick to decaffeinated tea and coffee or herbal teas. Keep off the cola drinks and watch out for sports drinks and so-called 'energy' drinks, many of which contain large quantities of caffeine.

■ Keep alcohol to a minimum. A glass or two of wine, no more than 500ml of beer or cider, and no spirits at all are best.

■ High-protein, low-carbohydrate diets increase mental activity so avoid them if you're stressed.

■ There is some good news. You can indulge in small helpings of good quality chocolate, the darker the better. It does contain very small amounts of caffeine, but it's also an excellent source of theobromine, a chemical which stimulates the release of the body's feel-good hormones, endorphins, from the brain.

is most likely to have serious detrimental effects on your health.

Our bodies' responses to stressful stimuli have always played a key role in mankind's survival. The 'Fight or Flight' response which our bodies produce without conscious effort or command and which prepares us for instant reaction at times of danger, lies at the root of our inability to cope with the stresses of living in an industrialised Western civilisation. When we can't choose either 'fight' or 'flight' and the only option is to 'grin and bear it' or 'grit our teeth' or 'soldier on' – all expressions which betray the emotions involved – the 'Fight or Flight' response becomes counter-productive and many of us find ourselves coping badly with the challenges of life. The result is an epidemic of stress-induced heart attacks, high blood pressure, insomnia, pre-menstrual syndrome, menopausal problems, sexual disorders, skin complaints, asthma, migraine and arthritis.

Stress and nutrition

But the way in which stress affects our nutritional status is, in some ways, the most important factor in the whole equation. Overproduction of stomach acid, which occurs when we are feeling stressed can lead to inflammation of the stomach lining, ulceration and poor absorption of the nutrients in our food. It also often results in gastric reflux and consequently oesophagitis, which in turn makes swallowing painful and has an adverse effect on eating. At the other end of the gut, excessive stress can shorten the time it takes for food to pass through the colon, either due to increased motility or inflammatory conditions like colitis. Many nutrients are absorbed in the lower end of the bowel and this is also where B vitamins are synthesised by the gut's natural flora. The end result is a general lowering of our nutritional status and a reduction in our B vitamins, which are among the nutrients responsible for the wellbeing of the nervous system.

So, stress and nutrition are inseparable and stress can trigger a self-perpetuating downward spiral – excessive stress–nutrient deficiency–worse nutrition–worse stress. It seems never-ending. But you can eat to beat stress and improving your diet should be your first step on the road to recovery. Naturally you also have to deal with the causes of the stress, too, perhaps making some lifestyle changes, perhaps just learning to say no without feeling guilty and perhaps doing some yoga or learning meditation or other relaxation techniques. But let's start with what you eat.

TOP 10 STRESS-BUSTING FOODS

What you need is a high-carbohydrate diet. This is rich in tryptophan which the body converts to serotonin, the mood-enhancing, tranquilising hormone.

BREAKFAST IS KEY and must include porridge, unsweetened muesli or a natural wholegrain breakfast cereal, plus some dried fruits and a little honey if you like. Add any fresh fruit or juice and a slice of wholemeal toast and you'll start your day happier and less stressed than you have for ages.

YOUR STAPLE FOODS SHOULD BE COMPLEX CARBOHYDRATES such as wholemeal bread, pasta, rice, beans and potatoes.

AIM FOR MODEST AMOUNTS OF PROTEIN from fish, cheese, eggs and poultry, and very little red meat.

EAT SEROTONIN-CONTAINING FOODS – bananas, pineapple, walnuts, figs, tomatoes, avocados, dates, papaya, passion fruit and aubergines.

EAT A CARBOHYDRATE SNACK EVERY TWO HOURS to keep your blood sugar on an even keel.

MAKE GENEROUS USE OF THE CALMING, RELAXING AND MOOD-ENHANCING HERBS like basil, rosemary, lemon balm, thyme, nutmeg, marjoram and lemon verbena.
Drink water and herbal teas

MID-LIFE CRISIS? WHAT MID-LIFE CRISIS?

It's towards the end of the middle years that most women will go through the menopause and that men and women will start to succumb to heart disease, high blood pressure and strokes. If you haven't taken sufficient care of yourself until now, don't despair. It's still possible to make dramatic changes. All that's needed is a close look at your eating habits.

The menopause

There's no need to dread the onset of the menopause. It's not a disease but is nature's way of preventing pregnancy when it's no longer a good idea. Some symptoms can be unpleasant and distressing, some may lead to medical problems, and some can be the cause of severe depression, but you can improve and control them all.

Understandably, many women are now refusing to take HRT, but there are parts of the world where they don't need it because the foods they eat – nature's own pharmacy – control the unpleasant symptoms. Include as many of these foods as often as you can in your daily diet. The more you eat, the fewer menopause problems you will have.

Beetroot is a traditional medicine for building up the run down and convalescent. It contains iron and is a good source of folic acid, which makes it a valuable addition to the menopause diet.

Chickpeas are a super menopause food as they supply protein, vitamins A, C and some of the B complex, and also calcium, iron, zinc, potassium, magnesium and phosphorus.

Fresh pineapple contains the natural enzyme bromelain, which improves digestion and the absorption of nutrients.

Ginseng has a powerful tonic and stimulating effect, so is great if you feel a bit down. Take it as a tea in small but regular doses.

Nectarines supply the essential Vitamin A.

Oats are a good source of easily digested protein, B complex vitamins, some vitamin E, calcium, magnesium, potassium and silica.

Red, green and yellow peppers are an excellent source of vitamin C, but the red and yellow ones also provide a good supply of vitamin A.

Sesame seeds are very rich in protein, iron and zinc.

Soya in all its forms is one of the richest sources of the phytoestrogens. These will help make up for your body's changing hormone patterns at this time

Spring greens are a real life-saver during the menopause. They contain potassium, calcium and iron, and are a very rich source of vitamins A and C.

Oily fish give essential fatty acids, vitamin D and lots of calcium (as long as you eat canned sardines with their bones).

Avocados offer masses of vitamin E for circulation and the skin, along with healthy fats that eliminate cholesterol and protect your heart and arteries.

Sage used generously in cooking helps to control hormonal fluctuations and reduces hot flushes.

Brittle bones

Whether you're male or female, it's never too late to improve your brittle bones. Calcium, magnesium, zinc and vitamin D-rich foods, sunshine and weight-bearing exercise will all make them stronger.

Skin problems

Skin is now likely to be a problem as oestrogen levels fall. Phytoestrogens, soya-based foods and all the other skin nutrients will help. A monthly facial scrub using a carton of natural yoghurt mixed with a heaped teaspoon of coarse sea salt makes an excellent, but gentle exfoliant.

Heart disease, high blood pressure and strokes

This unholy trinity of diseases linking the heart and circulation is the major cause of premature and preventable death in men throughout the Western world and once the menopause is reached, women are just as likely to suffer as the men.

The most important single factor in heart disease is smoking, so quit now if you haven't already. Being overweight is also a risk, so watch the scales, keep physically active and control your stress levels.

On the food front, start protecting yourself by following the Vitality Eating Plan on pages 112–13, but for the most secure life insurance possible, also cut down your consumption of fats, sugars and refined carbohydrates and increase the amount of fibre you get, particularly the soluble fibre that is found in oats, beans, apples, pears and cereals.

Eating lots of oily fish, good olive oil, fresh fruits, carrots and dark green leafy vegetables will increase your intake of the nutrients that protect your body against heart disease and keep your veins and arteries in good condition. Vitamin C is especially

important as it reduces the risk of blood clots, so eat plenty of red, green and yellow peppers, kiwi fruit, oranges and blackcurrants. Onions, garlic, leeks, chives and spring onions are good for reducing cholesterol, as is lecithin from eggs, soya beans and liver.

Throwing away the salt cellar and cutting down on all foods which contain salt or any additives with the word 'sodium' in the name will all help to reduce blood pressure too.

Finally, add a little healthy exercise – 20 minutes of brisk walking three times a week is enough to make a difference – take away the nicotine risk, stir in a little positive thought and relaxation, and you have the recipe for a healthy, happy and long life.

The Golden Years

Today you can expect to live until the age of 75 and more. In 1900, 4 per cent of Americans were over 65 but today the over-65s are 12 per cent of the population; that's more than 27 million people. Yet a mere 100 years ago the life span of women was seldom more than 50. They rarely reached the menopause and the prospect of another 25 golden years was not even a pipe dream. Now, statistically, the chances are that more women will be left to cope on their own.

Whether you are a man or a woman, though, your body changes quite dramatically now. Brain cells are lost, the muscles lose some strength, the joints some flexibility, the digestion some tolerance and the eyes and ears some sharpness.

Nutritionally this is a key time. It is essential to eat well even though your appetite may decrease. Single older women often start eating more convenience foods and snacks and do less real cooking. Older men on their own fall into two groups: those who depend on convenience foods and, surprisingly, those who develop an interest in food and take to cooking. They often do rather better nutritionally than the women who, having had a lifetime of shopping for and preparing three meals a day for the family, often give up.

Get your nutrients

If you have got this far in life, you can't have got it totally wrong and all you need now is a bit of fine tuning. The first thing to remember is that you're not just what you eat, you're what you absorb from what you eat, too.

Large-scale surveys show alarming deficiencies in the diets of older people in Britain, Australia and the USA, their intake of calcium, vitamins A,

B6, C, fibre and total calories giving the most cause for concern. Up to half of the elderly had low intakes of some of these nutrients, with older women being more at risk from nutritional deficiencies than men

Other factors play their part, too. Since digestion becomes less efficient in later years, there is a reduction in the amount of nutrients absorbed by the body. To make matters worse, more than a quarter of the people surveyed were taking supplementary bran to help with constipation. This further diminishes the amount of calcium, magnesium and zinc which they are able to absorb from their food. In addition, many of today's fruits and vegetables contain substantially fewer nutrients than they did 50 years ago. This, combined with reduced consumption, can result in very poor nutritional status.

Protect your bones

Medication for other ailments may further reduce the absorption of nutrients such as calcium, iron and vitamins C and D, and this may be critical for bone health. Osteoporosis isn't just a problem for women; around 1 in 10 men will get it too and in them it tends to develop more rapidly and is frequently severely disabling.

Vitamin D, for example, is essential for the body's use of calcium and is vital in the prevention and treatment of osteoporosis, but antacids containing aluminium and anticoagulants reduce its absorption. Similarly, aspirin, HRT, tetracyclines, 'sulpha' drugs, mineral oils and nicotine greatly reduce the effectiveness of vitamin C, which is necessary for the production of collagen, an important part of bone structure and essential for the body's immune system. Whether you use any of these medicines or not, take an extra 500g of vitamin C daily as a precaution. Look for the non-acidic form, ester-c, as this will not aggravate acidity and indigestion.

Magnesium deficiency is also a factor in osteoporosis and is commonly linked to diets that are high in salt. Yet another reason, in addition to controlling your blood pressure, for keeping your salt consumption to an absolute minimum.

Other factors such as drinking coffee and alcohol or large quantities of tea, as well as eating excessive amounts of refined bran, smoking and not doing enough weight-bearing exercise, also increase the rate of bone loss and the possibility of osteoporosis, as do diets that are low in calcium and high in phosphorus and protein. These are simple lifestyle factors which anyone can change if they choose to.

> **If you have got this far in life, you can't have got it totally wrong and all you need now is a bit of fine tuning.**

Supplements for your bones

Supplements are really important at this time but they must be in the right form. Up to 40 per cent of post-menopausal women have been found to have too little acid in their digestive juices and this drastically cuts the amount of calcium which can be absorbed from calcium carbonate supplements to a mere 4 per cent. Those with normal stomach acid absorb 22 per cent. This problem can be overcome by using soluble calcium citrate instead, which allows a 45 per cent uptake of calcium, even in those with reduced stomach acid.

At this age, important though healthy eating is, it's probably a good idea for most men and women to boost their bone protection with this simple daily supplement plan.

- Calcium citrate   1000mg
- Vitamin C with bioflavonoids   500mg
- Vitamin D   5mcg
- Magnesium   100mg

What to eat

As we have seen, now is the time to maximise your nutritional input. You need food bursting with nutrients that are easily absorbed, easily digested, and, most importantly, easily prepared.

You probably don't want to spend much time in the kitchen, but regular meals, no matter how small, are vital. Even if you're on your own, lay the table, add a few flowers, sit in comfort and enjoy a leisurely meal. It doesn't have to be cooked – a wholewheat roll, a piece of good cheese, some celery, raisins, nuts and an apple, make a nourishing lunch. During the winter months add a bowl of simple home-made vegetable soup to boost your protective antioxidants and help your immune system fight off the winter bugs.

Vital foods now should include small quantities of chicken (free-range is best if you can get it) to give you a low-fat and versatile source of protein, B vitamins, zinc and iron. Oats are one of the most protective foods, rich in fibre, minerals and protein, so start each day with porridge or muesli and you should also eat regular amounts of natural bio yoghurt (see right).

Eat chicory, endive, radishes and globe artichokes for the liver and digestive system; dried fruits for their high energy and fibre content, plus the added bonus of lots of beta-carotene in peaches and apricots; and garlic, onions and leeks to take care of your heart and circulation, as well as protecting against infection. Eat lots of these raw, in salads, or add them to vegetable soups, stews or casseroles.

In season you should be enjoying strawberries, raspberries, blueberries and blackberries, for their ability to remove uric acid from the system. Celery, cabbage and leeks do the same and these all help with arthritis, rheumatism and gout, too. Eat masses of dark green leafy vegetables, carrots, pumpkin and squashes, as these are an important source of beta-carotene, other essential carotenoids, minerals and vitamins.

To keep your brain active (see pages 170–71) the essential fatty acids in oily fish like salmon, sardines, anchovies and fresh tuna are vital and shellfish like mussels, especially the large New Zealand green-lipped variety, clams, scallops, oysters, cockles and winkles are also valuable. All these fish and shellfish are also good sources of zinc and iron and are easy to cook. With the exception of tuna, all other canned fish are a valuable addition to any Golden Years diet; their fatty acids help relieve joint pain and stiffness, too.

CHICKEN is a great low-fat protein which is good value, and quick and easy to cook. Use free-range birds if you can.

CHICORY stimulates the gall bladder to produce bile, which makes it an aid to liver function and digestion.

DRIED FRUITS Apricots, peaches and nectarines provide energy, fibre and vitamin A, while dates and figs are good sources of iron and calcium.

GARLIC is the great granddaddy of all the therapeutic food plants. Use it in savoury dishes each day. If you have a cold, eat some on toast.

MILLET is rich in protein, low in starch and contains silicon for skin, hair, nails and the health of the walls of the blood vessels.

OATS are an excellent source of soluble fibre to prevent constipation, are rich in B vitamins and provide slow-release energy without raising blood insulin levels.

PEARS have vitamin C in the skin and fruit sugar for quick-release energy. They are also rich in potassium – important if you are taking diuretic pills – and are a good source of the soluble fibre pectin.

STRAWBERRIES are a great help for all the joint diseases.

TURMERIC protects against stomach cancer and has an anti-inflammatory action on the entire digestive system.

TURNIPS are powerful eliminators of uric acid, so they help gout and other joint problems. They are also useful for the treatment of chest infections; puréed in a little milk they are a traditional European folk remedy for bronchitis.

MILK INTOLERANCE Natural bio yoghurt is easier to digest than ordinary milk, especially since lactose intolerance gets worse with age. Around 70 per cent of the American black and adult Jewish populations are affected by milk intolerance, and it's estimated that a maximum of 12 per cent of Caucasian Americans have this problem, too. It's equally common in the Asian population and is a growing disorder in the general population of the UK as well.

MOBILITY

There's no point having the extra years of life that the twenty-first century offers if you are suffering from painful and limiting conditions like arthritis, rheumatoid arthritis, rheumatism and damaged joints and haven't got the mobility to enjoy those years. In addition there is the mental distress which results from a loss of normal mobility – the lack of independence, the inability to perform the simplest task like putting on your own socks or picking up something you've dropped, the despair at not being able to walk your dog or go to the corner shop for your newspaper. By contrast, being active stimulates the cardiovascular system, maintains good muscle tone through exercise and good bone strength through weight-bearing. But there's no need to suffer stiff, aching joints in silence. There's plenty you can do to help yourself.

There are many reasons for loss of mobility; traumatic injury, temporary illness, chronic joint disease, chronic lung disease, post-operative recovery, severe obesity, and even depression – a commoner cause than most people realise. Whatever drug therapy may have been prescribed for you, regularly eating the Top 10 Foods for the Golden Years (see page 179) will help protect and maintain the integrity of your joint surfaces, build muscle strength, maintain good weight and nourish the mind and spirit, all of which are essential for both prevention and cure.

Joint and muscle problems at this age may require professional care or even surgery. Early treatment with physiotherapy, osteopathy, massage or acupuncture, can help reduce pain, improve mobility and result in the need for less medication, but following my dietary advice will enhance other treatments and produce considerable long-term benefits.

In addition, there is evidence that a diet low in the specific antioxidants, selenium, vitamins A, C and E, carotenoids and all the other phytochemicals, increases the likelihood of joint disorders, and can slow down the healing process.

Immobility and weight gain

Even short periods of immobility can lead to rapid weight gain which can, in turn, encourage more immobility. If this happens to you, then it's essential to make a reduction in calorie consumption without compromising good nutrition and the easiest way of achieving this is to cut down on all animal fats, except the oily fish.

MAKE SURE YOUR DIET AT THIS TIME OF LIFE INCLUDES

■ A weekly portion of liver – it helps prevent anaemia, too – plenty of carrots, broccoli, apricots, sweet potatoes and cantaloupe melon, all rich in vitamin A or beta-carotene.

■ Red and yellow peppers, kiwi fruit, oranges, Brussels sprouts and cabbage should all be eaten in abundance for their vitamin C.

■ Avocados, fresh nuts, asparagus, sunflower seeds and olive oil are rich in vitamin E.

■ Selenium is found in brazil nuts, and all fish, shellfish, meat, wholegrains and cereals and eggs.

Another major pitfall is comfort eating. Because you're immobilised you get miserable, being miserable can lead to depression, being depressed can lead you to the biscuit tin, the sticky bun and the chocolate cake. You must avoid these temptations.

A little exercise is all you need

In the elderly, immobility can become a habit which becomes a self-fulfilling prophesy – the less you do, the less you can do; the less you can do, the less you do. It is vital to encourage regular exercise; simply exercising arms, hands, shoulders, knees and ankles, whilst sitting, is a good start. Many studies have shown that even people who have been virtually chairbound for years, can soon be active and walking when encouraged into a regular exercise programme, combined with good nutrition. It's now certain that the discomfort of exercising painful joints is worthwhile; once you can work through the initial discomfort, the result will be a substantial reduction of the original pain.

MEMORY AND CONCENTRATION

One of the curses of growing old is the feeling that your memory is failing you and your powers of concentration are in decline. In the most severe cases, there is the spectre of Alzheimer's Disease lurking on the horizon. But, as with so many of the physical and mental problems that life throws at you, there are things you can do to overcome them, and the starting point is, as always, what you eat.

As with all bodily functions, a constant supply of glucose and oxygen is required for your brain cells to work at their optimum level. This means the regular consumption of balanced meals to provide a constant, even conversion of food into glucose, plus an adequate intake of easily absorbed iron in order to ensure the blood has adequate oxygen-carrying properties.

In addition, maintaining your IQ requires memory and concentration, both of which depend on good nutrition. Several studies of children have shown that those on the worst diets showed the biggest improvement in IQ and learning ability when they were given an all-in-one vitamin, mineral and fish-oil supplement. There's no doubt that boosting nutritional status with this type of pill is a good insurance policy for those of any age who may be having difficulty with memory or concentration, but taking a pill does not wholly compensate for bad diet. People have survived down the millennia by eating food, not by taking pills.

WHAT TO AVOID Watch out for animal fats which slow down brain function, and go easy on the drink. Whilst one glass of wine may relax your nerves and help you cope better with the mental stresses of difficult situations, be warned that alcohol is a depressant and at crucial times for memory and concentration it should be avoided.

Herbal supplements

The Chinese have used the leaves of the Ginkgo biloba tree for 5000 years to improve short-term memory and concentration. This herbal medicine increases the blood flow to the brain cells and there is considerable scientific evidence that it helps overcome the early signs of mental ageing.

Garlic, whether in food or as pills, also helps improve blood flow and reduces cholesterol, high blood pressure and the stickiness of blood. All these actions are good for the brain as well as for the rest of the body.

> "Maintaining your IQ requires memory and concentration, both of which depend on good nutrition."

TOP 10 FOODS FOR MEMORY

SHELLFISH is a particularly rich source of zinc, which is key for both memory and concentration and is commonly lacking in diets that consist largely of convenience foods. Oysters are the richest source of all, but there's plenty in crab, other fish, wholegrain cereals, beans and peas, mushrooms, wheatgerm, pumpkin and sunflower seeds.

ROSEMARY is the king of the memory-enhancing herbs. It stimulates the adrenal cortex and is of great value for memory loss, nervous tension, anxiety and general emotional debility. In ancient Rome rosemary wine was used to treat all these mental problems.

FRESH FRUITS, particularly grapes, pears and apples, and a handful each day of fresh unsalted peanuts, walnuts and almonds should be eaten to keep your boron levels up to scratch. Boron has not been thought essential for humans, but recent research suggests that it may play an important part in the transmission of electrical impulses in the brain.

DRIED FRUITS such as dates, figs and apricots, should be eaten every day, as they contain the minerals that prevent the body from absorbing aluminium. Aluminium is a possible factor in the onset of Alzheimer's Disease. Although not yet proven, there are enough question marks surrounding the toxicity of aluminium to make it better not to use aluminium cooking pans or deodorants and anti-perspirants containing aluminium.

CAN'T SLEEP?

'Sleep that knits up the ravell'd sleeve of care, The death of each day's life, sore labour's bath, Balm of hurt minds, great nature's second course, Chief nourisher in life's feast.'

No-one understood the importance of sleep better than Shakespeare, who wrote these words in his play, *Macbeth*. Insomnia and disrupted sleep patterns are one of the most common reasons why people in their Golden Years seek medical help. These problems cause high levels of stress and anxiety and can exacerbate pain, discomfort and other symptoms of a wide range of health problems.

As sleep descends, the activity hormones are switched off, making way for the growth and repair hormones to get to work. This is when your body sets about its nightly maintenance work, utilising the nutrients from your food. In other words, sleep is the prime example of the interaction between food, mind and body.

What to eat

Lots of foods help promote good sleep, especially those containing the sleep-inducing hormone, serotonin. Bananas, pineapple, walnuts, figs and tomatoes are common examples. Starchy foods contain the essential amino acid tryptophan, a precursor of serotonin, which is why malted-milk drinks help encourage better sleep. It seems to work especially well for people who drop off easily, but wake in the small hours. If that describes you, then try a malted-milk drink half an hour before bedtime.

The Ancient Romans used wild lettuce as an aid to sleep, and herbalists still use it today. Modern varieties of lettuce are all relatives of the wild plant, so a few lettuce leaves in a sandwich – the bread supplies tryptophan, too – makes a really good bedtime snack.

Honey has long been a favourite folk remedy for insomnia. Take it mixed with a little warm milk, a cup of chamomile tea or hot water with lemon.

Other herbal teas which help you sleep are lemon balm (melissa), crushed fennel seeds – especially when sleeplessness is caused by indigestion or wind – lemon verbena or lime blossom.

Lavender is another wonderful sleep-inducer. You can use the flowers in cakes and biscuits, sprinkle the essential oil on your pillow or, half an hour before bedtime, put a few drops into a fragrancer in the bedroom.

WHAT TO AVOID Hunger is the first factor in sleep deprivation. A rumbling stomach will surely wake you. You can lie there tossing and turning or you can mount a midnight raid on the fridge. If you're really hungry, then low blood sugar will add to your insomnia even more, ensuring that your brain doesn't produce sufficient of the sleep-inducing hormones.

On the other hand, going to bed after an enormous meal, lots of wine and several cups of black coffee will guarantee a night of little more than fitful dozing. Caffeine in any form, and for some people, even in tiny amounts, can drive away sleep for nights on end.

TROUBLES GALORE

As if brittle bones, declining mobility, memory loss and insomnia weren't enough to contend with at this stage of your life, along come digestive problems, constipation and heart and circulatory difficulties. As always, what you eat can help you find a cure.

Digestive problems

To improve your digestion you must eat at regular times and in sensible quantities. Four smaller meals a day are better than three big ones, and it pays to make mealtimes special, laying the table even if you are on your own, and taking your time over your meal. Chew your food well and don't forget to look after your teeth, seeing a dentist at least once a year if you have your own, every other year if you have dentures. Avoid fatty foods, eat some chicory, or globe artichoke each day to stimulate your liver and include lentils in your diet. These are an excellent form of protein, easy to digest without causing wind. Pears make a good end to a meal as they contain soluble fibre, vitamin C, and, like bananas, lots of potassium, which is important if you are taking 'water pills' (diuretics). Adding culinary herbs such as mint, fennel, dill, cumin and cloves to your cooking will also help to prevent and overcome digestive problems.

Constipation

This is an extremely common during the Golden Years, often caused by less exercise, poor diet and too much tea and coffee. Don't let it happen to you. Drink plenty of water and eat wholegrain bread and cereals, dried fruits, millet, greens and loads of fresh fruit and salads. If you worry that drinking a lot of water during the day will make you need to get up in the night, make sure you take a glassful as soon as you wake up, another during the morning, and at least two more before late afternoon, in addition to your other usual fluids. Add lots of garlic to your cooking; it is a good natural antibiotic and helps keep the bowels regular. Prunes are particularly beneficial; they contain plenty of fibre, a natural chemical which helps stimulate bowel function and, weight for weight, they provide higher levels of protective antioxidants than any other food.

Heart and circulatory problems

This is the time of life when these conditions can be a major problem. Follow the advice on page 175 and regardless of other problems like arthritis, it's essential to keep active. Most communities have exercise classes and swimming sessions designed specifically for older people, so get out there and find one.

Prostate problems

Nearly all men over the age of 50 are likely to suffer from enlargement of the prostate gland. It causes frequent trips to the toilet during the night which may involve difficulty in starting and stopping the flow of urine. There may be a constant dribble or repeated feelings of fullness of the bladder yet you only pass small quantities. There may be some discomfort in the area between the scrotum and the anus and eventually the gland may get large enough to completely obstruct the flow. This is a medical emergency.

Soya-based foods and others rich in phytoestrogens (see pages 80–81), together with the herbal remedy Saw palmetto help reduce the size. Prostate cancer is common, so problems in this area need immediate medical attention – I repeat, don't die of embarrassment.

THE RECIPES

All the foods referred to in Nutrition Made Simple and The Seven Ages of Life may sound a little worthy if you just see them as nutrients, proteins, fats, carbohydrates, vitamins and minerals that will help if you have a specific dietary need or are going through a certain stage in life. But that's not what food is all about.

It's about enjoyment, taking time to make food you like preparing, then sitting down with your friends and family and seeing how they appreciate it, too.

There are many foods which are super-charged with goodness, but just because they're 'nutritionally correct' doesn't mean they can't taste delicious, too. In this part of the book I'll be showing you how to use them to make tasty, nourishing meals.

Keep it seasonal

Much as I love strawberries, I'm appalled to see them on the supermarket shelves in Western Europe on Christmas Eve. Eating food out of season contravenes all the principles of healthy naturopathic eating.

It might seem extreme to some people, but we need to go back to the days of our ancestors – even to the Stone Age and agrarian times – when people ate what was readily available in their immediate area or what they'd saved and preserved from times of plenty. Just think of delicious chutneys, fruit preserves or of Christmas pudding, which makes use of all those wonderful dried fruits!

The problem started with the railways, when seasonal fruit was crated up, sent to cities for processing and then transported to areas that had never seen it before. Now we have air freight, when perfectly good produce is ripped off the trees or out of the ground before it's ripe, packaged and artificially ripened en route. Often it never even ripens properly. Just feel the skins of avocados or peaches in some of our supermarkets; if they feel really cool and the skin doesn't give to the touch, you can be almost sure they'll never ripen at home and even if they do, they'll taste of nothing. More importantly, by the time these fruits and vegetables have been freighted halfway round the world, deposited in a central dispatch warehouse, then driven to a shop near you, they will have lost at least half their nutritional value.

The simple fact is that the fresher the produce, the more goodness it has. In an ideal world we'd grow all the fruit and vegetables we need in our back gardens, but if you can't do that, look out for farmers' markets, pick-your-own farms or street markets which sell locally grown produce.

There are some exceptions to my rule against buying out-of-season produce: frozen pulses is one of them. Peas are the most famous, and although I love picking fresh peas from my garden, frozen are nearly as good nutritionally even if they don't have that slightly tough sweetness and wonderful aroma. They're usually put into a freezer within an hour of picking and so they lose practically none of their nutritional status. They certainly contain more goodness than fresh peas, broad beans or runner beans left for days in baskets by the side of a pollution-ridden road or under the hot lights of supermarket shelves.

Store it well

There's absolutely no point in buying good food then taking it home and storing it so that it loses all the goodness you bought it for in the first place. The most important thing is storage temperature, and this really is essential. I'm amazed at the number of people who buy wonderfully fresh fruit and vegetables then keep them in a warm room for the nutrients to oxidise and all the goodness to be lost. The main thing to remember then is keep it cool, but also follow these simple rules of good food hygiene:

- Always keep cooked meat separate from fresh meat. In the fridge always store raw meat below cooked so that there's no danger of blood from the meat dripping onto any other food.
- Use separate chopping boards for meat, vegetables and fish.
- Keep vegetables in a cool place – a larder or garage is ideal – and on a rack which allows the air to flow through.
- Salad stuff should be kept in a separate drawer in the fridge.
- If you use half a can of, say, tomatoes, put the remainder in a glass or plastic bowl, cover it and keep it in the fridge. Don't leave in the can.

THE RIGHT KIT

A bad workman always blames his tools, so the saying goes, and as far as cooking is concerned, choosing the right equipment is vital. You don't have to spend a fortune or have every gadget going – hands up those who've ever bought some fashionable piece of kit which is now stuck at the back of a cupboard and never used – but there are some essentials:

GOOD KNIVES Buy the best steel you can and your knives will last a lifetime. You could start with just four – one for carving, two for chopping and a paring knife.

THREE HEALTHY CHOPPING BOARDS – one each for meat, fruit and vegetables, and fish. Choose wooden boards as wood contains natural antibacterial chemicals and is less likely than plastic to harbour infections.

A SIMPLE HAND MOULI These are ideal for making purées and for preparing small quantities of fresh food for babies.

A POTATO RICER This is the best tool for making mashed potatoes and can also be used for other root vegetables. Again, it's ideal for making baby food.

GOOD SAUCEPANS I'm not a fan of non-stick, coated pans. No matter how careful you are, the surface always disintegrates and I worry about the toxicity of the coatings. Instead, buy the best stainless steel you can afford and, like good knives, they'll last at least one lifetime. I'm still using some of the pans my mother used when I was a boy. And that's a long time ago.

A HEAVY CAST-IRON GRIDDLE PAN These wonderful pans are perfect for low-fat cooking and are ideal for cooking fish, steaks, chicken breasts and chargrilled vegetables.

A WOK Get an old-fashioned steel wok. It works at far higher temperatures, which means quicker cooking and less absorption of fat. Kept properly seasoned, it will last for years. Another tip: always buy a wok one size larger than you think you'll need.

A JUICER Save yourself money and get the most from seasonal fruit by juicing it yourself. It tastes so much better than even the 'freshly-squeezed' juices that are sold in the shops.

A BLENDER They're essential for making delicious soups at home.

A GOOD FOOD PROCESSOR This isn't just a luxury; it's really useful for chopping, mixing, crushing, grinding and beating in seconds.

The KISS principle

I think it was some influential businessman who first coined the phrase Keep It Simple, Stupid (KISS), and when it comes to cooking at home, this couldn't be more true. Yes, it's great to go to a wonderful restaurant and see your food arrive looking as if it has been prepared for the cover of an expensive magazine, but home cooks don't have time to make sure every carrot is a uniform size and every mound of mashed vegetable perfectly moulded. I don't, anyway. Far more important, in my view, is the quality of ingredients, the way they're cooked and the impact they make on your tastebuds.

In preparing the recipes in this book, I used the freshest produce possible and cooked it very simply. What's the point in buying delicious food then drowning its flavour in a sauce which takes hours to make? Some of the dishes, like the Lamb, Lentil and Carrot Casserole on page 225, do take time to cook, but they're prepared in a matter of minutes then left to simmer or bake slowly to give the flavours time to arrive at their delicious best.

Other dishes, like Figs with Goat Cheese on page 23 take just a minute or two from start to finish. You simply don't need to spend a lot of time to make the most of a wonderful ripe fig.

You may be surprised to see that I've used some 'convenience' foods. Much as I like making things from scratch, there are days when I haven't got time to start right at the beginning. Canned tomatoes are one case in point. I love it when my tomatoes plants are groaning under their own weight and I have time to sit in the garden and skin and de-seed them myself, but more often than not I don't, so I buy good quality cans of organic chopped tomatoes, which lose very few of their nutrients in processing.

Pastry is another example. It's something I've never really mastered. I always end up with heavy pastry – and flour everywhere. I have fond memories of the light pastry my mother used to make, but she never passed that skill on to me. So I use frozen. It's quick, tastes fine, suits both sweet and savoury dishes – and I don't have to wash the kitchen floor afterwards.

Sometimes, when I'm pushed for time, I'll also use a stock cube rather than make my own stock from scratch. When I do, however, I always use a low-salt organic cube, to be sure I'm not over-dosing on sodium and other additives.

Cooking should be a joy not a chore, so keep it simple and use the best ingredients. That way you can enjoy great food without being a prisoner in your own kitchen.

The best vinaigrette ever

You'll see that I use vinaigrette in several of the recipes that follow. This truly is the best vinaigrette ever. I love it so much that I make a large quantity every weekend and keep it in a dark glass, stoppered beer bottle to use through the week. Keep it cool, but don't put it in the fridge; the oil will solidify.
(Makes 8 tablespoons)

Olive oil 3 tablespoons
Walnut oil 3 tablespoons
Red wine vinegar 2 tablespoons
Dry mustard 1/4 teaspoon

Whisk the oils, wine vinegar and dry mustard together in a jug / Serve immediately or store in a dark bottle and use within a week.

The chain gangs

In our 24/7 world, very few of us have time to make a 'proper' meal three times a day. But that doesn't mean you have to resort to takeaways or ready-prepared meals. There's nothing wrong with them occasionally and I, for one, don't know what I'd do without good ready-made ravioli when I'm really busy, but I worry when shop-bought food becomes the mainstay of family food. It's not only less nutritious than food made at home, but eaten all the time, it gives the wrong message to our children. How will they cope when they have to feed families of their own if all they've seen their parents do is open a can or put a ready-meal into the microwave?

Eating 'proper' meals doesn't have to mean shopping every day and spending hours preparing vegetables and making stews or casseroles. With a bit of foresight and planning, you can not only eat well, but save time and money, too. That's the principle behind Chain Cooking.

In our house, because there are usually just two of us, by using the Chicken Chain on pages 192–3, we can make a chicken last for four or five days. The recipes are a pretty good representation of what we eat if we have chicken for Sunday lunch. And before you ask, no, it doesn't get boring. You can stuff the chicken with different herbs for the roast, the salad variations are limitless, you can add different herbs and spices to the pilau and any seasonal vegetables can be included in the chicken soup.

Another advantage to cooking this way is that it also gives you a selection of family lunches. Most of the food in the Chains can be packed in containers and taken to work or school. You'll know your family's getting good nutrition in the middle of the day instead of relying on overpriced sandwiches, expensive pots of salad from takeaway bars or, heaven forbid, lunches consisting of packets of crisps and bars of chocolates.

We haven't left the babies out either. Many of the foods in the Chains are ideal for putting through a mouli or into a blender to give kids their first tastes of real food. It's far cheaper and more nutritious than relying on jars of baby food, you can be certain what you're giving them doesn't contain additives or artificial preservatives, and it introduces babies to a variety of tastes, which will make them more adventurous eaters later on.

As well as being good value and saving you time, Chain cooking can be very creative. The ideas I've given are almost off the top of my head, but once you start thinking of the many ways of using food, you can adapt my recipes to suit your family's tastes. The leftover chicken can be made into burgers, for example, or the fish into fish pie. Just by thinking ahead, you'll save hours of unnecessary shopping time, rather a lot of money – and you'll be giving your family food that's good for them.

A note about eggs

Whenever possible, you should use certified, salmonella-free eggs in your cooking, but especially when you are preparing food for babies and young children, if you are pregnant, or for the elderly.

Buy free-range, preferably organic, chicken and you'll be getting one of the most economical, plentiful and nutrient-rich foods around, plus you won't have meat injected with chemicals, hormones and antibiotics. Chicken gives you protein, iron and zinc. It's also amazingly versatile and can give a family several days of delicious healthy eating – as the following recipes based on two medium chickens show.

The roast

Simple roast chicken is a real family favourite. Here you get all the goodness in the meat, plus carbohydrates from the potatoes and vitamin C from the green vegetable. (Serves 4)

Medium chickens 2
Lemon or **orange** 1
Garlic 4 cloves, unpeeled
Unsalted butter about 50g, softened
Fresh herbs a selection, chopped
Boiled potatoes and **a green leafy vegetable** to serve

Cut off any surplus skin from the chickens / Rinse the cavities with cold water and put a halved lemon or orange and 2 split garlic cloves in each / Pull the skin gently off the front of the breasts and push in some softened butter mixed with a selection of chopped fresh herbs, such as rosemary, parsley, oregano, marjoram, sage, thyme or any others you have to hand/ Roast the chickens at 200°C/400°F/gas mark 6 until the chickens are tender and the juices run clear when a skewer is inserted into the thickest part of the thighs / Remove and reserve the breasts before carving / Serve one of the chickens with boiled potatoes and a green leafy vegetable / Keep the carcasses and any extra meat.

FIRST FOOD *Purée some of the chicken (without its skin) and vegetables with a little of the vegetable cooking water (but don't add salt to the water).*

Chicken and chickpea salad

This quick and easy light lunch or supper dish continues the story of the ever-adaptable chicken. Bursting with vitamin C from the salad vegetables, feisty with fibre, calcium and other essential minerals from the chickpeas, and still with the basic nutrients in the chicken, who could believe that something so quick to make and so delicious could do you so much good? (Serves 4–6)

Salad leaves 2 large handfuls of any you have available
Cherry tomatoes 6, halved widthways
Celery, peppers, radishes 2 handfuls of any mixture, sliced or cut into strips
Cooked chicken about 175g leftover meat (but leave some on the carcasses for the soup, below)
Chickpeas 2 x 400g cans, drained and rinsed
Cooked sweetcorn about 110g frozen or canned
Vinaigrette dressing about 125ml (see page 190 or use your own favourite)
Horseradish sauce 1 heaped teaspoon
Crusty wholemeal bread to serve

Put the salad ingredients into a large salad bowl / Tip in the chicken, chickpeas and sweetcorn / Mix together the vinaigrette and horseradish sauce / Pour the dressing over the salad and toss well / Serve with crusty wholemeal bread.

LUNCHBOX *This is great for lunch, but pack the dressing separately and pour it over just before you eat it.*

Coconut chicken pilau

This quick chicken dish uses the breasts of the chickens, which are particularly high in vitamin B6. The recipe's combinbation of protein, carbohydrates, very little saturated fat and the huge protective boost from the carotenoids in the peppers will make it a healthy family favourite. And, of course, the salad boosts your intake of vitamin C. (Serves 6–8)

Safflower oil a little

Onion 1, large, finely chopped

Garlic 3 cloves, finely chopped

Curry powder, mild, medium or hot according to taste
  1 tablespoon

Basmati rice 250g

Chicken stock 850ml (see page 214)

Creamed coconut 110g

Cooked chicken breasts 4, skinned and cubed

Broad beans 125g, cooked

Red pepper 1, large, chopped

Lemon juice 2 teaspoons

Raisins or **crushed hazelnuts** 1 tablespoon

Fresh chopped parsley to garnish

Mixed leaf salad to serve

Heat the oil, add the onion and garlic and cook until soft / Stir in the curry powder and cook for 1 minute / Add the rice, stock and creamed coconut, stirring well until the coconut is dissolved / Cover and simmer for 15 minutes, adding more water if the mixture starts to dry out / Add the chicken, broad beans, red pepper, lemon juice and hazelnuts (unless anyone has a nut allergy) and/or raisins and heat gently for a further 5 minutes/ Serve garnished with parsley, accompanied by a mixed leaf salad.

LUNCHBOX *Delicious cooled and packed in a large plastic container for the next day's office or school lunch.*

Chicken soup

Just when you thought there was nothing left to do with what's left of your two chickens, here's a meal in itself. It's such good value, so easy and as versatile as you want to make it. (Serves 4–6)

Safflower oil a little

Onion 1, large, finely sliced

Garlic 2 cloves, finely sliced

Celery 2 sticks, finely sliced

Bouquet garni 1

Bay leaves 3

Chicken carcasses 2, snapped into about 6 pieces each

New potatoes 6, halved

Other root vegetables about 225g, cubed. Any variety you
  like (mixed bags of frozen vegetables are fine)

Peas or broad beans 110g, fresh or frozen

Grated Parmesan cheese to serve

Heat the oil, add the onion, garlic and celery and sweat gently for a few minutes / Add about 1.2 litres water, the bouquet garni and bay leaves / Add the chicken – preferably in a pasta pan with a separate basket – bring to the boil and simmer for 1 hour / Remove the pasta basket or scoop out the chicken pieces with a slotted spoon, then leave until cool enough to handle / Fork any meat off the bones / Return the meat to the pan with the vegetables and simmer for 30 minutes (if using frozen vegetables, 15 minutes are sufficient) / Remove the bouquet garni and bay leaves / Pour into bowls and serve with Parmesan cheese.

FIRST FOOD *Simply mash the vegetables into the soup.*
LUNCHBOX *This soup survives well in a vacuum flask – great for those cold winter days when you need something warming in the middle of the day.*

MEAT CHAIN

Just the smell of a large joint of beef, lamb or pork roasting appetisingly in the oven means it must be Sunday or a special family occasion. Rightly so, since good organic meat gives you a cornucopia of essential nutrients, including protein, iron, potassium and B vitamins. If it's organic, it's also a good source of conjugated linoleic acid (see page 24). Then you have all the added benefits of the delicious, nutritious and vitamin-rich vegetables you serve with it. But be adventurous with the vegetables; adding herbs, honey and other unusual ingredients won't just make the meal more inviting, you'll get a health add-on, too.

The roast

To make the roast, plus the other recipes here, for four people, you'll need about 3kg of boned rolled sirloin of beef, boned rolled leg of lamb or boned leg of pork. Buy and cook two joints if you want to serve more.

Roast the meat in the usual way depending on how you like it cooked. For beef, rub a mixture of dry mustard and flour into the meat before roasting; lamb tastes delicious with a couple of cloves of garlic cut into slivers and inserted into the flesh; with pork, you need to be sure to score any rind correctly by making deep, even cuts at 2.5cm intervals.

Some unusual vegetable accompaniments include:

Sage roast potatoes Peel 4 large potatoes, cut a slice off one long side so that they sit on their backs and make 3–4 slits down the top edge, almost to their backs / Mix together about 6 teaspoons olive oil, 2 teaspoons chopped sage and 1 chopped garlic clove / Pour the mixture over the potatoes and into the slits / Roast for about 1 hour in the oven with the meat but in a separate pan until crisp.

Honey roast carrots Put 4 whole, scrubbed organic carrots into a roasting tin / Baste with a mixture of about 6 tablespoons melted butter and 2 tablespoons runny honey and roast for about 45 minutes in the oven with the meat.

Red cabbage with cassis Quarter and steam 1 red cabbage cut into quarters lengthways (it takes about 20 minutes) / Drain well and drizzle with cassis to taste before serving.

EAT IT COLD Many people – and I'm among them – prefer cold meat. It does need some dressing up, however, so try these additions, which will give you loads of vitamin C from the salad ingredients, plus antibacterial and cancer-fighting siligrin in the horseradish and antioxidants and healing enzymes in the tropical fruit:

• Warm new potatoes in melted butter with lots of freshly chopped parsley.
• A salad of crisp lettuce, spring onions and cubed beetroot with a dressing made with mayonnaise and 1 level teaspoon horseradish sauce.
• Tropical Salsa. Cut 2 oranges into segments, mix with cubes of 1 mango, 1 papaya and 2 finely sliced spring onions / Scatter torn rocket leaves on top.

LUNCHBOX *Leave a few potatoes aside before you add the butter. Cut the cold meat into shreds. Use all the ingredients, including the Tropical Salsa (left in a fridge overnight) to make a layered salad in a plastic container with a lid.*

Meat curry

Cayenne pepper is great for the circulation and lentils are a rich source of B vitamins, iron, zinc and calcium. Onions and garlic are antibacterial and diuretic. (Serves 4)

Rapeseed oil about 2 tablespoons

Onion 1, large, finely chopped

Garlic 2 cloves, finely chopped

Curry paste 1 tablespoon

Carrot 1, large, peeled if not organic and cubed

Red lentils 75g

Vegetable stock 600ml (see page 215 or use a commercially made cube or powder)

Cooked meat about 450g, cubed

Fresh coriander 1/2 handful of whole leaves

Naan bread 4 large slices, warm

Heat the oil, add the onion and garlic and sweat gently for 2 minutes / Add the curry paste, stir in then cook for a further 2 minutes / Stir in the carrot / Add the lentils and stock and simmer gently for 20 minutes / Tip in the cooked meat, increase the heat slightly and cook for 10 minutes / Scatter the coriander on top / Serve with the naan bread.

Quick meatballs

Rice gives slow-release energy, chilli, onion and garlic give a circulation boost. (Serves 4)

Cooked meat 450g, minced

Onion 1, minced

Chilli powder 1/2 teaspoon

Garlic 1 clove, finely chopped

Egg 1, large

Rapeseed oil for shallow-frying

Long-grain brown rice 225g

Passata 200g jar, warmed, to serve

Mix the cooked meat, onion, chilli powder, garlic and egg together in a bowl / Using your hands, form into 12 small flat balls / Chill in the fridge for about 30 minutes / Shallow-fry the meatballs in the oil for about 3 minutes on each side / Cook the rice according to the packet instructions / Arrange the meatballs on the rice and serve with the warmed passata poured on top.

LUNCHBOX *Hold the passata with these meatballs. It could get a bit messy in the workplace or on a school desk.*

Spiced meat with hummus

This dish combines stimulating paprika and cumin with healthy complex carbohydrates. The tomatoes and parsley also give you a good dose of vitamin C. (Serves 4)

Olive oil 2 tablespoons

Spring onions 2, very finely chopped

Paprika 1 teaspoon

Crushed cumin seeds 1 teaspoon

Cooked meat about 700g, cut into small cubes

Hummus 2 x 500g cartons

Tomatoes 4, cut into quarters lengthways

Fresh flat-leaf parsley about 1/2 handful chopped leaves

Crushed pine nuts 4 tablespoons

Pitta bread, to serve

Heat the oil, add the spring onions and sauté gently for 2 minutes / Add the spices and mix well / Tip in the meat and cook for about 5 minutes, stirring constantly / Spread the hummus onto 4 plates and arrange the tomatoes around the rims of the plates / Spoon the meat into the middle / Scatter the parsley and pine nuts on top / Serve with the pitta bread.

LUNCHBOX *Arrange as above, but pack in a plastic container with a lid.*

The wonderful texture of turnips, parsnips and swede, the crunchiness of peas, the fabulous smell and sweetness of summer's young tomatoes and peppers . . . vegetables are fantastic value and an amazingly flexible source of nourishment.

The basic ingredient for these recipes for four is about 2.25kg mixed root vegetables – fresh organic produce is better, but frozen casserole vegetables will do. If you are using fresh vegetables, peel, cube and parboil them, then store, covered, in the fridge or freezer. You can then add whichever green vegetables take your fancy.

Vegetable crumble

All the goodness of onion and garlic, with the diuretic properties of parsley and the vitamin C in peas, make this unusual vegetable dish health on a plate. (Serves 4)

Rapeseed oil 3 tablespoons

Onion 1, finely chopped

Garlic 2 cloves, finely chopped

Parboiled root vegetables 700g

Peas, fresh or frozen 350g

Red pepper 1, sliced

Fresh flat-leaf parsley ½ handful of whole leaves

Vegetable stock 600ml (see page 215 or use a commercially made cube or powder)

Oats 175g

Ground nuts 150g

Unsalted butter 75g

Tomato and onion salad to serve

Heat the oil, add the onion and garlic and sauté gently for 3 minutes / Put into a shallow baking dish with the root vegetables, peas, pepper and parsley on top / Warm the stock and pour over the vegetables / Mix together the oats and nuts / Sprinkle over the vegetables / Dot with the butter and cook at 180°C/350°F/gas mark 4 for 45 minutes / Serve with tomato and onion salad.

FIRST FOOD *Liquidise the vegetable mixture, leaving out the topping and mashing in the potato.*

Vegetable pasties

You don't have to be a Cornish coal miner to enjoy these fistfuls of convenient good nutrition. (Serves 4)

Cooked vegetables 600g

Worcestershire sauce 1 tablespoon

Frozen puff pastry 500g, thawed

Plain flour for dusting

Egg 1, beaten

Warm the cooked vegetables and add the Worcestershire sauce / Roll the pastry into 4 rounds on a lightly floured surface / Put the vegetable mixture onto one half of each round, leaving a 1cm gap around the outside / Moisten the edges of the pastry and fold over, enclosing the vegetable mix / Seal the edges by pressing with the tines of a fork / Make 2–3 fork pricks in each pasty to allow the air to escape / Brush with the beaten egg and bake at 220°C/425°F/gas mark 7 for about 30 minutes until the pastry is golden.

LUNCHBOX *The original lunchbox food, these pasties are just what you need when the lunchtime hunger pangs start.*

Bean casserole

Adding soya beans to our collection of healthy root vegetables makes this dish an excellent source of protein – often missing in a vegetarian diet. Of all the beans and pulses, soya beans are the richest in phytoestrogens, which protect against osteoporosis and other unpleasant symptoms of the menopause as well as helping to balance hormone levels. Because of the special fibre all beans contain, they help reduce cholesterol levels. (Serves 4)

Rapeseed oil 3 tablespoons

Onion 1, finely chopped

Garlic 2 cloves, finely chopped

Parboiled root vegetables 450g

Soya beans 400g can, drained and rinsed

Vegetable stock about 850ml (see page 215 or use a commercially made cube or powder)

Bouquet garni 1

Grated Parmesan cheese 4 tablespoons

Fresh wholemeal breadcrumbs, 4 tablespoons

Crusty bread to serve

Heat the oil, add the onion and garlic and sweat gently for 3 minutes / Add the root vegetables, soya beans, stock and bouquet garni and bring to a simmer / Continue cooking gently for about 20 minutes or until the vegetables are just tender / Mix together the cheese and breadcrumbs / Pour the vegetable mixture into bowls and sprinkle the cheese and breadcrumbs on top / Sear with a blowtorch until brown and crisp / Serve with crusty bread.

FIRST FOOD *Mash the vegetable mixture, leaving out the topping.*
FREEZING *This casserole freezes well, but don't add the topping until just before serving.*

Veggie baked potatoes

Ideal comfort food, this vegetarian dish has all the goodness of potatoes, which are high in fibre, B complex vitamins, minerals and vitamin C – and which aren't, let's get this straight, fattening. Oregano, a traditional Italian herbal accompaniment to tomatoes, is antiviral, antibacterial and, so they say, a strong aphrodisiac. (Serves 4)

Baking potatoes 4

Olive oil 3 tablespoons

Onion 1, finely sliced

Garlic 2 cloves, finely sliced

Parboiled root vegetables 450g

Tomatoes 2, cubed

Oregano 1 large fresh herb sprig or 1/2 teaspoon dried

Vegetable stock (see page 215 or use a commercially made cube or powder) or water about 300ml

Cheddar cheese 110g, grated

Put the potatoes on to bake at 200°C/400°F/gas mark 6 / Meanwhile, heat the oil, add the onion and garlic and sweat gently for 3 minutes / Add the root vegetables, tomatoes and oregano and just cover with stock / Simmer until tender, about 15 minutes, adding more stock or water as necessary / Mash coarsely, then increase the heat to evaporate any excess moisture / Make cuts crossways in the potatoes and pile the vegetable mixture into the opening / Sprinkle with the cheese and put under a hot grill until the cheese has melted.

FIRST FOOD *Mash well to serve.*

FISH CHAIN

Large wild salmon or sea trout are available from all fishmongers and most supermarkets these days. They are a marvellous source of B vitamins, essential fatty acids, protein and minerals, especially iodine.

A fish weighing around 4kg will be enough to serve six people with a stylish main meal as well as with all these other options for the leftovers – although 'leftovers' is a total misnomer as these dishes are equally delicious in their own right.

1 Poached fish

I think it's an insult to good warm poached salmon or sea trout to smother it in a fancy sauce. Serve it simply, with a mixture of unpeeled small new potatoes and broad beans cooked with fresh mint, braised celery hearts with caraway seeds – make more than you need and keep to serve cold – and baby spinach. (Serves 4–6)

Salmon or **sea trout** 4kg
Salt
Peppercorns 8
Bay leaves 3
Watercress, unpeeled boiled new potatoes, broad beans cooked with fresh mint, braised celery hearts with caraway seeds, baby spinach to serve

Get your fishmonger to gut, clean, scale and wash the fish / Put it into a fish kettle with about 2.5cm water, 1 teaspoon salt, the peppercorns and the bay leaves torn in half / Bring quickly to the boil / Cover and simmer for 20 minutes / Remove from the heat / Leave in the water for 5 minutes / Lift out and drain / Serve on a large oblong platter on a bed of watercress and cut from one end of the fish only.

FIRST FOOD *Make sure there are absolutely no bones left in the fish, then mash or liquidise it with all the vegetables except the celery. Babies almost certainly won't like the flavour and could choke on the caraway seeds.*

2 Simple fish salad

You'll love this impressive cold dish, which combines all the goodness of the fish with beta-carotene from the carrots, the crunchiness of the cold braised celery and the refreshing taste of cucumber. (Serves 4)

Cooked cold salmon or **sea trout** about 700g
Sliced cucumber, grated carrots with raisins in a mixed vinaigrette (see page 190 or use your own favourite) **and mayonnaise dressing, cold baby potatoes with sliced spring onions** to serve

Remove the head, bones and any remaining skin from the fish / Set aside about 700g, flake the rest and put it straight back into the fridge / Reassemble the reserved fish on a serving platter, covering any 'cracks' with finely sliced cucumber / Serve with the cold, braised celery from the poached fish recipe on the left, grated carrots with raisins in the vinaigrette and mayonnaise dressing and cold baby potatoes with sliced spring onions.

Fish cakes

These fish cakes are great hot or cold. They freeze well and just need to be brought to room temperature before serving. (Serves 4)

Cooked cold salmon or **sea trout** about 350g, flaked

Potatoes 450g, boiled and coarsely mashed

Spring onions 4, very finely chopped

Fresh parsley 2 tablespoons, finely chopped

Eggs 3 medium, lightly whisked

Matzo meal or **seasoned plain flour** about 6 tablespoons

Rapeseed oil for frying

Tartare sauce and **a large tomato and onion salad** to serve

Mix the fish with the potatoes, spring onions and parsley / Tip in a third of the whisked eggs and combine well / Using your hands, mould the mixture into 8 burger-shaped rounds and leave in the fridge for 30 minutes / Brush each cake with the remaining egg, then dip into the matzo meal or flour / Shallow-fry in the oil for 3–4 minutes on each side / Serve hot or cold, with tartare sauce and a large tomato and onion salad.

CHILDREN *Make the fish cakes into the shape of little fingers. They make a fun dish for a children's party, with a good, organic tomato ketchup served as a dip.*

LUNCHBOX *Delicious cold, these are ideal for taking to work or school.*

PARTIES *Bite-sized fish cakes make good canapés for a drinks party.*

Fish caesar

A fishy version of the traditional Caesar salad so loved by Americans. This dish combines the goodness of two healthy oily fish – salmon or sea trout and anchovies. It's a meal-in-itself for four people or a quick, stylish starter for six to eight. (Serves 4–8)

Cos lettuce 1, torn into large pieces

Extra-virgin olive oil 150ml

White bread 6 slices cut into 1cm cubes

Grated Parmesan cheese 2 heaped tablespoons

Canned anchovy fillets 4, drained

Egg yolk 1

Garlic 1 small clove, peeled and halved

Lemon juice 1 tablespoon

Worcestershire sauce 1 tablespoon

Cooked cold salmon or **sea trout** about 600g, flaked

Put the lettuce into a large bowl / Heat 2 tablespoons of the oil in a large frying pan / Add the bread cubes and cook until golden / Drain on kitchen paper and leave to cool / Put the cheese, anchovies, egg yolk, garlic and lemon juice into a food processor and whiz until well combined / Add 2 tablespoons iced water and whiz for a few seconds / Mix the bread croûtons with the lettuce / Stir in the Worcestershire sauce and cheese mixture / Serve with the flaked fish piled in the middle.

LUNCHBOX *Keep some of the dressing and salad, minus the croûtons, separately in the fridge. Before setting off for work or school, spread a baguette or ciabatta roll with the dressing, pile on the salad and wrap in greaseproof paper.*

Egg-stuffed tomatoes

Eggs are almost universally accepted as traditional breakfast fare. They are inexpensive and quick to prepare, and they are a good source of protein, vitamins A and B12 and zinc. You'll also get a good supply of calcium from the milk and cheese and vitamin C from the tomatoes. (Serves 2)

Large beef tomatoes 4
Extra-virgin olive oil
Salt and **pepper**
Unsalted butter 75g
Milk 200ml
Eggs 6, medium
Cheddar cheese 110g
Fresh parsley 4 sprigs

Halve the tomatoes widthways / Cut out the membranes and scoop out the seeds / Brush the insides with a little oil / Season and put into a low oven at 160°C/325°F/gas mark 3 for 10 minutes / Make the scrambled eggs using the butter, milk and eggs / Grate the cheese / Just as the eggs are about to set, stir in most of the cheese / Put the egg mixture into the tomatoes / Scatter the rest of the cheese on top and put under a very hot grill until the cheese browns, not more than 1 minute / Chop the parsley finely and scatter over to serve.

FIRST FOOD *Babies will love the scrambled egg, but leave out the cheese and parsley and don't serve in the tomato shells.*

Mushroom, herb and tomato crêpes

Crêpes and pancakes are so versatile. These use buckwheat flour, which improves circulation and fights high blood pressure. Then you have the calcium from the milk, the protein from the eggs and a host of health benefits in the herbs and vegetables. (Serves 4)

Plain flour 50g
Buckwheat flour 50g
Eggs 1, medium, plus an extra egg white
Milk 300ml
Tomatoes 2
Mushrooms 75g
Mixed fresh herbs 2 tablespoons
Unsalted butter about 100g

Sift the flours together / Whisk in the egg and egg white / Stir in the milk gradually / Leave to rest for 30 minutes / Skin the tomatoes by covering with freshly boiled water until the skins slide off easily / Remove the seeds and chop / Slice the mushrooms and chop the herbs / Melt 50g of the butter in a pan, add the mushrooms, herbs and tomatoes and sweat gently for 5 minutes until the mushrooms give out their brown colour / Melt the rest of the butter in another pan / Pour in just enough of the batter mixture to cover the base / Cook for about 3 minutes, then turn over and cook for a further 2 minutes / Keep warm and repeat using the rest of the mixture / To serve, put a little vegetable mixture on one half of each crêpe and fold over.

DESSERT *Make extra batter and fill the crêpes with sliced banana softened in butter and honey with a pinch of allspice. A good way to use bananas that are getting past their best.*

Soya sausages with cheesy beans

Soya has been a staple food in Asia for centuries, and it's now an accepted alternative to meat for vegetarians. Meat eaters may think it looks funny and tastes of nothing, but the wonderful thing about soya protein (often called TVP or textured vegetable protein) is that it takes on the flavour of the ingredients in which it's cooked or marinated, so it's amazingly adaptable. It's also high in phytochemicals, which protect against hormone-linked cancers in both men and women and which help to relieve the symptoms of the menopause. Here, I've combined soya with Tabasco, a wonderfully fiery sauce, plus the vitamins in tomatoes and the ultra-protective chemicals in onion. Baked beans are a fantastic source of fibre and the wonderfully creamy mozzarella gives you calcium, too. (Serves 4)

Onion 1

Unsalted butter 25g

Cherry tomatoes 3

Soya protein or textured vegetable protein (TVP) 110g

Cold vegetable stock (see page 215 or use a commercially made cube or powder) about 100ml

Egg 1, medium

Tabasco sauce 1 teaspoon

Fresh flat-leaf parsley 2 tablespoons, chopped

Low-salt, low-sugar organic baked beans 2 x 400g cans

Fresh buffalo mozzarella cheese 200g

Wholemeal breadcrumbs about 50g

Olive oil for frying

Chop the onion finely / Melt the butter in a frying pan, add the onion and sweat gently for about 5 minutes / Chop the tomatoes finely, add to the pan, cook, stirring occasionally, for a further 5 minutes and leave to cool / Mix the soya protein with the stock / Beat in the egg, Tabasco, parsley and onion and tomato mix / Form into 8 small sausages, flatten slightly with your hands and leave to cool slightly / Heat the baked beans and pour into an ovenproof dish / Cut the cheese into thin slices and arrange on top / Put into a 200°C/400°F/gas mark 6 oven until the cheese melts / Coat the sausages with the breadcrumbs then fry in the oil until slightly golden, about 3 minutes on each side / Serve with the beans.

LUNCHBOX *The sausages taste delicious hot or cold, so they are an ideal lunchtime treat.*

FIRST FOOD *Babies will love the sausages mashed in with the beans, but they might not be so keen on the cheese topping. And don't add the Tabasco to their portion.*

PARTIES *Roll the sausage mixture into small flattened balls before frying. Serve with tomato salsa, guacamole or any other favourite dip.*

Spicy chicken livers and grapes

Many people turn up their noses at eating liver but they are missing out on a wide range of nutrients as well as some delicious flavours. Livers are rich in easily absorbed iron, which is essential for healthy blood, and zinc, which is important for men's sexual health. They are also a good source of vitamin A, which helps keep the skin looking good and for night vision. (Serves 4)

Chicken livers (thawed frozen livers will do if you can't find fresh) 500g

Plain flour 4 tablespoons

Paprika 1 teaspoon

Black seedless grapes 250g

Unsalted butter 50g

Rinse, dry and snip any membranes off the livers / Cut into large, even-sized pieces / Mix together the flour and paprika and roll the livers in it / Halve the grapes / Melt the butter in a wide saucepan / Add the livers and sauté until they just become firm / Tip in the grapes and continue cooking for 5 minutes / Pour some of the butter over the toast and pile the livers and grapes on top.

PARTIES *Put one piece of liver and half a grape on cocktail sticks for drinks-party nibbles.*

Summer fruit salad on cinnamon toast

This really is a sweet-and-sour wake-up morning call, with the fresh tangy taste of the fruit and the buttery sweetness of the cinnamon bread. All fruits are high in vitamin C and fibre. They also contain small amounts of minerals, which are better absorbed by the body because of the fruits' vitamin C content. They go well with this version of French toast, which contains cinnamon, which helps to relieve coughs, digestive problems and fatigue. (Serves 4)

Mixed summer berries and **currants** (any combination – and frozen berries will taste just as good) 450g

Eggs 3, medium

Wholemeal bread 4 thickish slices

Unsalted butter 75g

Ground cinnamon 1 level teaspoon

Brown caster sugar 1 heaped teaspoon

Poach the fresh fruit lightly in a little water, or thaw the frozen berries and poach in the water they release in thawing / Beat the eggs / Cut the crusts off the bread / Melt the butter in a large frying pan / Dip the bread in the egg mixture and fry in the butter over a medium-high heat until golden on both sides / Keep warm until all the bread is fried / Warm the berries if necessary / Mix together the cinnamon and sugar and serve sprinkled on the toast with the berries on top.

FIRST FOOD *Teething babies will like the toast cut into fingers, but leave out the cinnamon and sugar.*

Haddock with bacon

This high-protein dish is ideal for those lazy Sundays when you get up late and don't want to eat again until the evening, or when friends come round for brunch. All fish is high in nutrients – particularly iodine, some vitamins and protein – but although eating large amounts of smoked fish has been linked to cancer, it's perfectly healthy for an occasional treat. Do go for the paler, undyed smoked haddock, however – the buttercup-yellow variety is practically swimming in chemicals. (Serves 2)

Undyed smoked haddock 350g

Unsalted butter 50g

Milk about 110ml

Cayenne pepper a pinch

Natural live yoghurt 2 tablespoons

Unsmoked back bacon 2 rashers

Wholemeal bread 2 slices

Skin and flake the haddock / Melt the butter in a pan and add the haddock, milk and cayenne / Simmer for 2 minutes, stirring to break up the fish and adding more milk if it seems to be drying out / Remove from the heat and stir in the yoghurt / Keep warm while you grill the bacon and toast the bread / Serve the haddock on the toast with the bacon on top.

Soufflé baked potatoes with prawns

Facts first: potatoes aren't fattening and prawns don't increase your cholesterol level. Potatoes are high in fibre and vitamin C and baked potatoes are particularly nutritious because of the potassium in their skins. Prawns are very low in calories and rich in zinc, iron and protein. Put them together in this delicious dish and you'll be set up for the day – whatever time it starts. (Serves 2)

Large old potatoes 2

Unsalted butter 50g

Mascarpone cheese 2 tablespoons

Egg 1, medium

Cooked peeled prawns 110g

Prick the potatoes all over with a fork and bake at 200°C/400°F/gas mark 6 for about 1 hour / When they are just about cooked, remove them from the oven, halve and scoop out the flesh / Melt the butter in a saucepan, add the flesh of the potatoes and beat thoroughly / Beat in the mascarpone / Whisk the egg and add to the potatoes / Carefully stir in the prawns / Pile the mixture back into the potato skins, cover with foil and return to the oven for 15 minutes or until piping hot.

FIRST FOOD *Babies with adventurous palates might enjoy the filling if it's well mashed and left to cool slightly.*

Emmenthal fritters with marmalade

Marmalade and cheese make a good sandwich combination. Just like chutney, the marmalade gives a distinct tang to many cheese dishes. Here we serve it with melt-in-the-mouth fritters made with Swiss Emmenthal, which, like all cheeses, is high in calcium, vitamins A, D and some B vitamins, and zinc. Yes, these fritters are fried, but I'm using rapeseed oil, which, like most vegetable oils, has high levels of vitamin E and not much saturated fat. Rapeseed oil is ideal for frying because it has little flavour and, because it has a high smoke point, it fries quickly so less fat is absorbed by the food. It also has an excellent ratio of Omega-3 and Omega-6 fatty acids. (Serves 4)

Plain flour 110g
Milk 200ml
Emmenthal cheese 110g
Dry mustard ½ teaspoon
Cayenne pepper a pinch
Egg whites 4, medium
Rapeseed oil for frying
Bitter, chunky marmalade 4 large tablespoons

Beat the flour and milk together / Grate the cheese and stir thoroughly into the mixture with the mustard and cayenne / Whisk the egg whites until stiff and fold into the mixture / Fry in batches in the oil, using dessertspoon-sized quantities of the batter until golden / Drain on kitchen paper / Warm the marmalade and serve with the fritters.

PARTIES *These fritters are delicious served cold and without the marmalade for party or buffet nibbles.*

Vegetable frittata

There are many variations of this dish, and in Mediterranean countries most families have their favourite. You can use almost any vegetables – boiled potatoes that weren't eaten at a previous meal, that odd spear of broccoli you didn't get round to cooking, the remains of a pack of stir-fry vegetables that you didn't really need. This variation gives you lots of vitamin C and natural resistance in the peppers, folic acid and potassium in the courgettes, and the calming and digestive effects of basil. (Serves 4)

Onion 1
Unsalted butter 75g
Small green pepper 1
Small red pepper 1
Courgettes 2
Eggs 8, medium
Fresh basil 8 large leaves

Chop the onion finely / Melt the butter in a large non-stick frying pan, add the onion and sweat gently for 5 minutes / De-seed the peppers, cut into small cubes, add to the pan and continue cooking for a further 5 minutes / Slice the courgettes finely, add to the pan and cook for 10 minutes / Beat the eggs well and add the basil leaves, torn roughly / Tip the egg mixture onto the vegetables, tilting the pan so that it runs right to the edges / Cook over a medium heat until starting to set, about 5 minutes, occasionally loosening the sides with a palette knife / If the middle still hasn't set, put the frittata under a hot grill for a few minutes / Leave to cool slightly / Put a large plate over the pan and, very quickly, turn them both upside down to turn out the frittata / If you don't feel brave enough to chance that, cut into slices to serve.

Potato and broccoli cakes with poached eggs

The beauty of this dish is that you can make it totally from the leftovers of a previous meal. You can use any green vegetable – even the unjustifiably maligned Brussels sprout takes on a new lease of life finely chopped to take the place of broccoli. I've specifically used broccoli, however, because it's a rich source of beta-carotene, which is known to help prevent and restrict the growth of many types of cancer. Anyway, I like it. (Serves 4)

Onion 1

Unsalted butter 50g

Mashed potato about 175g

Cooked broccoli about 110g

Eggs 6, medium

Fresh breadcrumbs about 6 tablespoons

Sunflower oil for frying

White wine vinegar a dash

Chop the onion finely / Melt the butter in a frying pan, add the onion and sweat gently for 5 minutes / Put the mashed potato and broccoli into a wide bowl and mix well / Tip in the onion and butter and mix again / Beat 1 egg and add it to the bowl, mixing again / Make 4 cakes out of the mix and leave in the fridge for 15 minutes / Beat the second egg in a small bowl / Tip the breadcrumbs onto a plate / Heat the oil in a clean frying pan / Dip each cake into the egg, then into the breadcrumbs and fry in the oil for about 4 minutes on each side / Keep warm while you make the eggs.

To make perfect poached eggs Bring a saucepan of water to a simmer and add the wine vinegar / Put the remaining 2 eggs, in their shells, carefully into the pan for about 30 seconds (this helps hold the whites together) / Remove with a slotted spoon, then crack into the simmering water / Leave for 4 minutes before removing again with a slotted spoon / Serve the cakes with the eggs on top.

LUNCHBOX *Without the poached eggs, these savoury cakes are a perfect takeaway for school or the workplace.*
FIRST FOOD *Try mashing half of one cake into the poached egg yolk and baby might not even notice that he or she is eating something as healthy as broccoli.*

Greek pitta parcels

Pitta bread is a brilliant 'container' for lunchtime snacks. It's strong, easy to pack and holds its shape, particularly in children's hands. This filling is simplicity itself and gives you protein from the hummus and falafel, plus vitamin C from the tomatoes. (Makes 4)

Wholemeal mini pitta breads 4

Hummus (see page 207 or buy a commercial variety) about 200g

Cherry tomatoes 4, halved

Gherkins 2, large, sliced

Falafel (make your own, use a commercially made packet or buy from any deli) 4

Split the pitta breads almost in half lengthways and spread the bottom halves with the hummus / Layer on the tomatoes and gherkins / Add the falafel and close the parcels / Wrap in foil for a lunchtime takeaway.

FIRST FOOD *Babies will love chewing on the pitta bread, especially if they're teething, but the filling has too much fibre – and they probably won't like the taste of it anyway.*

Garlic ciabatta with mozzarella and lettuce

Ciabatta is one of my favourite breads. It's light and has all the goodness of olive oil, with which it's made. This lunchtime munch contains even more olive oil, as well as calcium from the wonderfully smooth mozzarella, important volatile oils and a brilliant aroma from the basil, protective and mood-enhancing chemicals in the garlic, and vitamin C from the lettuce. (Makes 4)

Ciabatta bread 4 rolls

Garlic 2 cloves, peeled and halved

Extra-virgin olive oil 4 tablespoons

Fresh buffalo mozzarella cheese 275g (drained weight)

Fresh basil 8 large leaves

Little Gem lettuce 1, leaves separated

Split the rolls and rub the cut sides with the garlic / Brush with the oil / Slice the mozzarella and divide between the rolls / Put the basil, then the lettuce on top and close the rolls / Wrap in foil to serve.

FIRST FOOD *Ciabatta is too crusty for babies. They may like the mozzarella, but leave out the herbs.*

Stilton salad

The mildness of melon is a wonderful accompaniment to the strong taste of Stilton, one of the best English cheeses. All cheese is a good source of calcium – particularly important for growing children and especially for girls, who need to start protecting themselves against bone-thinning osteoporosis as soon as they are in their teens. (Serves 2)

Cucumber ½, peeled, de-seeded and cubed

Melon ½, cubed

Cherry tomatoes 6, quartered

Stilton cheese 175g

Vinaigrette dressing (see page 190 or use your own favourite) 4 tablespoons

Crusty bread to serve

Put the cucumber, melon and tomatoes into a bowl / Crumble over the Stilton / Pour on the dressing / Pack in small containers to be served with chunks of crusty bread.

CHILDREN *Even though the strong flavour of Stilton is softened by the melon, this may not be to all children's tastes, so substitute the Stilton with cubes of a milder cheese like Edam.*

Hummus and dips

Dips are a great choice if you're looking for a simple lunchtime food. If you (or the kids) get peckish mid-morning you can always dip in to keep those hunger pangs at bay and protect yourself from the temptations of chocolate biscuits or a sticky Danish pastry. Hummus is one of the healthiest of dip foods. The chickpeas and tahini provide energy and calcium, while the vegetables give copious amounts of vitamins and minerals. (Serves 4–6)

Canned chickpeas 250g (drained weight), rinsed

Garlic 2 cloves, roughly chopped

Lemon 1, juiced

Tahini 2 tablespoons

Cumin seeds 1 teaspoon, crushed finely in a pestle and mortar

Extra-virgin olive oil 125ml

Cucumber ½, peeled, de-seeded and cut into strips

Celery 2 sticks, hard membranes removed and cut into strips

Red pepper 1, cut into thin strips

Carrot 1, cut into thin strips and peeled if not organic

Fennel 1 bulb, leaves separated and cut into thin strips

Drain the chickpeas / Put into a food processor or blender with the garlic, lemon juice, tahini and crushed cumin seeds / Whiz slightly then start adding the oil in a steady stream until smooth / Put into small containers with the prepared vegetables packed separately.

PARTIES *Excellent for passing round at drinks parties.*

LUNCHES

Tuna pasta

If you end the morning feeling drained, maybe because you haven't eaten a proper breakfast, you'll need an energy boost at lunchtime. This is it. There are complex carbohydrates in the pasta, protein, minerals and vitamin D in the tuna, and vitamin C in the peppers and spring onions. Add a helping of fruit and you have all you need to see you right through until the evening. (Serves 2)

Pasta spirals, fresh or dried 200g
Extra-virgin olive oil about 1 tablespoon
Tuna canned in brine or **olive oil** about 150g
(drained weight)
Red pepper 1, cut into small cubes
Spring onions 2, sliced
Mayonnaise 4 tablespoons
Fresh fruit to complete the meal

Cook the pasta according to the packet instructions / Drizzle with a little oil, mix well and leave to cool / Drain and flake the tuna / Stir in the peppers and spring onions, then blend in the mayonnaise / Pack into small containers and serve followed by fresh fruit to complete the meal.

Penne with peas and rocket

Made in 10 minutes, this simple pasta could be served hot for a family supper and any leftovers could be eaten cold for next day's lunch. The pasta provides energy, the cheese gives calcium and protein, the peas (even if they are frozen) are a good source of vitamin C and rocket gives a wonderful peppery flavour to the whole dish. (Serves 2)

Penne, fresh or **dried** 200g
Peas, fresh or frozen 100g
Extra-virgin olive oil 1 tablespoon
Rocket leaves 1 handful, roughly torn
Freshly grated Parmesan cheese 2 tablespoons

Cook the pasta according to the packet instructions / Cook the peas / Allow both to cool, then mix together / Stir in the oil, then the rocket and finally the cheese / Pack in small containers.

FIRST FOOD *Before you add the rocket and cheese, put the pasta and peas into a blender and pulse with a little of the pasta water to produce a smooth paste.*

Chicken thighs with chestnut dip

Chicken is a wonderful source of protein – essential when you or the kids are in the middle of a busy day. Chicken thighs have the added advantage of being really easy finger food if you're having lunch at your desk (which, incidentally, I don't advise – everyone needs a break and some fresh air at lunchtime). This dish combines chicken with chestnuts, which are high in starch but contain virtually no fat. They also have a certain amount of potassium and some B vitamins. (Serves 2)

Unsalted butter 60g

Onion 1, small, finely sliced

Garlic 1 clove, finely sliced

Chicken thighs, skinned 2

Chicken stock (see page 214 or use a commercially made cube or powder) 150ml

Fresh rosemary 1 large sprig

Chestnut purée 200g

Clear honey 2 tablespoons

Melt 50g of the butter in a large frying pan / Add the onion and garlic and sauté for 2 minutes / Add the chicken thighs and cook, turning occasionally, until gently browned all over / Pour in the stock, add the rosemary, cover and simmer gently until all the juices from the chicken run clear, about 25 minutes / Remove the chicken and leave to cool / Heat the chestnut purée / Add the honey and the extra 10g butter / Leave to cool / Dip the chicken into the purée and wrap in kitchen foil.

PARTIES *Use chicken legs instead and pass around with the chestnut dip while you're having drinks before dinner.*

Herb risotto

Risotto is a fabulously versatile food. You can add almost anything to it, savoury or sweet. This dish contains a generous helping of herbs, with their cornucopia of soothing and healing volatile oils. You'll also get the heart-protective properties of the onion and garlic, plus some calcium from the crème fraîche. (Serves 2)

Olive oil 2 tablespoons

Onion 1, finely sliced

Garlic 1 clove, finely sliced

Carnaroli or **arborio rice** 150g

Hot vegetable stock (see page 215 or use a commercially made cube or powder) 450ml

Fresh herbs 2 tablespoons, chopped

Freshly ground black pepper 3 large twists

Crème fraîche 4 tablespoons

Mixed fruit salad to complete the meal

Heat the oil, add the onion and garlic and sweat gently for 5 minutes / Tip in the rice and stir until covered with the oil / Add the stock, a ladleful at a time, stirring until all the moisture is absorbed and the rice is just tender, about 20 minutes, adding extra water if it looks as if it's drying out / Off the heat, stir in the herbs, black pepper and crème fraîche / Leave to cool, then pack in small containers and add another container of mixed fruit salad to complete the meal.

Almond fingers

Children of all ages love something sweet at the end of a meal. In these wheat- and gluten-free biscuits we use almonds, a traditional festive treat throughout Europe and the Middle East. Almonds contain more calcium and protein than any other nut and they are also a good source of heart-protective monounsaturated fats, potassium, iron and some B vitamins. (Makes about 12 fingers)

Brown caster sugar 60g
Icing sugar 60g
Ground almonds 150g
Lemon juice 1 teaspoon
Egg yolk 1, small
Plain flour for dusting
Unsalted butter for greasing

Sift the sugars into a bowl / Add the almonds and lemon juice / Stir in the yolk and knead to a dough / Turn onto a floured board and mould into a long bar about 1cm thick / Put onto a greased baking tray and bake at 190°C/375°F/gas mark 5 for about 25 minutes or until set / Cut into 12 portions before cooling.

TEATIME *These biscuits make a welcome addition to afternoon tea.*

Honey shortcakes

An unashamed indulgence, these honey cakes taste delicious. Honey gives you energy and boosts immunity, the lemon rind adds some vitamin C and the wholemeal flour is a good complex carbohydrate. Excellent after a lunch high in other ingredients containing richer sources of vitamin C. (Makes about 10 cakes)

Unsalted butter 225g
Runny honey 6 tablespoons
Lemons 2, grated rind
Wholemeal flour 350g, plus extra for dusting
Eggs 1 or 2, depending on size

Warm the butter gently in a large bowl set over a saucepan of water / Beat in the honey / Add the lemon rind and sift in the flour / Mix to a paste with 1 egg, adding a second egg if the mixture seems too dry / Roll on a floured surface and cut into 5cm squares / Bake at 160°C/325°F/gas mark 3 for about 30 minutes / Leave to cool on a wire rack before serving.

TEATIME *Shortcakes are a favourite afternoon tea treat.*

Rosehip raisin bread

This quick and easy teabread makes an excellent addition to any lunchbox but is perfect at any time of day. Keep a loaf or two in the freezer for a quick snack. They thaw sufficiently to slice after about 10 minutes. Just put the slices into a warm oven, spread with butter and serve. There are lots of carbohydrates and energy from the raisins and complex starch in the wholemeal flour. (Makes enough for one 1.2 litre loaf tin.)

Rosehip tea bags 6

Raisins 450g

Dark demerara sugar 200g

Egg 1 medium, beaten

Wholemeal self-raising flour 250g

Soak the tea bags in 300ml boiling water / Leave until cold then remove and discard the tea bags / Mix the tea with the other ingredients and leave in the fridge for at least 6 hours / Line the loaf tin with greaseproof paper / Pour in the bread mixture and bake at 180°C/350°F/gas mark 4 for 30 minutes / Turn out and cool on a wire rack.

TEATIME *Home-made teabread will impress guests who drop in for tea.*

Pepper tarts

If you want to show off at lunchtime, look no further. These tarts look great and taste delicious. They are also extremely healthy, low in calories, rich in vitamin C and an important source of vitamin A, folic acid and potassium. (Makes 4)

Shortcut pastry (frozen is fine) enough to line 4 x 10cm diameter loose-bottomed flan tins

Olive oil about 75ml

Spring onions 3, sliced

Peppers 1 large red, 1 large green, cut into fine slices

Single cream 100ml

Egg 1, medium

Fresh herbs 1 tablespoon, finely chopped

Line 4 x 10cm diameter loose-bottomed flan tins with the pastry and brush with a little of the oil / Heat the rest of the oil in a pan, add the onions and sweat gently for 2 minutes / Add the peppers and continue cooking for a further 5 minutes / Meanwhile, whisk together the cream, egg and herbs / Put the onion and peppers into the flan cases / Pour over the cream mixture / Bake at 200°C/400°F/gas mark 6 for about 30 minutes until set / Leave to cool before turning out.

PARTIES *Made in tiny flan tins, these tarts are perfect to serve at a drinks party.*

Courgette and cranberry soup

Don't use cranberry sauce just alongside roast turkey. Cranberries have far more to offer than that. They are one of the most cancer-protective foods around and are excellent for the prevention and treatment of urinary infections. Here the sauce is combined with a feast of delicious vegetables. (Serves 4–6)

Olive oil 3 tablespoons

Leek 1, finely sliced

Celery 2 sticks, finely sliced

Onion 1, medium, finely sliced

Paprika 1 teaspoon

Courgettes 4, large, cubed

Fresh chervil 1 tablespoon, freshly chopped leaves

Vegetable stock (see page 215 or use a commercially made cube or powder) 1 litre

Cranberry sauce 250g

Heat the oil in a large pan, add the leek, celery and onion and cook to soften / Sprinkle on the paprika and continue cooking for 1 minute, stirring constantly / Tip in the courgettes and chervil and cook until the courgettes are just breaking up / Pour in the stock, cover and bring to the boil / Put into a blender or food processor, whiz until smooth and then return to the pan / Tip in the cranberry sauce and heat through, stirring / Serve.

Curried parsnip and carrot soup

Carrots and parsnips are wonderful nutritional bedfellows. Not only does their colour and texture combine brilliantly, carrots are rich in beta-carotene and help protect your eyesight – the old wives' tale is absolutely right – and parsnips are full of fibre, folic acid and potassium. Incidentally, old carrots are far better nutritionally than the prettier, younger ones often sold with the leaves still attached. (Serves 4–6)

Olive oil 4 tablespoons

Onion 1, finely sliced

Garlic 2 cloves, finely sliced

Curry paste 1 heaped tablespoon

Parsnips 2, cubed

Carrots 4, sliced and peeled if not organic

Vegetable stock (see page 215 or use a commercially made cube or powder) 1 litre

Heat the oil, add the onion and garlic and cook gently to soften, about 3 minutes / Stir in the curry paste and continue cooking, stirring, for 1 minute / Add the parsnips and carrots and stir to mix in the paste / Pour in the stock and simmer for 20–25 minutes until the vegetables are tender / Tip all the ingredients into a food processor and whiz until smooth.

LUNCHBOX *This soup is wonderful as a winter warmer in a vacuum flask for lunchtime or chilled for summer.*

Roast pepper soup with cumin and prawns

This soup has so few calories, you'll probably burn them up just digesting it. Despite that, peppers are a good source of vitamins A and C, and prawns are rich in protein, essential fatty acids, iron and zinc. This recipe also gives you a basic fish stock recipe. (Serves 4–6)

For the fish stock (makes 1.2 litres)

Fish trimmings (most supermarkets these days will keep them for you if you ask in advance) 110g

Carrots 2, peeled if not organic and sliced

White onion 1, chopped

Leek 1, chopped

Fresh parsley 3 large stems

Fresh tarragon 3 large stems

Bay leaves 2

White peppercorns 8

For the soup

Red peppers 8

Olive oil 4 tablespoons

Ground turmeric 1 teaspoon

Fresh breadcrumbs 4 tablespoons

Fish stock 1.2 litres

Cooked peeled prawns 175g

To make the fish stock, put all the ingredients into a large saucepan or ideally, a pasta pan with a separate basket / Add 2 litres water / Bring to the boil then simmer for 30 minutes / Lift out the pasta basket or strain through a sieve.

To make the soup, put the peppers into a hot oven at 200°C/400°F/gas mark 6 until charred, about 15 minutes / When just cool enough to handle, rinse slowly under cold running water, peel away the skins, then de-seed them / Put into a blender or food processor with the oil, turmeric, breadcrumbs and fish stock / Whiz until smooth then put into a saucepan / Rinse the prawns, add to the pan and heat through / Serve.

Watercress wizard

Watercress is often just used as a garnish but it's rich in vitamins A, C and E and iodine, and is good for stomach infections and thyroid deficiency. Research also shows that three average portions a day can neutralise the carcinogens responsible for lung cancer in those people still stupid enough to smoke. (Serves 4–6)

Unsalted butter 50g

Watercress 5 tablespoons, freshly chopped leaves

Olive oil 2 tablespoons

Onion 1, finely chopped

Potatoes 110g, peeled and cubed

Vegetable stock (see page 215 or use commercially made cube or powder) 1 litre

Single cream 300ml

Soften the butter in a bowl set over a saucepan of simmering water / Stir in the watercress and leave to cool / Heat the oil, add the onion and cook to soften / Tip in the potatoes and stir until just golden / Pour in the stock and simmer for about 15 minutes, until the potatoes are just tender / Add the cream / Put into a blender or food processor and whiz until smooth / Return the soup to a clean saucepan, bring to a simmer and then whisk in the watercress butter / Serve.

SOUPS

Chicken and dumpling soup

There are many variations on chicken soup
(see page 193) that I couldn't resist another. This is
a light soup, which gives you a chicken stock that's
useful for many other recipes in this book. And the
dumplings, made with extremely low-fat matzo
meal, are deliciously light, too. Anyone with a gluten
allergy can use gluten-free crackers whizzed in a
food processor instead. (Serves 4–6)

For the soup and stock (makes 1.2 litres)

Chicken carcass 1 (get your butcher to save you one
after he or she has removed the breasts, thighs and other
parts he can sell separately. Cut it into pieces if it won't fit
into the pan)

Onion 1, skin left on

Leek 1, roughly chopped

Celery 2 sticks, chopped

Fresh rosemary 1 large stalk

Fresh chervil 4 stems

Fresh thyme 1 large stalk

Bay leaves 3

Peppercorns 6

For the dumplings

Unsalted butter 110g

Eggs 2, medium beaten

Fresh parsley 2 teaspoons, chopped leaves

Fresh mint 2 teaspoons, chopped leaves

Matzo meal 100g

Put the chicken carcass into a large saucepan or,
ideally, a pasta pan with a separate basket / Add
2 litres water, bring to the boil and simmer,
uncovered for 30 minutes / Add the onion, leek,
celery, rosemary, chervil, thyme, bay leaves and
peppercorns / Simmer for a further 40 minutes
then remove the pasta basket or put through a
fine strainer.

To make the dumplings, mix together all the
ingredients and leave in the fridge for about
2 hours / Roll into balls (don't worry if they seem
quite moist) / Drop into the stock and simmer for
about 15 minutes / Serve.

Rocket vichyssoise

Even if you've only got a small garden, I insist you
plant some rocket. It grows like a weed – roadsides
in southern Italy are rampant with it – and I can't
believe the ridiculous prices charged for a small
packet in supermarkets. Its wonderful peppery
flavour makes this soup really special. (Serves 4–6)

Unsalted butter 50g

Leeks 3, large, finely sliced

Potatoes 350g, peeled and diced

Vegetable stock (see opposite or use a commercially
made cube or powder) 1 litre

Fresh marjoram 1 tablespoon freshly chopped leaves

Rocket l large handful

Single cream about 4 tablespoons

Heat the butter in a large pan / Add the leeks and
cook to soften, about 3 minutes / Tip in the
potatoes, pour in the stock and add the marjoram /
Simmer for about 10 minutes until the potatoes
are tender / Add the rocket, remove from the
heat and leave to cool / Put into a blender or
food processor, whiz until smooth and leave to
chill / Serve with a swirl of cream floating on top
of each bowl.

Mmm . . . minestrone

This recipe gives you the basic vegetable stock used for many of my soups. I make mine in large batches and freeze it. This stock is nutrition in a bowl. When you add the wonderful vegetables for this classic Italian soup, it becomes the epitome of eating well and staying healthy. (Serves 4–6)

For the vegetable stock (makes 1 litre)

Onions 2, 1 peeled and quartered, I with the skin left on

Celery 3 large sticks, halved

Carrots 3, roughly sliced and peeled if not organic

Leek 1, large, sliced and with the green part left on

Parsnip 1, large, cubed

Fresh sage 2 sprigs

Fresh thyme 3 sprigs

Bay leaves 6

Fresh parsley 4 stalks

Mushrooms 110g

Black peppercorns 6, crushed

For the soup

Onion 1, finely sliced

Garlic 2 cloves, finely sliced

Olive oil 3 tablespoons

Celery 1 stick, finely chopped

Carrot 1, cubed

Red pepper 1, cubed

Vegetable stock (see below) 1 litre

New potatoes 8, quartered

Fresh or frozen peas 110g

Frozen sweetcorn 110g

Freshly grated Parmesan cheese 4 tablespoons

Crusty bread to serve

To make the vegetable stock, put all the ingredients into a large saucepan or a pasta pan with a separate basket / Add 1.5 litres water and bring to the boil / Simmer, uncovered for 1 hour, then strain or remove the pasta basket and push the cooked vegetables through a sieve with a wooden spoon.

To make the soup, put the onion and garlic into a large saucepan, add the oil and cook to soften, for about 3 minutes / Tip in the celery, carrot and pepper and continue cooking for a further 3 minutes / Add the vegetable stock and potatoes and simmer for 20 minutes or until the potatoes are almost tender / Tip in the peas and sweetcorn and continue simmering for 10 minutes / Stir in the Parmesan / Serve with crusty bread.

FIRST FOOD *Liquidise for babies but omit the Parmesan.*

Kale and sausage soup

Cabbage soups have been peasant food in Europe for many centuries. This uses curly kale, a member of the cabbage family, which has been shown to reduce the severity of many cancers, particularly of the colon. The garlic sausage makes it a meal in itself. (Serves 4)

Old potatoes 700g, peeled and cubed

Garlic 2 cloves, very finely chopped

Vegetable stock (see recipe above or use a commercially made cube or powder) 1 litre

Tomato purée 2 tablespoons

Worcestershire sauce 1 tablespoon

Curly kale 350g, very finely chopped

Garlic sausage 110g, cubed

Put the potatoes, garlic, stock and tomato purée into a large pan and bring quickly to the boil, stirring so that the tomato purée is well combined / Mash roughly / Add the Worcestershire sauce / Tip in the curly kale and garlic sausage and simmer for 5 minutes / Serve.

Broad bean and sorrel soup

Broad beans are one of God's gifts. I love the smell of the young flowers and the velvety touch of the insides of the pods. As long as you buy them young enough, you don't have to throw the pods away – they work brilliantly here, cut very finely with scissors. Sorrel is another herb sadly forgotten by most people. Similar to spinach, it helps clean the blood and is a reasonably good source of vitamin C. (Serves 4)

Unsalted butter 25g
Onion 1, finely chopped
Young broad beans 700g, beans removed and pods snipped into very fine slices
Vegetable stock (see page 215 or use a commercially made cube or powder) 1 litre
Powdered saffron a pinch
Fresh sorrel 1 handful, leaves
Natural live yoghurt to serve

Melt the butter in a large pan, add the onion and cook until soft, about 5 minutes / Tip in the beans and pods and continue cooking gently for a further 5 minutes / Pour in the stock and saffron and simmer for 20 minutes / Put into a blender or liquidiser with the sorrel leaves and whiz until smooth / Serve with a dollop of yoghurt on top.

LUNCHBOX *This soup is just as good cold. To pack in a vacuum flask, however, leave out the yoghurt.*

Ginger chicken soup with pak choi and noodles

Thank goodness wonderful pak choi is so much more widely available these days. I love its delightfully light texture, which goes perfectly with this oriental-style soup. The ginger makes it beneficial for soothing coughs and colds, and it is excellent for relieving all types of nausea – including morning sickness in the early stages of pregnancy. (Serves 4–6)

Fresh root ginger 2.5cm piece, peeled and finely grated
Unsalted butter 25g
Chicken breasts 2
Chicken stock (see page 214 or use a commercially made cube or powder) 1 litre
Pak choi 4 bulbs, finely sliced lengthways
Egg noodles, fresh or **dried** 175g

Put the ginger into a frying pan with the butter and soften gently for 5 minutes / Cut the chicken breasts along the grain into fine slithers / Add to the pan with about 125ml of the stock / Boil quickly for 5 minutes or until the chicken is tender / Tip into a saucepan containing the rest of the stock and bring to a simmer / Stir in the pak choi and noodles and simmer until the noodles are cooked, about 5 minutes / Serve.

Smoked fish and mussel soup

This variation on the Scottish classic, Cullen Skink, is a meal in itself. One bowl will give you carbohydrates from the potatoes, cancer-protective nutrients from the onion, protein from the mussels and a range of volatile oils from the herbs and nutmeg. And it tastes wonderful too. What more can you ask? (Serves 4)

Unsalted butter 50g

Onion 1, finely chopped

Milk 600ml

Bay leaf 1, snapped along the spine

Nutmeg ½ teaspoon, ground or freshly grated

New potatoes 350g, peeled

Undyed smoked haddock 450g, skinned and
　all bones removed

Double cream 150ml

Fresh mussels 20, cleaned thoroughly and 'beards' removed

Fresh parsley 2 tablespoons freshly chopped leaves

Melt the butter, add the onion and cook for about 3 minutes until soft / Add the milk, bay leaf, nutmeg, potatoes and 300ml water / Simmer for 10 minutes or until the potatoes are nearly cooked / Add the haddock and simmer for a further 10 minutes until both fish and potatoes are cooked / Scoop out the fish and leave to cool until you can break it into pieces / Remove and discard the bay leaf/ Lightly mash the potatoes into the soup and add the flaked fish and cream / Keep warm / Put the mussels into a large saucepan / Shake, covered, over a high heat until the shells open (discard any which don't) / When they are just cool enough to handle, open the shells and add the flesh to the soup / Scatter with chopped parsley to serve.

LUNCHBOX *Leave out the mussels and this soup is great to take from home for lunch. You don't need to keep it hot – it tastes just as good cold.*

Spinach and fennel soup

Rich in chlorophyll and folic acid, spinach is an essential food for women who are, or are thinking of becoming pregnant. It has also been shown to protect against age-related macular degeneration, the biggest cause of sight problems in the elderly. The wonderful aniseed taste of fennel not only adds flavour to this soup, it also helps relieve digestive problems and … excuse me! … flatulence. (Serves 4–6)

Olive oil 2 tablespoons

Fennel 2 small bulbs, very finely chopped

Garlic 2 cloves, very finely chopped

Fresh green chilli 1, de-seeded and chopped

Ground turmeric 1 teaspoon

Vegetable stock (see page 215 or use a commercially
　made cube or powder) 1 litre

Baby spinach 700g, very finely chopped

Fresh young mint leaves 3 tablespoons,
　finely chopped

Natural live yoghurt 275g

Heat the oil, add the fennel, garlic and chilli and cook to soften, about 5 minutes / Stir in the turmeric and cook for 1 minute / Pour in the stock and simmer for 20 minutes / Add the spinach and mint and continue simmering for 5 minutes / Stir in the yoghurt and mix well to serve.

Grilled turbot on broad bean and fennel mash

A top chef once told me that when he and his foodie friends eat fish, it's always turbot. You'll see why when you taste the melting succulence of these simply steamed fillets, which, like all fish, are rich in vitamins A, D and E, together with Omega-3 fatty acids. Fennel adds a slight aniseed flavour to the broad beans. It's also a useful diuretic and helps the digestion. (Serves 4)

Olive oil about 4 tablespoons
Fennel 1 bulb, very finely chopped
Vegetable stock (see page 215 or use a commercially made cube or powder) about 250ml
Broad beans shelled, 450g
Natural live yoghurt about 5 tablespoons
Turbot fillets 4
Salt and pepper
Fresh dill to garnish
Rice to serve

Heat 3 tablespoons of the oil, add the fennel and sweat until very soft, about 10 minutes / Add the stock and broad beans and simmer until the beans are tender / Pour off any excess stock and mash roughly with a potato masher / Stir in the yoghurt and keep warm / Brush the fish with the rest of the oil, season and cook under a very hot grill for about 5 minutes / Serve on top of the broad bean mash, garnished with dill and with the rice on the side.

Baked plaice with hazelnuts

Hazelnuts are a real powerhouse of nutrition. They add to the protein content of the fish and also contain fibre, magnesium, iron and zinc. But their greatest nutritional benefit is vitamin E; the amount specified here will give almost a quarter of of one person's vitamin E needs for a week. That's good news for your skin, muscles, nerves, blood vessels and heart. (Serves 4)

Unsalted butter 75g
Mushrooms 75g, sliced
Roasted chopped hazelnuts 75g
Skinned plaice fillets 4
White wine 4 tablespoons
Little Gem lettuces 4, halved lengthways
Vegetable stock (see page 215 or use a commercially made cube or powder) 300ml
New potatoes to serve
Fresh mint 2 sprigs

Melt half the butter in a small saucepan and gently sauté the mushrooms for 5 minutes / Add the hazelnuts and stir well / Divide the mixture between the fillets and roll into parcels / Put each fillet onto a piece of kitchen foil large enough to enclose it completely / Add a knob of the remaining butter and a tablespoon of wine to each parcel / Close and bake at 200°C/400°F / gas mark 6 for 15 minutes / Meanwhile, braise the lettuce in the stock for 15 minutes / Tip the fish with its juices onto plates and serve with the lettuce and new potatoes cooked in their jackets with the mint.

Grilled chicken with chervil and raspberry vinegar

As you can see from The Chicken Chain on page 192, chicken is versatile and nutritious. It goes perfectly with chervil, and raspberry vinegar – available in most shops – which adds a beautiful sweet-and-sour flavour. The mushrooms are a modest source of protein, with plenty of phosphorus, potassium and vitamin E. (Serves 4)

Olive oil about 5 tablespoons

Chicken thighs 4

Onion 1, finely sliced

Garlic 4 cloves, finely sliced

Fresh chervil 2 tablespoons, finely chopped

Raspberry vinegar 3 tablespoons

Chicken stock (see page 214 or use a commercially made cube or powder) about 300ml

Unsalted butter 25g

Mushrooms 75g, finely sliced

Plain flour 2 tablespoons

Rice and steamed broccoli florets to serve

Heat the oil in a large frying pan, add the chicken pieces and cook for about 5 minutes until browned all over / Set aside and add the onion and garlic to the pan / Sweat gently for 5 minutes then add the chervil and cook for a further 1 minute / Return the chicken pieces to the pan, add the vinegar and stock, cover and simmer until the chicken is tender, about 30 minutes / Remove the chicken and keep warm / In another pan, melt the butter, add the mushrooms and soften for 5 minutes / Sprinkle in the flour and cook for 3 minutes, stirring constantly / Tip the mushroom mixture into the stock and simmer until the sauce thickens, about 3 minutes / To serve, put the chicken on a platter, pour the sauce on top and serve with rice and steamed broccoli florets.

LUNCHBOX *Any leftover chicken thighs can be eaten cold and will make a welcome addition to a snack in the middle of the day.*

Rack of lamb with rosemary and cranberry sauce

This dish is perfect when you are entertaining, want to show off a little, but don't have a lot of time. It cooks in 20 minutes. Lamb is an excellent source of protein, and thanks to the cranberries in the sauce, this delicious recipe helps protect against cancer, too. (Serves 4)

Racks of lamb 2 or 3, 12 cutlets altogether

Olive oil 2 tablespoons

Sea salt and black pepper

Fresh rosemary 4 large sprigs

Fresh cranberries 110g

Brown caster sugar 1 tablespoon

Boiled new potatoes in their jackets and **shredded steamed curly kale** to serve

Rub the lamb with the oil, season with sea salt and pepper / Put into a roasting tin and roast at 230°C/450°F/gas mark 8 for 20 minutes / While it's cooking, prepare the sauce / Put the rosemary into a pan with the cranberries and 3 tablespoons water / Simmer until the cranberry skins soften / Remove the rosemary with a slotted spoon, stir in the sugar and simmer until completely dissolved / Carve the lamb into cutlets, pour over the sauce and serve accompanied by boiled new potatoes and shredded steamed curly kale.

LUNCHBOX *Any leftover cutlets make a delicious lunchtime treat*

Sweet and sour duck with French peas

Duck can be very fatty. That's why I start by steaming it so the fat falls into the pan below and you are left with lovely crisp skin. OK, it's not very healthy, but life is for enjoyment and roast duck wouldn't be the same without the skin. Having said that, duck is an excellent source of protein, iron, zinc and most of the B vitamins. It's complemented here not only by the sour taste of the gooseberries, but by their extremely high vitamin C content. Gooseberries are also helpful in the treatment of urinary infections and constipation. (Serves 4–6)

Duck 1, weighing about 1.8kg

For the sauce
Gooseberries 225g
Fresh mint 1 large stalk
Runny honey 1 tablespoon

For the peas
Rindless back bacon 3 rashers, cut into small cubes
Unsalted butter no more than 25g
Spring onions 4, large, finely sliced
Peas, fresh or frozen 200g
Lettuce 1, small
Natural live yoghurt 2 tablespoons

Boiled new potatoes to serve

Prick the duck all over, cover loosely with foil and put on a grill pan or trivet inside a roasting tin / Pour about 2.5cm of water into the tin / Put into an oven at 200°C/400°F/ gas mark 6 for 20 minutes / Remove, increase the heat to maximum and discard the water / As soon as the heat reaches maximum, return the duck to the oven, turn the heat down to its previous temperature and roast for 1 hour.

To make the sauce, put the gooseberries and mint into a saucepan with just enough water to cover and simmer until soft / Strain to remove the skins / Return the pulp to the saucepan, add the honey and heat until combined.

To make the French peas, put the bacon into a deep-sided frying pan and sweat for 3 minutes with a little butter if necessary / Tip in the spring onions and continue cooking for 5 minutes / Pour in the peas and just enough water to cover / Simmer until the peas are almost tender / Add the lettuce and bring quickly to the boil to reduce any excess water / Stir in the yoghurt.

To serve pull the duck flesh off the carcass and arrange on 4 plates / Pour over the sauce / Put pieces of crispy skin on top / Serve with boiled new potatoes and the peas on the side.

Cod niçoise

This popular dish from the south of France has almost as many variations as there are good cooks in that part of the Mediterranean, and that's a lot. Here I've chosen to include okra, which adds a slightly more robust feel to the dish, as well as the other vegetables that are essential to anything 'niçoise'. This dish gives you protein and B vitamins from the cod, masses of vitamin C from the vegetables and antioxidant lycopene from the tomatoes. Incidentally, although good fresh tomatoes undoubtedly have that special flavour and aroma, tomatoes lose very few of their nutrients in canning. There should always be a few cans in your cupboard. (Serves 4)

Olive oil 4 tablespoons

Onion 1, finely chopped

Garlic 2 cloves, finely chopped

Chopped, canned organic tomatoes 700g

Okra 10, sliced

Green pepper 1, de-seeded and finely cubed

Aubergine ½, peeled and cubed

Fresh herbs 2 tablespoons, chopped

Cod steaks 4

Fresh breadcrumbs about 4 tablespoons

French bread to serve

Heat the oil, add the onion and garlic and sauté for about 3 minutes until soft / Add the tomatoes, okra, pepper, aubergine and herbs and simmer for 15 minutes / Arrange the cod in a single layer in a large ovenproof dish / Pour over the tomato mixture and sprinkle on the breadcrumbs / Bake at 200°C/400°F/gas mark 6 for 20 minutes / Serve with crusty French bread.

Asparagus tart

The star of this simple tart is asparagus, a gourmet delicacy in many parts of the world. Apart from tasting divine, it can help relieve urinary infections, constipation, arthritis, rheumatism and water retention. (Serves 4–6)

Unsalted butter for greasing

Ready-made puff pastry 500g

Fine asparagus spears 20–30, depending on thickness

Eggs 2 medium, plus 1 extra yolk

Mascarpone cheese 300g

Fresh dill or frond fennel 3 tablespoons finely chopped herb, plus about 6 complete fronds to garnish

Celeriac 1 medium root, cubed, boiled and mashed with carrots 2, peeled if not organic, sliced and boiled

Mixed leaf salad with vinaigrette dressing (see page 190 or use your own favourite) to serve

Lightly grease a 28 x 20cm or 28cm diameter loose-bottomed flan tin / Roll out the pastry to fit / Arrange the asparagus spears attractively on the pastry / Whisk together the eggs and mascarpone / Stir in the dill or fennel / Pour the mixture over the asparagus / Bake at 200°C/400°F/gas mark 6 for 30 minutes / Garnish with the herb fronds and serve with the celeriac and carrot mash and salad.

FIRST FOOD *Babies will certainly like the mashed carrot, but some may not take so easily to the taste of celeriac. Adventurous characters may also like the flan filling well mashed, but don't hold your breath and be prepared for their urine to smell slightly strange afterwards.*

LUNCHBOX *This tart is delicious hot or cold and makes a great lunchtime snack. The mash tastes great cold, too, so pack it in a plastic container.*

MAIN COURSES

Bean and chickpea curry with fruit rice

Like all pulses, chickpeas are powerhouses of nutrition, rich in protein, manganese, iron, folic acid and vitamin E. They are inexpensive, filling and so versatile. Here they are combined with vitamin C-rich French beans. Raisins give cancer and heart protection and the avocado in the salad give more heart protection, plenty of potassium and vitamins A, B, C and E. PS to women who think avocados are fattening: they are not. (Serves 4)

Olive oil 3 tablespoons
Onion 1, finely sliced
Garlic 2 cloves, finely sliced
Thai green curry paste 1 level tablespoon
Vegetable stock (see page 215 or use a commercially made cube or powder) 500ml
French beans 450g, cut into 2.5cm lengths
Chickpeas 2 x 400g cans, drained and rinsed
Unsalted butter 50g
Plain flour 2 tablespoons
Long-grain rice 250g
Raisins 2 heaped tablespoons
Salad leaves 4 handfuls
Avocado 1, medium
Vinaigrette dressing (see page 190 or use your own favourite) about 6 tablespoons

Heat the oil, add the onion and garlic and sweat until soft, about 5 minutes / Add the curry paste and continue cooking for 1 minute, stirring constantly / Pour in the stock, add the beans and chickpeas and simmer for 10 minutes or until the vegetables are tender / Melt the butter gently in a small frying pan/ Add the flour and stir until well combined / Transfer about 150ml of the stock to the butter and flour roux and heat, stirring constantly, until thickened / Return the mixture to the curry, stir well and keep on a very low heat, stirring occasionally for about 10 minutes / Cook the rice according to the packet instructions / Steep the raisins in freshly boiled water for 5 minutes / Drain and add to the cooked rice / Put the salad leaves into a bowl / Scoop the flesh out of the avocado and mix into the lettuce / Drizzle with the dressing / Serve the curry on the rice, with the salad on the side.

Linguine with no-cook anchovy dressing

This really is a main course made in minutes and it always amazes me that a sauce based on quite severe ingredients tastes so sweet when warmed by the pasta. It's full of goodness, too – essential oils from the anchovies, the heart-protective qualities of garlic, vitamin C from the lemon, tomatoes and herbs and slow-release protein from the linguine. (Serves 4)

Anchovies 50g can

Garlic, 1 clove, finely chopped

Capers 1 tablespoon, rinsed

Lemon 1, grated zest and juice

Extra-virgin olive oil 6 tablespoons

Linguine, fresh or dried 275g

Cherry tomatoes 6

Fresh flat-leaf parsley 2 large sprigs, finely chopped

Chives ½ handful, finely snipped

Put the anchovies, with any of the oil still clinging to them, but not the whole canful of oil, into a mortar / Add the garlic, capers and lemon zest and crush until they start to become smooth / Pour in the lemon juice / Add the oil a little at a time until the mixture combines / Cook the pasta according to the packet instructions / Tip the pasta into a bowl / Pour in the dressing / Tip on the tomatoes, parsley and chives and mix well / Serve.

Penne with spinach, blue cheese and almonds

This simple pasta is full of goodness: the spinach is rich in folic acid (essential for any woman who is, or who's planning to become, pregnant); the cheese and almonds are wonderful sources of calcium; tomatoes give you masses of vitamin C; and the pasta will provide lots of slow-release energy. (Serves 4)

Fresh young spinach 1kg

Mild blue cheese Irish Cashel Blue or Italian dolcelatte are excellent 110g

Natural live yoghurt 3–4 tablespoons

Flaked almonds 2 heaped tablespoons, toasted in a little butter until golden

Fusilli or other short pasta, fresh or dried 450g

Tomatoes 4, sliced

Spring onions 4, large, sliced

Capers 1 heaped teaspoon, rinsed well

Vinaigrette dressing (see page 190 or use your own favourite) 3–4 tablespoons

Steam the spinach, drain well and put into a blender with the cheese, yoghurt and almonds / Whiz until smooth, adding more yoghurt if the mixture seems too thick / Cook the pasta according to the packet instructions / Drain, put into a large bowl, add the almonds and sauce immediately and stir – the heat of the pasta will warm the sauce / Arrange the tomatoes and onions on a plate / Squeeze the capers between your fingers, arrange on the salad and drizzle with the dressing / Serve.

LUNCHBOX *This pasta tastes good cold. Pack it in a small container to take to work or school.*

Apple chicken

Nothing could be easier than this quickly assembled chicken casserole. And you'll be amazed at the way the flavour of the cider or apple juice permeates the vegetables, particularly the potatoes. All root vegetables are rich in fibre and a range of vitamins, and the bay leaves contain volatile oils, which help the digestion. (Serves 4)

New potatoes in their jackets 225g
Other root vegetables about 450g, peeled and cubed
Chicken 1, weighing about 1.3kg, excess fat removed, but left whole
Apple juice or cider to half cover the chicken, about 1 litre
Bay leaves 3

Put the potatoes and other vegetables into a large casserole / Place the chicken on top / Pour over the apple juice or cider and add the bay leaves / Cook, covered, for 2 hours at 220°C/425°F/gas mark 7 / Take the chicken out and remove the skin / Pull off the bone into manageable pieces – it will be too tender to carve / Serve with the vegetables and sauce spooned over the top.

Mussel and clam risotto

I love cooking shellfish and this is one of my very favourite dishes. Apart from the fact that is has a delicious taste and texture, there is an important health reason for eating shellfish, and that's its high selenium and zinc content. Most people in the Western world are very deficient in these important minerals, which have been shown to protect against heart disease and cancer of the oesophagus and prostate. They are also known to increase male fertility. (Serves 4)

Fresh mussels and/or clams about 2.25kg, cleaned thoroughly and 'beards' removed
White wine 200ml
Unsalted butter 50g
Onion 1, finely sliced
Carnaroli or **arborio rice** 400g
Bay leaves 2
Fresh herbs a small handful, chopped
Vegetable or fish stock (see page 215 or page 213 or use a commercially made cube or powder) about 850ml
Single cream 3 tablespoons
Tomato and spring onion salad to serve

Put the shellfish into a large saucepan / Pour in the wine and heat, covered, until the shells open (discard any which don't) / Take the fish out of their shells, set aside and strain the liquid / Melt the butter in a separate saucepan, add the onion and cook for 5 minutes until soft / Tip in the rice and stir until coated with the butter / Pour in the reserved fish liquid and add the bay leaves and herbs / Simmer until the liquid is almost absorbed, then, adding a little warm stock at a time, continue simmering and stirring until the rice is just tender, about 20 minutes / Stir in the cream, carefully add the fish and warm through / Serve with the tomato and spring onion salad.

Calves' liver with sage and mustard mash

Liver doesn't come high on most people's culinary choice list. Maybe it's something to do with its texture, but calves' liver really is the king of this part of the butcher's counter. It's quick to prepare, melts in the mouth and is rich in vitamins A and B, iron and zinc. It goes perfectly with sage, which stimulates digestion and is also a good antiseptic and anti-inflammatory. Pregnant women, however, shouldn't eat liver or liver products because liver is exceptionally high in vitamin A, which can cause birth defects. (Serves 4)

Potatoes about 900g, mashed with milk and butter
Mustard 1 tablespoon ready-made Dijon or other smooth mustard
Calves' liver 450g, cut into thin slices
Unsalted butter 50g
Fresh sage 8 leaves
Young boiled carrots to serve

Mix together the mashed potato and mustard and keep warm / Rinse the liver and dry on kitchen paper / Heat the butter in a frying pan until just steaming / Add the liver, in batches if necessary, cooking for 1 minute on each side / Put the sage in a slotted spoon and immerse in the hot butter for 2 seconds / Serve the sage on the liver with the mash and boiled carrots as accompaniments.

Lamb, lentil and carrot casserole

It always surprises me how people shun cheaper cuts of meat. Shank of lamb is so delicious – that's because so much of the meat is near the bone – and it is amazingly good value. It's also rich in protein and B vitamins and an excellent food for those with anaemia. Here, it's served with those wonderful Puy lentils, little sparks of energy, which contain iron, zinc and calcium, made more easily absorbed by the small amount of vitamin C in the carrots. (Serves 4–6)

Olive oil a little
Lamb shanks 2–3 (about 1.5kg in weight)
Onion 1, finely chopped
Garlic 2 cloves, finely chopped
Carrots 3, peeled if not organic and sliced
Vegetable stock (see page 215 or use a commercially made cube or powder) 700ml
Bay leaves 2
Bouquet garni 1
Puy lentils 275g

Heat the oil in a large, ovenproof casserole, add the lamb and brown all over / Remove and set aside / Put the onion, garlic and carrots into the casserole and cook gently for 5 minutes / Return the lamb to the casserole, pour in the stock, add the bay leaves, bouquet garni and lentils / Cover and cook for 2 hours at 200°C/400°F/gas mark 6, adding more stock or water if it starts to dry out / To serve, arrange the lamb on top of the lentils and vegetables on a large platter / Everyone can then pull the meat off the bone and help themselves to the delicious vegetable sauce.

FIRST FOOD *Put some carrot, meat, stock and a small amount of lentils into a blender and whiz until smooth for weaned babies.*

Mediterranean vegetarian medley

This combination of herbs, tender vegetables and soft mozzarella just oozes summertime. It's light, aromatic, fantastic to look at and tastes wonderful. It's perfectly complemented by a salad with the strong tastes of rocket and watercress softened by sumptuous grapes. One point though, make sure you get fresh, soft mozzarella; the blocks often used to make cheap pizzas just won't give you the look, the smell or the flavour. (Serves 4)

Olive oil 4 tablespoons

Onions 2, finely chopped

Fresh chopped herbs (must include oregano) 3 tablespoons

Tomatoes 4, medium, sliced

Courgettes 3, medium, sliced

Fresh buffalo mozzarella cheese 400g (drained weight)

Freshly grated Parmesan cheese 3 tablespoons

Fresh breadcrumbs 3 tablespoons

Watercress 2 handfuls

Black grapes 110g

Rocket 1 handful

Vinaigrette dressing (see page 190 or use your own favourite)

Heat the oil, add the onions and sweat gently for about 5 minutes, add half the herbs and use the mixture to layer the base of a shallow flan dish / Arrange the tomatoes, courgettes and mozzarella slices alternately, standing upright, on the onions / Sprinkle over the rest of the herbs and squash the vegetables down slightly with your hands / Cover with kitchen foil and bake at 200°C/400°F/gas mark 6 for 25 minutes / Remove the foil / Mix together the Parmesan and breadcrumbs / Sprinkle over the dish and return to the oven for 10 minutes / Put the watercress, grapes and rocket in a bowl and toss in the vinaigrette dressing.

LUNCHBOX *This dish is delicious cold for the following day's lunch.*

Pork with prunes, noodles and green salad

Many people consider pork a fatty meat. Not true – especially when you choose ultra-lean pork fillet. The B vitamins make pork particularly helpful for those with stress problems, and B6 together with zinc helps control the symptoms of PMS. The prunes are here not only because they give such a deliciously sweet flavour but because they are one of the most protective foods against cancer. (Serves 4)

Pork fillet 500g

Ready-to-eat prunes 50g

Unsalted butter 75g

Onion 1 medium, finely chopped

Red wine 2 glasses

Fresh sage 1 large sprig

Noodles, fresh or dried, and a green salad to serve

Flatten the fillet by hitting with a rolling pin or meat mallet / Cut into 5cm slices / Squash the prunes with your fingers / Put onto the pork slices, roll up and secure with cocktail sticks / Melt the butter, add the onion and pork and cook until browned all over, about 7 minutes / Add the wine and sage / Cover and simmer for about 20 minutes / Cook the noodles according to the packet instructions / Serve the pork on the noodles with a mixed green salad on the side.

Tofu and vegetable kebabs with rosemary chips

Most good vegetarians will know the health benefits of tofu. It's an excellent high-protein alternative to meat, protects against hormone-related cancers, relieves the effects of the menopause and has a significant anti-cancer action. Latest research also shows that it protects men against heart disease and – amazingly – baldness. It has very little taste, but is excellent at absorbing the flavours around it. Here we leave it to marinate in soy sauce, ginger and garlic to make a wonderful addition to a healthy kebab. The kebabs can be cooked in the kitchen or on a barbecue. (Serves 4)

Olive oil 6 tablespoons
Soy sauce 1 tablespoon
Fresh root ginger 1cm piece, grated
Garlic 2 cloves, finely chopped
Bay leaves 2
Peppers 1 red, 1 green, cut into 2cm squares
Baby mushrooms 12
Red onions 2, cut into quarters with the layers separated
Tofu 250g (drained weight), cut into 2cm cubes
Cherry tomatoes 8

For the rosemary chips
Old potatoes 3
Olive oil about 125ml
Fresh rosemary the leaves of 2 large sprigs

Mix together the oil, soy sauce, ginger, garlic and bay leaves / Put into a wide bowl, add the tofu and vegetables (except the tomatoes) and leave to marinate in the fridge for at least 2 hours / Thread the tofu and vegetables, with the tomatoes, alternately onto metal or pre-soaked bamboo skewers / Grill or barbecue for 8 minutes, turning occasionally and basting with the marinade.

To make the rosemary chips, halve the potatoes, slice thinly, rinse and dry thoroughly / Brush a large roasting tin with the oil / Place the potatoes in the tin, brush with more oil and scatter over the rosemary leaves / Roast at 200°C/400°F/gas mark 6 until crisp, about 20 minutes.

Juniper pheasant with artichoke mash

Juniper is a much-neglected spice, but its fruity flavour goes well with all game, particularly pheasant. The birds themselves love eating Jerusalem artichokes – I know from the number I see having breakfast on my artichoke patch – and the pheasant taste delicious with this unusual artichoke mash accompaniment. From a nutritional point of view, pheasant is rich in protein, iron and vitamins and low in fat, and artichokes promote the growth of good bacteria in the gut. (Serves 4)

Olive oil 3 tablespoons
Pheasant breasts 8
Shallots 8
Red wine 375ml
Chicken stock (see page 214 or use a commercially made cube or powder) 200ml
Crushed juniper berries 6
Unsalted butter 50g
Field mushrooms 50g, finely chopped
Plain flour 2 tablespoons
White grapes 110g

For the artichoke mash
Jerusalem artichokes about 300g
Old potatoes about 300g
Olive oil 3 tablespoons
Fresh chives, a handful, snipped

Heat the oil in a large casserole / Add the pheasant breasts and brown all over, then remove from the casserole / Add the shallots to the casserole and cook until browned / Return the pheasant breasts to the casserole, add the wine, stock and juniper berries / Simmer for 20–30 minutes until the pheasant is tender / Remove the pheasant and shallots and keep warm / Heat the butter in a separate pan, add the mushrooms and sauté gently until they start to give off their juices – about 5 minutes / Sprinkle in the flour and stir to make a roux / Add a ladleful of stock to the mixture and stir until combined / Return to the rest of the stock and simmer gently, stirring constantly, until starting to thicken, about 3 minutes / Tip in the grapes and heat for a further 5 minutes / Pour the sauce over the pheasant and shallots to serve.

To make the artichoke mash, Peel, cube and boil the artichokes and potatoes for about 15 minutes until tender / Drain and mash over a low heat / Add the oil and continue mashing over the heat / Mix in the chives and serve.

Poussins with tarragon

These small chickens look very stylish when you are entertaining, and you don't have all the bother of carving a larger piece of meat either. Poussins have all the nutritional benefits of their larger cousins – particularly protein, B vitamins, iron and zinc. They are cooked here with tarragon, a traditional component of many chicken dishes. (Serves 4)

Poussins 4, small

Fresh tarragon 8 large sprigs and 2 tablespoons chopped leaves

Unsalted butter 110g

Olive oil 6 tablespoons

Garlic 2 large cloves, crushed but not peeled

New potatoes 8 medium, scrubbed

Celery 4 sticks, cut into julienne strips

Baby courgettes 6, quartered lengthways

Rinse the poussins and put 2 large sprigs of tarragon in each cavity / Smear with half the butter / Put the oil and garlic into a large roasting tin / Add the scrubbed but not peeled potatoes and turn until covered in the oil / Add the poussins / Put into a very hot oven at 230°C/450°F/gas mark 8 and immediately turn down to 220°C/425°F/gas mark 7 / Roast for about 45 minutes, basting occasionally / Mix the tarragon with the rest of the butter / Put a knob of tarragon butter on each poussin and serve with the potatoes, celery and courgettes, all steamed together for 10 minutes.

Stir-fried warm beef salad

What an abundance of well-balanced nutrients! There is masses of vitamin C in the salad vegetables and good carbohydrates in the potatoes. Too much red meat can mean your diet is high in saturated fat, but here we are using fillet. Yes, it's expensive, but it's high in protein and B vitamins and contains substantially less fat than, say, mince. (Serves 4)

Mixed salad leaves, 3 large handfuls of varied Mediterranean leaves

Cucumber ½, peeled and cubed

Red onion 1, finely sliced

Yellow pepper 1, membranes removed and cut into fine strips

Vinaigrette dressing (see page 190 or use your own favourite) 150ml

Horseradish sauce 1 level teaspoon

Asparagus tips 12

Beef fillet 450g

Olive oil about 4 tablespoons

Boiled potatoes to serve

Put the salad leaves, cucumber, onion and pepper into a large bowl / Mix together the vinaigrette and horseradish sauce and pour over the salad / Steam the asparagus tips until just tender, refresh in cold water and add to the salad / Flatten the beef with a rolling pin or meat mallet and cut along the grain into thin strips / Stir-fry in the hot oil, stirring constantly, for about 3 minutes / Remove from the oil with a slotted spoon and drain on kitchen paper / Tip into the salad bowl and toss well with the salad / Serve with boiled potatoes.

Chocolate-covered prunes

OK, eating loads of chocolate isn't the best way to better health, but we all need to succumb once in a while. Food is for enjoyment, after all. Here I've used modest amounts of the best chocolate available – and good chocolate contains chemicals, which release the feel-good factor in the brain. The chocolate is also combined with ultra-healthy prunes, one of the richest sources of cancer-protective nutrients. (Serves 4)

Top quality plain dark chocolate 110g
Top quality milk chocolate 110g
Stoneless California prunes about 350g (32 prunes)
Fresh mint 3 tablespoons, finely chopped leaves

Melt both chocolates separately in bowls set over saucepans of simmering water / Dip half the prunes one at a time in each of the chocolates / Arrange alternately on a large platter / Scatter over the mint to serve.

PARTIES *These make an unusual addition to cocktail party nibbles.*

Winter pudding

Rich and filling, this winter version of traditional summer pudding is bursting with goodness. All the nutrients in the fresh fruit are concentrated when they are dried, so you get huge amounts of iron and potassium and valuable amounts of selenium. As they are so high in fibre, they are a natural cure for constipation and a great source of natural energy. In addition, this makes a quick, healthy alternative to Christmas pudding. (Serves 4–6)

Dried fruit (any but try to include cranberries, apricots, figs and mangoes. Cut them all into a uniform size) 350g
Prune juice 600ml
Ground cloves $1/2$ teaspoon
Slightly stale white bread about 7 thinnish slices, crusts removed
Brandy to taste
Hot custard to serve

Put the fruit, prune juice and cloves into a saucepan and simmer for 20 minutes / Reserving 2 slices of bread, use the rest to line a 600ml pudding basin (the bread will stick more easily if you rinse out the basin and leave it slightly damp) / Pour some of the hot fruit juice into the base of the basin / Spoon in the fruit and pour over the rest of the juice / Use the reserved bread to cover the top of the fruit / Cover with a tea plate and weight (a large can of beans is perfect) / Leave until cold then chill in the fridge for at least 2 hours / Carefully upturn the fruit pudding onto a serving dish (if it gets a bit misshapen re-form it with damp hands) / Serve with the brandy mixed into the hot custard.

Orange-flower sorbet with mint biscuits

Sorbets are deliciously refreshing, particularly after a robust main course. Although this dish has quite a large amount of sugar, it also contains masses of vitamin C from the home-squeezed juices. And you wouldn't believe how quick, easy and healthy it is to make biscuits with mint, a herb normally associated with meat dishes. These biscuits are far better for your digestion than after-dinner mint chocolates. (Serves 4)

For the sorbet

Brown caster sugar 200g

Orange-flower water 250ml

Home-squeezed orange juice 350ml

Home-squeezed lemon juice 3 tablespoons

For the mint biscuits

Unsalted butter 110g, plus extra for greasing

Caster sugar 50g

Fresh mint 2 tablespoons, finely chopped leaves

75% wholemeal self-raising flour 175g, plus
   extra for dusting

To make the sorbet, mix the sugar thoroughly into the orange-flower water / Bring to a simmer and continue cooking for 5 minutes, then cool / Pour in the orange and lemon juice and stir until well combined / Put into an ice-cream or sorbet-maker if you have one / If not, pour into a freezerproof container and put into the freezer until almost firm, then break up the chunks as they are about to freeze / Repeat until the sorbet becomes slush-like / Put it back into the freezer until firm.

To make the mint biscuits, cream the butter with the sugar / Add the mint and flour and knead into a dough / Roll onto a floured board and cut with a pastry cutter into small rounds / Bake on a greased baking tray at 230°C/450°F/gas mark 8 for about 10 minutes.

LUNCHBOX *The biscuits are great for a lunch or teatime snack.*

....

Figs with goat cheese

That wonderful purple flesh! The way the fruit bursts in your mouth and the juice dribbles down your chin! Stop me before I get carried away. Figs are such a treat, and they are full of goodness, too, with lots of iron, potassium, beta-carotene, fibre and energy. I normally wouldn't do anything other than eat them raw, but this combination of figs quickly grilled with creamy goat cheese is a culinary marriage made in heaven. (Serves 4)

Fresh figs 8, halved lengthways

Goat's cheese 1 cylindrical roll, weighing about 150g,
   cut into 8 round slices

Runny honey about 4 tablespoons

Toasted pine nuts 4 teaspoons

Natural live set yoghurt to serve

Put the figs, cut-side up, into an ovenproof dish just large enough to hold them / Put a slice of cheese on each fig half / Put under a very hot grill until the cheese starts to melt, not more than 1 minute / Put onto individual plates / Drizzle with the honey / Sprinkle the pine nuts on top / Serve a heaped tablespoon of yoghurt on the side.

PUDDINGS

Poached peaches

Apart from containing a good quantitiy of vitamin C, peaches aren't particularly rich in many other nutrients. But as they are almost completely free of salt and fat, they make a good filling food for anyone suffering with high cholesterol or blood pressure and they do contain some protective antioxidants. They taste and smell brilliant too – particularly with the soft aromas of rose water and star anise. (Serves 4)

Unsalted butter 50g
Ripe peaches 4, small, cut in half
Sweet white wine 150ml
Rose water 125ml
Star anise 2
Brown caster sugar 1 tablespoon
Orange juice 4 tablespoons
Ricotta cheese 200g

Melt the butter in an ovenproof dish just large enough to hold the peaches / Put the peach halves, cut-side down, into the dish / Pour over the wine and rose water and add the star anise / Sprinkle with the sugar / Poach, uncovered, in the oven at 180°C/350°F/gas mark 4 for about 25 minutes until the peaches are tender / Serve with the orange juice beaten into the ricotta.

Steamed apricot pudding

Because of their high fibre content, dried apricots are one of the best cures for constipation. But let's not dwell on that! This satisfying alternative to a traditional steamed pudding is extremely light, and the ginger essence gives an extra zing to the sumptuous sweetness of the fruit. (Serves 4)

Ready-to-eat apricots 225g, snipped into quarters
Wholemeal bread 5 slices, without crusts
Eggs 2 medium
Milk 250ml
Ginger essence 3 drops
Unsalted butter for greasing
Hot custard to serve

Mix together the apricots and bread / Beat together the eggs, milk and ginger essence / Pour over the apricot mix and set aside for 20 minutes / Put into a 600ml greased pudding basin, cover with greaseproof paper and tie with string / Put the basin into a large saucepan and add enough water to come roughly half way up the sides / Steam for 1½ hours, checking occasionally to make sure the water hasn't boiled away / Serve with hot custard.

Blueberry jelly with scented geranium

If jellies remind you of thick, gelatinous mounds of sweet chewy nothingness, you are in for a surprise. These are deliciously sophisticated berry desserts that look really stylish at the end of a dinner party. You'll get loads of protective chemicals from the blueberries, volatile oils from the geranium leaves and calcium and good bacteria from the live yoghurt. (Serves 4)

White caster sugar 110g
Sweet geranium leaves 10, large
Sweet white wine 200ml
Lemon juice 1 tablespoon
Powdered gelatine 2 teaspoons
Fresh blueberries 225g
Natural live yoghurt 275g
Runny honey 3 tablespoons

Put the sugar and half the geranium leaves into a saucepan with the wine / Bring slowly to the boil and simmer for 2 minutes / Cool, remove the geranium leaves and add the lemon juice / Put the gelatine into a bowl and add water according to the packet instructions / Put the bowl over a saucepan of simmering water and stir until dissolved / Pour the syrup onto the gelatine and add the blueberries / Ladle the mixture into 4 moulds or ramekin dishes and leave to set in the fridge for 2 hours / Put the rest of the geranium leaves in the small bowl of a blender and whiz until fine / Add the yoghurt and honey and whiz until combined with the leaves / Pour some of the yoghurt mix onto 4 plates and turn out the jellies on top.

FIRST FOOD *Babies will love their own version of this dessert, but make theirs with water rather than wine, make sure the blueberries are well mashed and that there are no large pieces of herb in the yoghurt.*

Summer fruit vol au vents

There is an important thing to remember about summer berry-type fruit: the darker their colour, the more protective they are against a range of modern diseases, including cancer. So try to include blackcurrants, blackberries, blueberries, black cherries and loganberries in this melt-in-the-mouth recipe. (Serves 4)

Summer berries (fresh are better, but frozen work just as well) 225g
Agar agar $1/4$ teaspoon
Runny honey about 2 tablespoons
Small vol au vent cases (ready-made are fine) 8
Single cream to serve

Put the fruit into a saucepan and add 150ml water / Bring quickly to the boil, add the agar agar, stir in gently but thoroughly and leave to cool slightly / Melt the honey and use it to brush the tops of the vol au vent cases / Spoon in the fruit and leave to cool / Serve drizzled with the cream.

PARTIES *These vol au vents make an excellent sweet addition to canapés for a drinks party.*

Just a word before we start … all the suggestions here contain juice of some sort and I can't emphasise strongly enough that home-made juices are definitely the best, particularly if you use organic produce. Juicing your own fruit and vegetables means you have the freshest possible end product with all its natural nutrients still intact. Even supermarkets' 'freshly squeezed' juices start to lose their goodness the second they are processed.

In the long term, juicing at home also turns out infinitely cheaper. Just compare the price of a bag of oranges and the juice you get from that with the supermarket bill when you buy a litre of ready-made juice. You do have to invest in a juicer, of course, but citrus fruit machines are very inexpensive and even machines which can cope with vegetables and non-citrus fruit aren't that pricey. Yes, you do have to clear up the mess and wash the machine, but there's no waste; just put any peel, pips, pith, and so on in a compost bin and you'll have your own garden soil nutrients, too.

In any case, there's nothing like making your own juice. You can experiment with your own mixtures – and I've made a few decidedly dodgy ones in the past – and children love doing the same. It's a fail-safe way to get reluctant kids to eat fruit and vegetables; if they've made a juice themselves, they are far less likely to turn their noses up and scream, 'I don't like that'.

Here are some super-nutritious ideas to get you started. But before you start, remember to try to buy organic. If you're going to make your own juices, it really is worth the extra expense.

Tomato tang

For this recipe, you'll need a proper juicer but the reward will be a cornucopia of delicious nutrition. Tomatoes will give you a large dose of lycopene, one of the most powerful weapons against prostate cancer and heart disease. Carrots come with a huge dose of beta-carotene. Radishes improve digestion and help with gall bladder and liver problems. And coriander, apart from its deliciously peppery flavour, cleanses the system, calms you down – and is also known as an aphrodisiac. (Serves 2)

LUNCHBOX *Warm the juice well and pour into a vacuum flask for a deliciously different lunchtime soup.*

Carrot 1
Radishes 4
Tomatoes 4
Celery 1 stick
Fresh coriander ½ handful
Lemon 1

Put the carrot, radishes, tomatoes, celery and nearly all the coriander through a juicer (no need to peel any of them if they are organic) / Put into a jug and stir well / Juice the lemon and add about 2 tablespoons to the jug / Finely chop the reserved coriander and sprinkle on top of the juice / Serve.

Plum and apricot smoothie

Dried apricots are action-packed food – filling, nourishing and full of both instant and slow-release energy. Because of their high fibre content, they are excellent if you're prone to constipation and their vitamin A makes them essential for keeping immunity levels high and for protecting against skin and sight problems. Oranges are, of course, extremely rich in vitamin C. The added bonus for women in this smoothie is the soya yoghurt, which contains hormone-like substances to relieve PMS, hot flushes during the menopause and to protect against osteoporosis. (Serves 4)

Ready-to-eat apricots 6
Plums 4
Oranges 2
Soya yoghurt 500g

Put the apricots into a bowl, cover with freshly boiled water and leave to cool / Remove the stones from the plums and put into a blender / Juice the oranges and add the juice to the blender / Tip in the apricots and their water / Blend until smooth / Add the yoghurt and blend again / Serve.

Strawberry and vanilla smoothie

Who can resist the soft red colour and succulent smell of good strawberries? But in the height of summer, even the most ardent fan might groan inwardly at the thought of yet another bowl of strawberries and cream, so here's a different way to take advantage of this fabulous fruit. Strawberries contain large amounts of malic acid, one of nature's ant-inflammatories. They also contain beta-carotene, iron and vitamin C, which makes them good for anaemia, and they help the body get rid of uric acid, so they are a deliciously beneficial food for those with arthritis and other joint problems. And the fromage frais and milk give you a good supply of calcium, too. (Serves 4–6)

Strawberries 450g
Fromage frais 400g
Milk 300ml
Vanilla essence 4–8 dashes (or to taste)

Wash and hull the strawberries / Put them into a blender with the fromage frais and milk and blend until smooth / Pour into glasses and stir in vanilla essence to taste / Serve.

Blueberry and crème fraîche smoothie

Blueberries are without doubt my favourite fruit – worth every penny of their rather expensive price in the super-market. I'm lucky that they grow well in my garden, so I can be as self-indulgent as I like when late summer comes – as long as the hens haven't got to them first. I revel in the knowledge that these dusky little beauties are one of the most protective foods of all; they help every single cell in the body ward off the effects of free-radical chemicals and pollution. (Serves 2)

Blueberries 200g
Crème fraîche 250g
Milk about 150ml

Wash the blueberries and hull if necessary / Put them into a blender with the crème fraîche and blend until smooth / Add the milk and blend again until you get the required consistency / Serve.

Carrot and apple juice

Along with Brussels sprouts, carrots don't enjoy a place of affection in most people's minds. But if your heart sinks at the thought of an over-cooked, mushy orange mess sitting at the side of your dinner plate, give carrots a chance with this filling and nutritious drink. You'll get vitamin A, cancer protection and skin-friendly nutrients from the carrots, plus cholesterol-lowering, heart-protective and digestion-improving substances from the apples. (Serves 2)

Carrots 2, large or 250ml commercial carrot juice
Eating apples 2 or 250ml commercial apple juice

Wash and juice the fruit (there is no need to peel them if they are organic) / Mix together well before serving.

Hot apple and peppermint tea

Loads of vitamin C and fibre from the apples, plus stress-relieving and digestion-improving chemicals in the mint, make this a deliciously nutritious warming drink. Yes, this is a juice which is served warm, giving the mint a chance to fill your kitchen with its wonderful aroma. (Serves 2)

Eating apples 4–5 or 500ml commercial apple juice
Fresh peppermint 1 large stem, plus 2 sprigs to garnish

Wash and juice the apples (there is no need to peel them if they are organic) / Bruise the peppermint stem by pressing with the back of a large wooden spoon / Put the juice and mint into a saucepan and warm gently (don't allow to boil) / Scoop out the mint / Serve with the mint sprigs on top.

LUNCHBOX *Poured into a vacuum flask, this juice is warming in the middle of the day.*

Cranberry and prune juice

This deep red delicious juice is bursting with goodness. There is masses of vitamin C in cranberries and some in the prunes and they both contain specific nutrients which help regulate the bowels and protect against urinary infections. They are also both among the top ten foods which have been proved to neutralise free radicals in the body and protect against ageing, heart disease, cancer and other degenerative conditions. (Serves 4)

Cranberry juice 500ml
Prune juice 500ml
Fresh mint sprigs 4

In a large jug, mix the juices together well / Serve with a sprig of mint in each glass.

LUNCHBOX *This juice is equally delicious hot or cold and could easily be taken to work or school in a vacuum flask.*

Spicy orange and grapefruit juice

All citrus fruits contain huge amounts of vitamin C, which helps guard against infection by both bacteria and viruses. They are also a good source of fibre and potassium. In fact, simple fruits like oranges and grapefruit have more medicinal benefits than practically any other food. This juice combines the two with help for the digestion – and a slightly dry and spicy flavour – from the cardamom. It's a brilliantly refreshing start to the day. (Serves 2)

Cardamom seeds 1 level teaspoon
Oranges 4 or 300ml commercial orange juice
Grapefruit 1 or 200ml commercial grapefruit juice

Crush the cardamom seeds finely / Put into a small cup and just cover with freshly boiled water / Leave to cool completely / Juice the oranges and grapefruit / Pour the cardamom seeds and water into the juices and serve.

DESSERT *Don't waste the fruit skins. Scoop out any remaining pith and fill them with Orange-Flower Sorbet (see page 231).*

HOME PRESERVES *Alternatively, if you're into making home preserves, here's a simple marmalade recipe that uses the same fruits. Weigh the fruit before juicing. Measure how much juice you extract. Put that amount of water into a saucepan with the sliced orange and grapefruit skins and any pith still attached, plus the juice and sliced skin of a lemon. Scoop any pips out of the juicer, tie up in a muslin bag and add to the fruit. For every 450g of whole fruit, add another litre of water. Leave for about 8 hours. Bring to the boil and simmer until the skins are very tender, about 1$\frac{1}{2}$ hours. Again for every 450g of whole fruit, add 900g preserving sugar, warmed for 10 minutes in a medium-hot (180°C/350°F/gas mark 4) oven. Stir until the sugar is dissolved, then boil until the liquid is reduced by half and the marmalade sets on a cold spoon. Pour into sterilised jars – straight from a hot wash in a dishwasher will do. Each 450g of fruit will give about 1.6kg of marmalade.*

A passion for pineapple

The stinging sweetness of pineapple, the aromatic pepperiness of passion fruit … this drink will turn any drizzling summer afternoon into a day on a Caribbean beach. With or without the rum, it makes a wonderful party punch – and with specific health benefits, too. Pineapple contains an important enzyme called bromelain, which helps disperse blood clots and heal damaged skin and injured muscles. It has also been shown to be an effective anti-inflammatory. Passion fruit is rich in vitamin C and also contains phytochemicals, which are antiseptic, sedative and mildly laxative. (Serves 4)

Passion fruit 3 or 75ml commercial passion-fruit juice
Pineapple 1 medium or 400ml commercial pineapple juice
White rum (optional) 4 standard measures
Ice cubes
Lemon 1
Fresh mint a few leaves

If using fresh fruit, scoop the flesh out of the passion fruit / Peel the pineapple (unless your juicer instruction book says it can cope with robust peel like this) / Put the passion fruit and pineapple through the juicer and pour into a jug (if using commercial juices, simply mix them together) / Mix in the rum and add the ice cubes / Slice the lemon / Serve with the lemon and mint leaves floating on top.

Index

Author's Acknowledgements

Extravagant gratitude is due to Hilary Mandleberg,
editor, Amanda Lerwill, designer, Jane O' Shea
and all at Quadrille, and to my secretary, Janet Betley.

Picture Credits

1–8 Digital Vision; 10 © Archivo Iconográfico, S.A./CORBIS; 11© Bettmann/CORBIS; 13 The Culture Archive;
14 Digital Vision; 19–20 Geoff Wilkinson/The Organic Picture Library Ltd; 25 & 28 Digital Vision; 29 The Image Bank/
Getty Images; 31 Digital Vision; 32 Photolibrary.com; 33 Imagesource/Imagestate; 34 ABPL/PFT
Photography/Steve Lee; 35 John Foxx/Alamy; 37 (main) Digital Vision; 37 (inset) Photodisc Green/Getty Images; 38
www.fabfoodpix.com; 41 © Zefa/R.James; 42 Ian Hooton/Mother & Baby Picture Library; 45 Ian Hooton/Mother & Baby Picture
Library; 46 Photolibrary.com; 49 Photodisc Green/Getty Images; 51 Stone/Getty Images/Laurence Monneret; 52 Photolibrary.com;
55 Photodisc Green/Getty Images; 57 Taxi/Getty Images/Tony Anderson; 58 The Image Bank/Getty Images/Julie Toy; 60 Digital
Vision; 61 © Getty Images; 63 Paul Mitchell/Mother & Baby Picture Library; 64 ABPL/Joy Skipper; 65 Stone/Getty Images/Andrea
Booher; 67 Allsport Concepts/Getty Images/Mike Powell; 69 ABPL/Tim Hill; 70 ABPL/PFT Photography; 71 Photodisc Green/Getty
Images; 72 Imagestate; 74 ABPL/Maximilian Stock Ltd; 77 Geoff Wilkinson/The Organic Picture Library Ltd; 79 Photodisc
Green/Getty Images; 81 Mother & Baby Picture Library; 83 Photodisc Green/Getty Images; 87 Geoff Wilkinson/The Organic Picture
Library Ltd; 89 ABPL/William Shaw; 91 ABPL/Joff Lee; 92 ABPL/Joy Skipper; 94 ABPL/Joy Skipper; 96 ©Zefa/Sucré Salé/Pierre
Desrieux; 98 Photodisc Blue/Getty Images; 101 Geoff Wilkinson/The Organic Picture Library Ltd; 103 Geoff Wilkinson/The Organic
Picture Library Ltd; 104 Digital Vision; 107 Geoff Wilkinson/The Organic Picture Library Ltd; 108 ABPL/Gerrit Buntrock; 110 Digital
Vision; 114 Paul Mitchell/Mother & Baby Picture Library; 119 The Image Bank/Getty Images/Daly & Newton; 121 Ian
Hooton/Mother & Baby Picture Library; 122 The Image Bank/Getty Images/Juan Silva; 125 & 127 Ruth Jenkinson/Mother & Baby
Picture Library; 128 Paul Mitchell/Mother & Baby Picture Library; 131 © image100; 132, 134 & 137 Ian Hooton/Mother & Baby
Picture Library; 139 Photolibrary.com; 140 Paul Mitchel/Mother & Baby Picture Library; 142 Ian Hooton/Mother & Baby Picture
Library; 144 Photoalto/Imagestate; 146 Taxi/Getty Images/Gen Nishino; 149 www.Stockbyte.com; 150 © image100;
155 © Iconica; 156 Taxi/Getty Images/Matthew Brookes; 165 Photolibrary.com; 167 Imagestate; 169 Taxi/Getty Images/Steven
Lam; 171 © Iconica/Barry Rosenthal; 172 Photolibrary.com; 175 The Image Bank/Getty Images/Anne-Marie Weber; 176
Stone+/Getty Images/Kevin Mackintosh; 179 Photolibrary.com; 181 Taxi/Getty images/Frederic Lucano; 183 Taxi/Getty
Images/Christopher Thomas; 186 Digital Vision; 190 www.Stockbyte.com; 189 Hugh Threlfall/Alamy